PLANNING A DISTRIBUTION SYSTEM

PLANNING A DISTRIBUTION SYSTEM

Peter R Attwood

Gower Press

First published in Britain in 1971 by Gower Press Limited
140 Great Portland Street, London W1N 5TA

© Peter Attwood 1971

ISBN 0 7161 0090 8

Set in 10 on 12 point Times and printed in England by
Clarke, Doble & Brendon Ltd
Plymouth

CONTENTS

Foreword		xiii
Acknowledgements		xv
1	**THE DISTRIBUTION SYSTEM**	**1**
1:1	Functional distribution	1
1:2	Organising management functions	4
1:3	Objectives of distribution	7
1:4	Distribution operations	8
1:5	Influence of warehousing factors on plans	8
1:6	Warehousing example	10
1:7	Influence of delivering on distribution planning	12
1:8	Distribution planning principles	13
1:9	Systematic method of distribution resources planning	18
2	**STRATEGIC PLANNING FOR DISTRIBUTION**	**21**
2:1	Need for strategic planning	21
2:2	Scale of planning	23
2:3	Objectives of strategic planning	24
2:4	Future of distribution	25
2:5	Coordinated centres of demand	28
2:6	Planning deliveries	30
2:7	Synthetic planning standards	33
2:8	Budgetary control in distribution	38
3	**ANALYSING MARKET DEMAND**	**40**
3:1	Market demand	40
3:2	Value analysis	43
3:3	Ordering cycle	47
3:4	Distribution logistics	51
3:5	Customer rationalisation	53
3:6	Planning for market demand	54
3:7	Analysing delivery problems	55

CONTENTS

4	**SITING SUPPLY POINTS**	**61**
4:1	Locating supplies for distribution	61
4:2	Methods of siting	66
4:3	Siting according to demand	69
4:4	Solving complex siting problems	71
5	**DECIDING THE BEST SUPPLY SITES**	**75**
5:1	Number of supply sites	75
5:2	Number of sites and distribution costs	77
5:3	Variable factors of siting	82
5:4	Depot siting	85
5:5	Best site for a supply point	86
6	**ROUTING DELIVERY VEHICLES**	**95**
6:1	Scientific routing	96
6:2	Factors that affect vehicle routing	98
6:3	Developing vehicle routes	99
6:4	Computerised routing	102
6:5	Estimating route distances	103
6:6	Journey planning	105
6:7	Assigning vehicles to routes	106
7	**SCHEDULING DELIVERIES**	**111**
7:1	Scheduling delivery vehicles	112
7:2	Methods of scheduling delivery vehicles	112
7:3	Variable factors of scheduling	114
7:4	Vehicles required for deliveries	115
7:5	Requirements of goods scheduling	116
7:6	Journey scheduling	118
7:7	Operational programming	120
8	**PREPARING DISTRIBUTION PLANS**	**125**
8:1	Planning economic deliveries	125
8:2	Planning trunking deliveries	128
8:3	Local delivery resources planning	132
8:4	Selecting the vehicles	150
8:5	Transport manning	153
9	**CONTROLLING DISTRIBUTION**	**157**
9:1	Tripartite organisation of distribution	157
9:2	Controlling distribution costs	159
9:3	Controlling distribution stocks	162
9:4	Controlling results graphically	167
9:5	Work study for controlling deliveries	171

CONTENTS

10	A SUCCESSFUL DISTRIBUTION SYSTEM	179
10:1	Successful control of distribution	180
10:2	Successful warehousing plans	186
10:3	Successful distribution cost reduction	190
10:4	Monitoring delivery service	193
10:5	From plan to reality	197

APPENDIX: FORMS FOR MONITORING DELIVERIES		203
APPRECIATION		213
INDEX		215

ILLUSTRATIONS

1:1	Distribution chain	2
1:2	Functional management structure for distribution	3
1:3	Members of an organisation	4
1:4	Lines of management	5
1:5	Circle of communication	5
1:6	Relationships between warehousing costs and throughput	9
1:7	Throughput/cost graph for a cased goods warehouse	11
1:8	Different types of distribution system	14
1:9	Schematic distribution resources planning	19
2:1	Strategic planning graph	22
2:2	Scale of planning	24
2:3	Bar chart of distribution trends	26
2:4	Map of European demand coordinates for automobiles	28
2:5	Table of latitudinal coordinates	29
2:6	Table of longitudinal coordinates	30
2:7	Strategic planning for distribution	33
2:8	Truck movement average times	34
2:9	Truck handling and movement times	35
2:10	Additional handling times	36
2:11	Schematic warehousing system	37
3:1	Table of demand coefficients for distributing cakes	42
3:2	Procedure for the Darsiri method of value analysis	44
3:3	Procedure for the Darsiri method of value analysis	48
3:4	Ordering cycle	49
3:5	Distribution network	52
3:6	Analysing order processing	54
3:7	Reducing delivery time	59
4:1	Distribution system	63
4:2	Iso-cost contour map	67
4:3	Analogue siting simulator	68
4:4	Two demand locations system	70
4:5	Three demand locations system	70
4:6	Branch line system	70
4:7	Loop line system	70
4:8	Complex distribution system	72
4:9	More than two supply sites	74
5:1	Cost variations and the number of warehouses	78
5:2	Delivery costs data	79

ILLUSTRATIONS

5:3	Optimising distribution costs	80
5:4	Relationships between costs and lead time	81
5:5	Optimising overhead costs	84
5:6	Depot siting procedure	87
5:7	Florida Ice Company: first system	88
5:8	Florida Ice Company: second system	88
5:9	Florida Ice Company: third system	89
5:10	Florida Ice Company: fourth system	89
5:11	Florida Ice Company: complex system	90
5:12	Table of distribution cost vectors	92
6:1	Route optimisation with coordinates	104
6:2	Time matrix	107
6:3	First revised time matrix	107
6:4	Second revised time matrix	108
6:5	Third revised time matrix	108
6:6	Final time matrix	109
7:1	Schematic scheduling	117
7:2	Sequence matrix	121
7:3	Basic time chart	122
7:4	Partially completed time chart	122
7:5	Final time chart	123
8:1	Rationalisation process	128
8:2	Scheduling chart	130
8:3	Standard offloading times	135
8:4	Capacities of vehicles	136
8:5	Coded delivery areas in the Midlands	137
8:6	Cases delivered to the region of 1970	138
8:7	Estimated cases for delivery in 1971	139
8:8	Delivery planning standards	140
8:9	Map of the delivery area SH	141
8:10	Estimated monthly requirements	142
8:11	Local delivery vehicles in area SH	147
8:12	Vehicle requirements for the three areas	147
8:13	Journeys to the Midlands region: off-peak month	148
8:14	Journeys to the Midlands region: peak month	149
8:15	Monthly vehicle requirements	150
8:16	Operating costs for 10-ton tipper truck	153
8:17	Staff organisation for distribution	154
9:1	Organisation for cost control	160
9:2	Stock levels	163
9:3	Stock behaviour pattern with constant demand	165
9:4	Controlling stock-outs	166
9:5	Economic order quantity	167
9:6	Z-chart for wheat distribution	169
9:7	Warehouse flow lines	170
9:8	Methodical procedure	172
9:9	Traffic congestion problem	173
9:10	Standard depot times for a vehicle driver	176
9:11	Standard drop times for a 5-ton van	178

ILLUSTRATIONS

10:1	Distribution information system	182
10:2	Checklist for improving distribution	183
10:3	Total cost of distribution	187
10:4	Sensitivity analysis chart	188
10:5	Distribution wheel	191
10:6	Monitoring delivery costs	195
10:7	Monitoring delivery service	196

FOREWORD

Physical distribution is a matter of economic priority on a national scale and its importance is increasing. It can account for upwards of 25 per cent of the total cost of goods at the point of sale. Not surprisingly it has been the focus of an enormous amount of research and development in the past decade resulting in fundamental changes in total strategy, operational techniques, and design of equipment and transport. This book illustrates the application of modern management services and particularly highlights the value of operational research techniques in the rapid solution of seemingly complex problems.

In the past, cost reduction effort tended mainly to be directed to the control of direct labour and production plant cost in manufacturing and processing. Modern techniques, such as value analysis, have demonstrated the relative economic significance in the different functional areas; in the more progressive firms, top management is now directing attention to the greater economies to be derived from well-planned warehousing and transportation.

The distribution system covers the whole range of operations and movement of goods between the producer and the consumer. The requirements for maximum performance in each different area of activity are often conflicting and the operational system will be that compromise which produces the best overall result. This is achieved when a distribution system automatically co-ordinates the actions of the managers controlling each area of activity and can test the effect of changes in one area on the performance of others.

The main function of a distribution system is to provide the customer with goods in the right condition, at the right time, at the right place, in the right quantities and at an economical cost. As the market is likely to be continuously changing, the performance of the system in this dynamic situation should be tested at regular intervals for efficiency in operation and for "robustness" against predictable and unforeseen changes. Only in this way can the investment be safeguarded.

Distribution systems can be greatly affected by both internal and external

FOREWORD

changes, often outside the control of management. Typical internal changes are growth, change in commodity mix, technological opportunity and rationalisation after take-over or merger. External changes can be caused by national and international legislation, technological development, competitors' activities and market shift. There is therefore a need for a planning, design, management and communication system which will detect these changes and react to them as they occur.

Peter Attwood deals comprehensively, lucidly and in depth with all these aspects of this highly complex subject. He has achieved the distillation of principles from his own and his associates' wealth of experience and has presented and explained these in an intelligible and uncomplicated way. His book is a standard work of reference on distribution and is commended to strategic planners and managers at all levels. It will be of particular interest to directors of logistics, distribution managers, transport managers and warehouse managers.

C G Chantrill
Chairman, C G Chantrill & Partners Ltd

1 THE DISTRIBUTION SYSTEM

The fundamental aim of a distribution system is to transfer products from the place of manufacture to the place of consumption. In practice, this statement is too general because it says nothing about keeping customers happy or costing money. It is necessary to qualify the fundamental aim by adding to it the reason for distribution, which is to provide a service to customers who pay to receive goods as ordered.

Distribution contributes no profit to a company; however, without satisfactory distribution there is unlikely to be an income from sales. This paradox faces all marketing-oriented companies, because a successful distribution system must provide the best service to customers for the least cost to the company. Optimising these conflicting objectives will produce a satisfactory balance which is acceptable to both customers and the company.

1:1 FUNCTIONAL DISTRIBUTION

The objective of a distribution system is to match the production output to the market demand by holding goods until they are required and delivering them when they are. It follows that there are two basic functions of distribution, warehousing and delivering products. Both functions require dynamic management because they are subject to continual change, being dependent upon both production and marketing for their existence; however, there is a general concept that warehousing is static while delivering is mobile, but it is wrong.

Whenever a function is affected by change, it is necessary to be prepared for it, and this means being flexible and fully understanding the basic principles. The first need for understanding distribution is to identify its elements and to put them into perspective by developing a functional organisation. Distribution must be viewed as a whole before it can be organised into specific duties which can be fitted into a management structure that will help to determine their true relationships.

Distribution chain

Production and marketing are linked together in Figure 1:1 by distribution

THE DISTRIBUTION SYSTEM

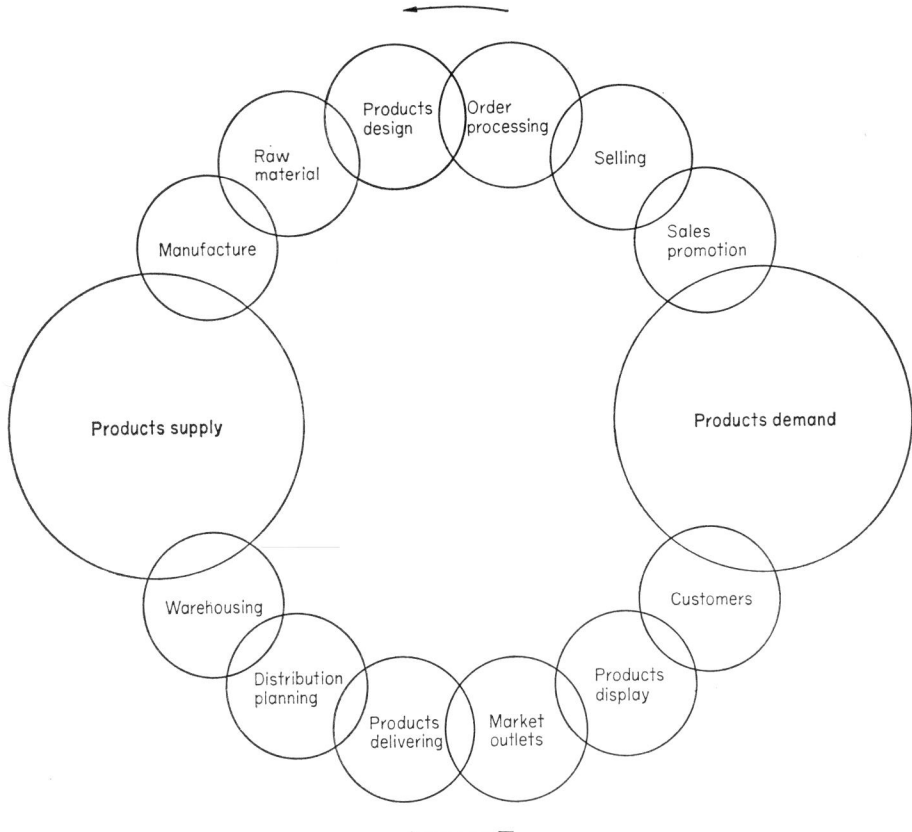

Figure 1:1 DISTRIBUTION CHAIN

which is responsible for matching the supply to the demand for goods in terms of quantity and location. Essentially, distribution is a service that must be an overhead cost on both production and marketing. Reducing distribution costs will increase company profits, but it is easiest to reduce costs when their sources have been recognised. Structuring the functions of distribution will show where costs can be reduced.

Value of distribution

A company must measure distribution value in terms of the service offered and its cost. Value can be increased by providing a better service or by reducing the cost. In a marketing-oriented company, the service is mainly for the benefit of customers and it is advisable to give marketing authority over distribution. Although this applies in most cases, it is unwise to genera-

THE DISTRIBUTION SYSTEM

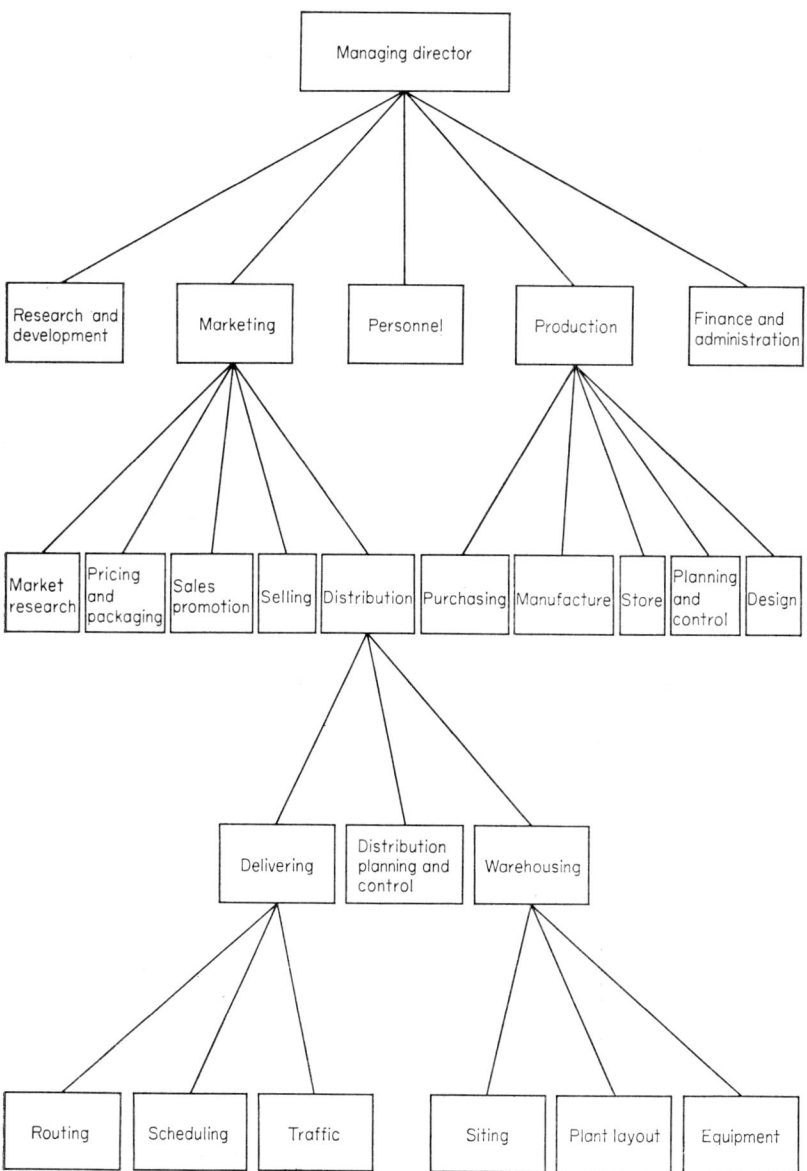

Figure 1:2 FUNCTIONAL MANAGEMENT STRUCTURE FOR DISTRIBUTION

THE DISTRIBUTION SYSTEM

lise, because distribution may provide a greater service to production through warehousing in some instances. A truly functional organisation structure provides each man with one superior so that authority is related directly to responsibility and loyalties are not divided. It is difficult to relate services to different departments in a functional management structure, but it is essential that this is done in order to prevent monopolisation. Normally, distribution is included in the marketing function on the principle that people who take orders must be responsible for seeing that the goods are delivered satisfactorily. The relationships between functions in an ideal management structure are illustrated by Figure 1:2.

1:2 ORGANISING MANAGEMENT FUNCTIONS

Ideally, each person in an organisation must know the lines of authority and responsibility, and realise that his job is linked to that of the managing director promotion-wise. Such an organisation will take the form of a pyramid which is composed of smaller pyramids of decreasing size. The smallest pyramid at the bottom comprises only three persons, as shown in Figure 1:3. A person with authority controls the operations of persons below him and they are responsible for carrying out his instructions, which keeps him in command over them. Communication is the coordinating medium that binds together persons with authority and responsibility to form the framework of management (see Figure 1:4).

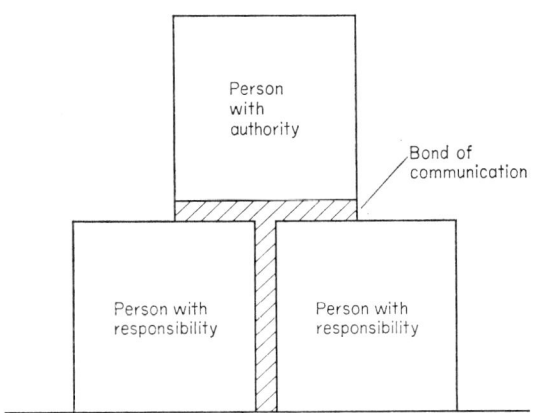

Figure 1:3 MEMBERS OF AN ORGANISATION

Bond of communication

After a clear and well-defined organisation has been established, it is vital to bond it into a coordinated structure with sound communications. The

THE DISTRIBUTION SYSTEM

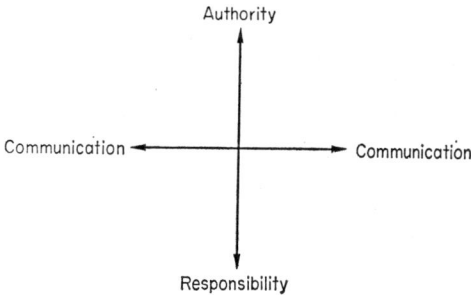

Figure 1:4 **LINES OF MANAGEMENT**

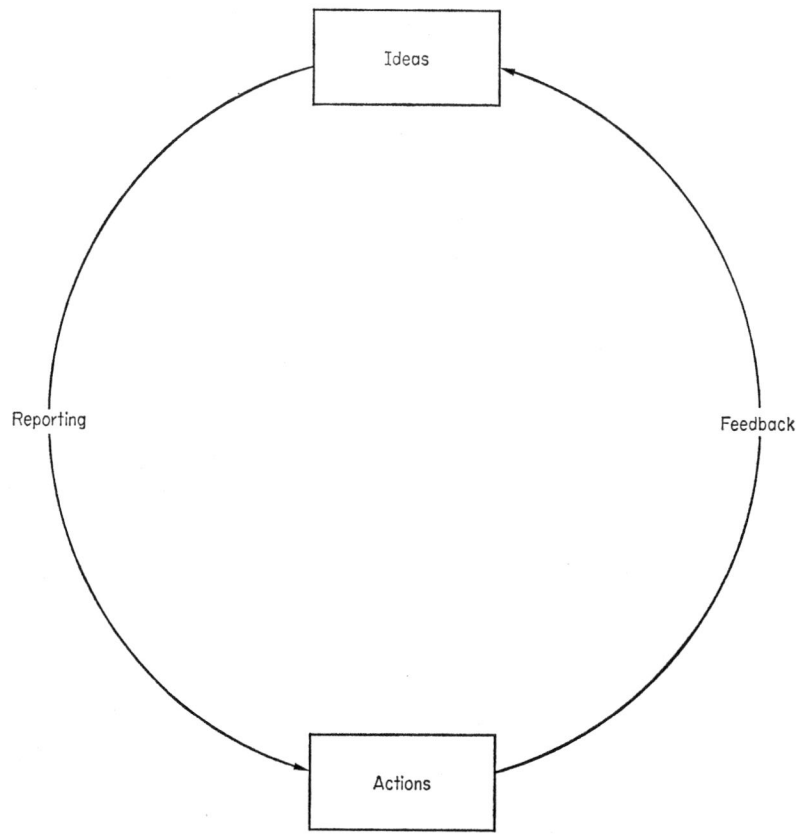

Figure 1:5 **CIRCLE OF COMMUNICATION**

aim of communication is to transmit instructions and information which will provide the basis for control.

Good communication starts at the top of any management structure with the managing director interpreting the company policies laid down by the board of directors and delegating authority down through the organisation. Usually, it is advisable for the managing director to get together with his senior managers periodically for the triple purpose of explaining, shaping and regulating operating policies and analysing ideas for developing plans. Depending upon the size of the organisation, successive meetings between superior and subordinates will keep each person informed of progress and help them to feel that they are part of a team.

In general terms, a company must have an official communication system that circulates factual information and combats the grapevine; the circle of communication is suggested in Figure 1:5. Additionally, communication must be planned and encouraged to develop as the recognised procedure for issuing orders and instructions. It must be quite clear who is the issuing authority and who is responsible for executing orders. They must be recorded and everyone concerned made aware of them. Recorded instructions must be kept to a minimum, but they should be compiled into a carefully indexed manual which serves as the operating code for all to follow.

It is important to stress that campaign plans are best prepared with the aid of such a code provided that the instructions have been written briefly, clearly and concisely. It is particularly important that the manual is kept up to date as new instructions are issued or old ones are reviewed or cancelled. The greatest benefit from an effective communications bond is that everyone in the organisation is aware of the picture as a whole and not merely as a small jigsaw piece. At any level, a person will function more intelligently when the full implications of his own job are understood and good communications help to do this.

Leadership

The oldest, most natural and greatest asset of a manager is leadership. It is a projection of personality which is a combination of persuasion, compulsion and setting examples that encourage others to react in a respectful way. Organisation is a science, but leadership is an art.

Art is the manifestation of personality; therefore, leadership is personal regardless of an organisation's size. The boss must be seen and recognised as a person who understands what is happening on lower levels. Electronic communications cannot replace personal contacts in an organisation and impersonal plans will be only partially successful. The human touch in leadership breaks down barriers to communication and resistance to change so that trust will replace fear.

THE DISTRIBUTION SYSTEM

The qualities of a good leader are courage, willpower, judgement, knowledge and broadmindedness. Each of these qualities combines to make the personality necessary for a leader to engender respect and create confidence that his plans are for the benefit of all. A manager must be both leader and organiser, and a true manager is a product of the environment that provided him with the knowledge and experience of his job. Maturity is a gift of time that must be repaid by making certain that others are trained to succeed. The basic qualities of a distribution manager are the same for all managers anywhere in the world.

1:3 OBJECTIVES OF DISTRIBUTION

The overall objective of distribution is to provide a service to the marketing and production functions by holding and delivering products efficiently and economically. Secondary objectives can be related to warehousing, delivering and planning the distribution system.

1 *Warehousing* is principally a service to production, being designed to hold products of manufacture, to transform stocks from production units into marketing units and to assemble loads for delivering to customers.
2 *Delivering* is a marketing service, being designed for transporting products according to orders and delivering them into the hands of customers.
3 *Planning the distribution system* must be designed to coordinate warehousing with delivering, to advise on siting factories, warehouses and depots, to route delivery vehicles, to schedule deliveries and to control operations in accordance with requirements.

The costs of distribution are related to these three objectives, but they will vary according to the number, sizes and locations of warehouses which, in turn, influence the numbers, sizes and types of vehicle and the personnel employed.

1 *Numbers of warehouses.* Transport costs and delivery delays will decrease as the number of warehouses increases, but stockholding and operating costs will rise.
2 *Sizes of warehouses.* The unit cost of distributing goods will decrease as the size of a warehouse increases, but capital and land costs will increase.
3 *Locations of warehouses.* Transport costs depend upon the location of a warehouse in relation to the source of the greatest volume of products to be distributed.
4 *Vehicles.* The number of vehicles required will increase with the number of warehouses; as vehicle size increases the product unit operating cost will

THE DISTRIBUTION SYSTEM

reduce, while different vehicle types will be required for different products or routes.

1:4 DISTRIBUTION OPERATIONS

Operations are of two kinds in distribution, those relating to the physical movement of products, or the transmission of information for the purpose of control. Planning the movement of products includes routing the vehicles; scheduling deliveries in order to provide a satisfactory service; assessing the merits of owning, hiring or contracting vehicles for delivering to customers; and recording all transport costs. The transmission of information is necessary for stock control, processing orders, invoicing customers and controlling operations.

An effective distribution organisation will provide for the coordination of these operations and forecast the future requirements according to predetermined service levels and distribution costs. As a result, there will be lower stock levels, fewer stock-outs or delivery delays, shorter delivery times and a more reliable service to customers.

An analysis of the distribution operations will identify their purpose, increase their effectiveness and reduce their costs. This is most important where objectives conflict, which is quite common in distribution since a better service usually costs more money.

1:5 INFLUENCE OF WAREHOUSING FACTORS ON PLANS

The major objective of warehousing is to provide the "surge capacity" that is needed to overcome fluctuations in supply or demand. When supply equals demand exactly, no storage capacity is required; however, high volume or continuous production is less costly than low volume or batch production and, very often, a warehouse can be justified on these economic grounds only.

Planning the number and locations of warehouses will depend upon the distribution objectives and the different variables of a system. Normally, warehouses will be located in areas of heavy demand, but their number depends upon the total surge capacity required and economic warehouse capacities. The best combination of warehouse number and locations will depend upon the factors that affect the distribution system most, as a whole, including the location of customers, the size of orders, the frequency of deliveries and delivery times.

Strategic plan. This considers the achievement of operating objectives under a range of conditions; it will provide flexibility and give the best chance of success regardless of throughput. The strategic planning of warehousing operations must proceed after analysing the market demand; then the number and locations of warehouses can be decided. The cost of operating a warehouse will be dependent upon the throughput of products and the relationship between costs and throughput of products. The relationship between costs and throughput will be a straight line for most warehouses. The rate of increasing costs will differ with warehouse types and it can be represented by the slope of the throughput line plotted as a graph (see Figure 1:6).

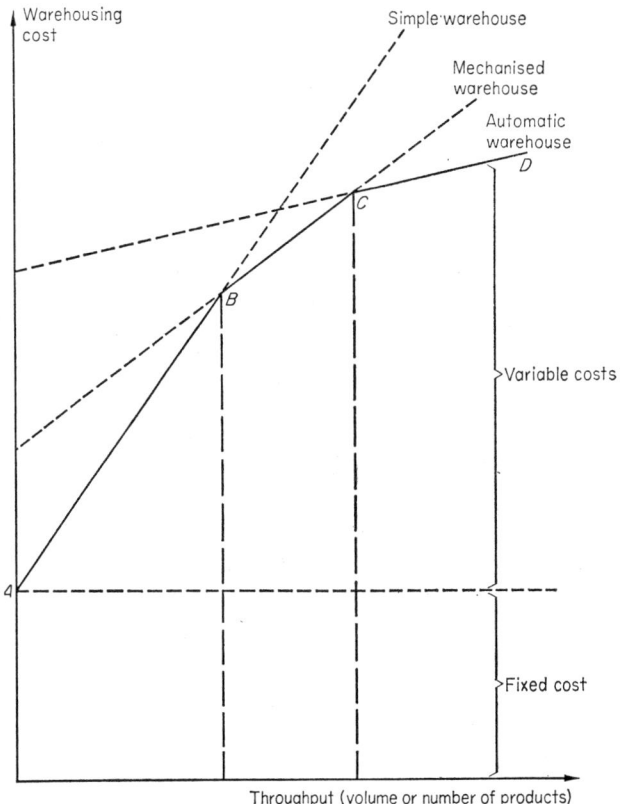

Figure 1:6 RELATIONSHIPS BETWEEN WAREHOUSING COSTS AND THROUGHPUT

Ideal solution. An ideal solution to problems of variable warehouse throughputs is to consider more than one type at each site. The three different warehouse types in the graph (Figure 1:6) are each represented by a straight line, but give a more reasonable simulation of actual costs when shown as the composite line *ABCD*. The operating costs of a warehouse are both fixed

THE DISTRIBUTION SYSTEM

and variable, but they differ with the type of warehouse as shown in the graph. The basic fixed cost is common to them all. The variable costs depend upon the rate of increase with throughput and they vary with warehouse type. The combined costs can be illustrated in the following equation:

$$C = mV + F$$

where
C = total operating costs
m = slope of line (rate of increase)
V = variable costs
F = fixed costs

Simple warehouse. This is suitable for small throughputs of products and the variable costs are little more than the basic fixed cost initially (point A).

Mechanised warehouse. This has a higher capital cost, but it costs less than a simple warehouse to operate in the middle throughput range (between points B and C).

Automatic warehouse. This is sophisticated and expensive to set up, but it is the most economic to operate when throughput is very high (above point C).

In practice, the same basic fixed cost applies regardless of the number of warehouses of the same type and the variable costs are shared between them.

$$C_n = n\frac{(mV+F)}{n}$$

where
C_n = total cost of n warehouses
   = $n \times$ (mean variable costs + fixed cost)
   = variable costs + $n \times$ fixed cost
That is $C_n = mV + nF$

1:6 WAREHOUSING EXAMPLE

The relationships between costs and throughput of a warehouse for cased goods were plotted on a graph over a period of time and are shown in Figure 1:7. The throughput/cost ratios were representative of a straight line in which:
F = £15 000
m = £0.30 per ft^3 throughput increase

THE DISTRIBUTION SYSTEM

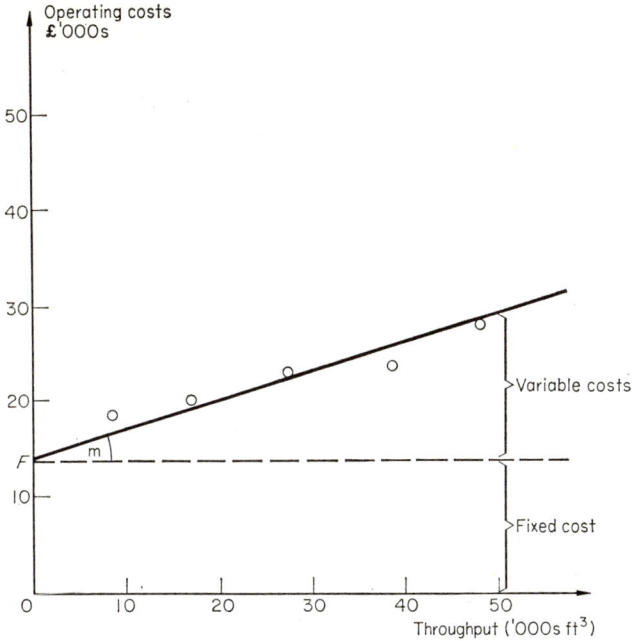

Figure 1:7 THROUGHPUT/COST GRAPH FOR A CASED GOODS WAREHOUSE

The volume of cased goods was expected to increase to 120 000 ft³ over the next ten years and it had to be decided if it was more economic to operate one large warehouse or three of the same size?

Assuming that the capacity of the one warehouse was 40 000ft³ increasing its size three times would affect only variable costs. The total operating costs for one large warehouse could be calculated from the equation:

$C = mV + F$
  $= £0.3 \times 120\ 000\text{ft}^3 \times £15\ 000$
  $= £36\ 000 + £15\ 000$
  $= £51\ 000$

Operating three warehouses of 40 000ft³ capacity would affect the fixed cost too and the total operating costs would be greater.

$C_n = mV + nF$
  $= £0.3 \times 120\ 000\text{ft}^3 + 3 \times £15\ 000$
  $= £36\ 000 + £45\ 000$
  $= £81\ 000$

The choice between one large and three small warehouses would be based upon the most economic operation, with reference to both warehousing and delivering costs. Increasing the number of warehouses would reduce the cost of making local deliveries; in this example, the savings from reduced delivery costs would have to exceed £30 000 in order to justify three warehouses instead of one. Trunking costs would depend upon the distances between warehouses and the supply point, but they were likely to increase; consequently, the savings from local deliveries would have to be even greater.

Generally speaking, the number of warehouses affects local delivery costs and the location of warehouses affects trunking costs. When deciding the number and locations of warehouses, it is necessary to compare all the costs of alternative configurations and then to choose the least costly.

1:7 INFLUENCE OF DELIVERING ON DISTRIBUTION PLANNING

The major objective of a delivery system is to transport goods from the point of supply to the locations of demand. The supply point may be a factory warehouse when delivering will be direct to customers; or it may be from a central warehouse, or a number of regional depots. Planning a distribution system will depend upon the overall objective and normally this will be to provide a certain level of service to customers; therefore, plans must start with the customers.

Customer research will determine the number and locations of customers, the sizes and frequencies of their orders and the delivery lead times expected. The distances between factory and customer locations determine the need for intermediate warehouses; transport times are fairly constant since the maximum driving hours are fixed by law at ten hours in any twenty-four. Also goods vehicles are limited by Trade Union rules to an average speed of 28 mile/hr (45km/hr) on open roads and 22 mile/hr (35km/hr) in built-up areas.

Simplest delivery system. This is direct from a factory warehouse to customers and it will be feasible if their distance apart is less than ten times the permitted average speed. On open roads and allowing for return trips in the same day, the maximum distance between the supply and delivery points will be:

$$\frac{10\text{hrs} \times 28 \text{ mph } (45\text{km/hr})}{2} = 140 \text{ miles } (225\text{km})$$

The size of vehicles to be operated will depend upon the volume of goods to be delivered to an area. The unit cost of delivering goods is least for large vehicles which are recommended wherever possible. The maximum feasible distance to and from an area will reduce as the number of customer drops per journey increases; each drop will involve an unloading time, while each additional drop will entail an extra transport distance, both of which reduce the time available for driving to and from the area.

Number of vehicles required. This will depend upon the customer order frequencies expected and the length of the delivery cycle. When the order frequency of a product is daily, one vehicle journey will be required for each demand load. But when the frequency is once every two days, one vehicle journey will be required for every two demand loads, or one every second day.

It is impossible to devise a simple formula for solving problems that involve different numbers and sizes of warehouse or delivery vehicles, because so many variables will apply that there will be countless alternative solutions. However, a systematic method for solving problems will ensure that all the steps are logical and it will prevent any important factors being overlooked.

1:8 DISTRIBUTION PLANNING PRINCIPLES

The purpose of a distribution system is to move products from the point of manufacture to their market for the least cost consistent with providing good service.

Distribution systems

The character of the products and the geographical area served will determine the type and size of the distribution system. Different systems range from direct distribution to complex multi-purpose systems. The simplest example is hardly a system at all; for instance, supplying large expensive items like ships or power generators. On the other hand, consumer goods have small value but large volume and distributing them represents a major part of their total cost. The different types of system are numerous and some idea of the range is shown in Figure 1:8.

Basic components

Basically, the products for distribution are either static in warehouses, or mobile during delivery. Most systems start with a central warehouse that is associated with the place of manufacture; the end is at the market. Between the factory and the market there are depots, delivery vehicles and distribution routines.

THE DISTRIBUTION SYSTEM

Type of business	Normal level of service required by customers	Components needed						Cost of system
		Factory	Central warehouse	Depot	Transit depot	Wholesaler	Retailer	
Heavy engineering	Make to order	✓						No system
Small components	Batches to order	✓	✓					Small cost
Instruments or tools	Available from stock	✓	✓	✓				Moderate cost
Domestic hardware	Available from stock	✓	✓	✓	✓	✓	✓	Moderate cost
Canned foods	Regular deliveries			✓	✓	✓	✓	Moderately high
Perishables	Daily delivery	✓						High
Electricity	Instantaneous	✓						Very high

Figure 1:8 DIFFERENT TYPES OF DISTRIBUTION SYSTEM

THE DISTRIBUTION SYSTEM

The choice of system depends upon a number of factors including the following:

1. The types of product
2. The range and volume of products
3. The geographic spread
4. The level of service expected
5. The number and types of customer
6. The relative costs
7. The finance available for investment

Distribution performance

The performance of a distribution system depends upon two things, the service level and the operating cost. The type of product and the time for delivering it determines the service level. A long wait is normal before a ship is delivered, but not a cauliflower.

One measure of distribution performance is the analysis of the average and greatest length of time that elapses between an order being placed and the goods being received. Relatively speaking, the shorter the lead time the greater the cost of distribution.

The general relationship between speed of delivery and its cost is given in Figure 1:8. Beyond a certain point, the extra cost of improving service increases disproportionately.

Improving the distribution service

The structure of a system is important when determining the quality of service that it provides. Some examples are illustrated in the next few paragraphs showing the different ways that service levels can be improved.

1 *Direct delivery from factory to customer.* Stocks will need to be held in a warehouse near the factory and frequent deliveries made to the whole market. Speedy deliveries and widespread delivery areas are characteristic of this type of distribution; consequently, delivery costs will be high and warehousing costs low.

2 *Trunking delivery to warehouses.* This is a more practical arrangement when distribution areas are large in terms of area or volume of goods. It is cheaper to operate than direct delivery and it is suitable for a wide range of non-perishable consumer goods.

3 *Local delivery to retail outlets.* Depot costs are more expensive, but the opportunities for providing regular deliveries and ready availability of goods are excellent. It is suitable for distributing a diverse range of spare parts or staple consumer goods. A variation to this system includes transit depot facilities, or a combination of the local sales office with the depot.

THE DISTRIBUTION SYSTEM

4 *Intermittent deliveries to the public.* National forms of public delivery service include the post office, railways and national carriers. They are valuable for serving sparsely populated areas, because their costs are balanced economically over the whole country or subsidised by the government.

5 *Continuous delivery direct to customers.* The ultimate in distribution service is provided by the public utilities such as water, gas and electricity companies. However, the nature of these services underlines the reason for nationalisation.

It is usual to combine more than one of the methods into a specific distribution system so that it can take into account the variety of characteristics that occur in practice. Also, it is common to find that different service levels have to be provided by the same system.

Analysing distribution

The design of a distribution system must start with the consumer needs and they can be analysed into three broad production categories:

1   Group manufacture of a wide range of products
2   Group manufacture of a narrow range of products
3   Sole manufacture of a single product

In the first category, the main problem is to decide which distribution facilities can be made common to all factories or to all products. There are limits to the extent that distribution can be standardised, but sharing warehouses and vehicles is possible in many cases.

In the second category, a unified distribution system is essential for reducing costs. Characteristically, a narrow range of products can be manufactured at any of the factories in a group and they will be sited in direct relationship to the markets that they serve. Examples include cigarette manufacture, newspaper publishing and brewing. The choice of product manufacture will be integral with decisions regarding the design of the distribution system.

Generally speaking, single product factories need a specific distribution system designed for the product manufactured. The factory site is often dictated by the source of raw materials or tradition, rather than the location of the market.

Production considerations. Production costs are least when the factory is sited near the raw materials, because of reduced transport costs. Continuous or large batch production is less costly from the manufacturing viewpoint, but more expensive from the point of inventory carrying. It is important to

THE DISTRIBUTION SYSTEM

design both the production and distribution systems at the time in order to optimise costs and savings.

Marketing considerations. An efficient distribution system is necessary for promoting more sales and there must be a mutual design bond between the marketing and distribution systems too. The distribution manager must be prepared for increased market demand which can result from the efficiency of his organisation. Unfortunately, sales promotion campaigns are mounted without his cooperation. Sometimes, therefore, the results will be detrimental to marketing as well as distribution.

Planning a distribution system must be a joint venture that considers the overall needs rather than individual needs alone. In this way production and marketing needs can be satisfied optimally. The design of a distribution system must be treated as part of the company policies, then planning will be unbiased. Policies must be established before planning integral systems within the company, because they determine the relative importances of the systems.

Long-term planning

After establishing the company policies, long-term plans for distribution can be made. Factors that must be considered include the number and range of products to be handled; the distribution area to be covered; the structure of the system; and the forecasts of demand for the life of the system.

Long-term planning has to provide answers to questions concerning the type of system to be operated, the sites for supply points, the allocation of manufacturing plants to factories and goods to warehouses. Provisions have to be made for supplying remote areas and small market demands, for determining the stocks to be held and for delivering to customers in the appropriate manner.

The plans must be adaptable in order to cope with long-term contingencies such as the effects of changing production volumes, merging production lines together or enlarging distribution areas to include exports.

Short-term planning

The near future will be considered in short-term plans. A detailed examination of operations over the length of a cycle, a season or a year comes under the heading of short-term planning. This examination must consider the questions of stocks to be held at each depot, the frequency of deliveries along each route, the layout and handling equipment for each warehouse or the schedules for each vehicle. Contingencies that have to be overcome

THE DISTRIBUTION SYSTEM

include changes in vehicle operating legislation, new types of transportation and the effects of bad weather, strikes or breakdowns.

Designing a distribution system

A systematic approach is essential for coping with the large number of factors and the variety of principles that affect distribution. The design of a system can be thought of in four stages, as follows:

1   The policy-making stage
2   The long-term planning stage
3   The short-term planning stage
4   The controlling stage

Policy making is the province of directors and general management, since it covers the overall plan for distribution. Policies must be based upon sound forecasts for the whole company and they will be economic in the main. A distribution system requires great flexibility in order to be economic.

Long-term planning has to start with the concept that there are many different types of system that can be implemented and the first task will be to decide the feasible ones. The only systematic way of exploring the alternatives available is to find the most flexible and least costly system for the circumstances. Then an operational model can be designed on paper for comparing the effects of different factors, the costs and the ultimate performance.

The short-term planning stage develops from the long-term planning stage which determined the operating restrictions to the system. For example, fixing the sites and sizes of depots will restrict the choice of warehouse layout or vehicle turnround time.

Finally, day-to-day control procedures have to be designed and installed according to the restrictions laid down by both the long- and short-term plans. Most transport managers are concerned with controlling daily routines and their efforts will be most effective if the plans have been made according to their operating resources.

1:9 A SYSTEMATIC METHOD OF DISTRIBUTION RESOURCES PLANNING (Figure 1:9)

1   Forecast *market demands* for the planning period under consideration and set the *distribution objectives*
2   Calculate the *production capacities* available at *factories*
3   Decide the *production facilities* required in order to meet the *total market demand*

THE DISTRIBUTION SYSTEM

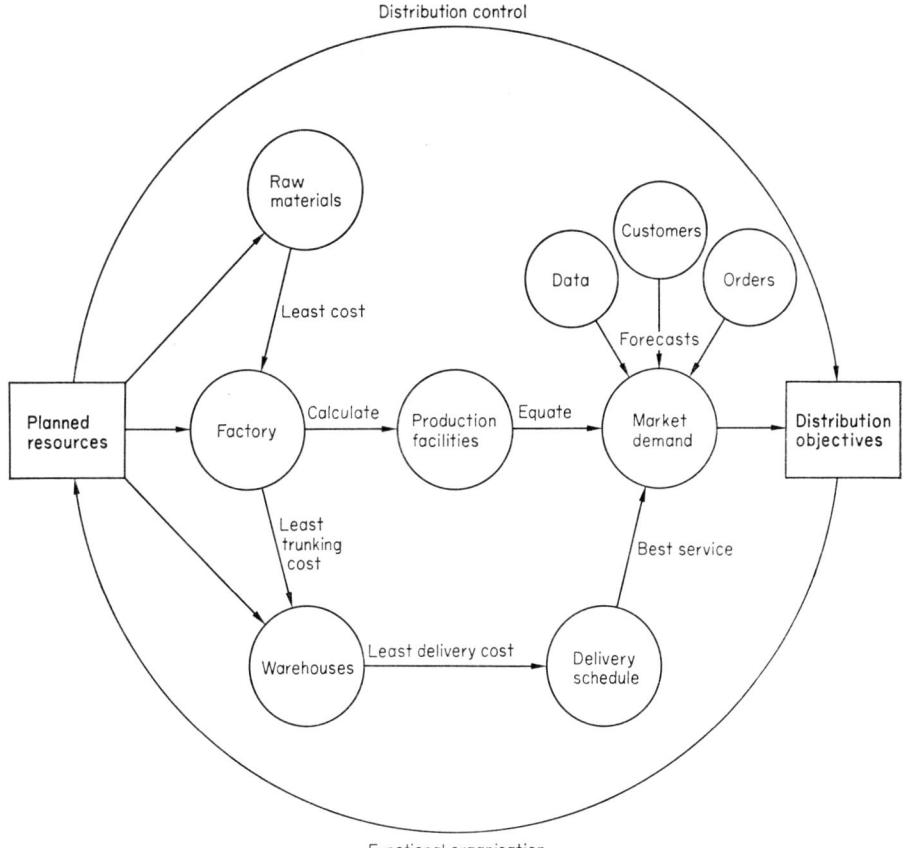

Figure 1:9 SCHEMATIC DISTRIBUTION RESOURCES PLANNING

4 Site the *factories* near to the sources of raw materials or locations of demand so that *overall delivery costs* will be minimal
5 Develop the *demand data* in terms of number and locations of *customers*, sizes and frequencies of *orders* and delivery lead times
6 Decide the *warehousing* requirements and site the *warehouses*
7 Determine the need for *trunking* and decide the *vehicles* and *routes* required if it is necessary
8 Determine the *vehicles* and *routes* needed for *local deliveries* to customers
9 Prepare *delivery schedules* for the vehicles
10 Analyse the *functional distribution* requirements and structure a *management organisation* for the distribution system

THE DISTRIBUTION SYSTEM

11 Decide the *control* procedures needed for the system in order to satisfy *customers*
12 Implement the *planned resources* and operate the system according to *strategic plans* for achieving the *distribution objectives*

2 STRATEGIC PLANNING FOR DISTRIBUTION

The first stage of planning a distribution system is to define the system in broad outline so that strategies for the overall plan can be developed. This outline must consider both the present conditions and the expected future trends. Future trends will be approximate until confirmed, but incorporating them will suggest the best general strategies to be employed.

A strategic plan must be flexible so that it can allow for a considerable variation in operating characteristics from the original specification. It is in this area of operations that scientific planning can be of great value for deciding the most suitable strategy.

2:1 NEED FOR STRATEGIC PLANNING

Distribution is a dynamic function because it is affected by environmental factors. Quite often, these factors are out of the control of the persons responsible for distribution, yet plans must consider any likely effects they may have on distribution. Strategic planning is designed to take these effects into account.

The first condition of an effective plan is that the overall objective has been defined in terms that describe the general requirements. These terms must have been discussed in detail by all the people concerned. The overall objective will form the framework for developing the strategic plans.

The variable factors that affect a distribution system include consumer attitudes and preferences, competitive activities, market legislation, new products development and traffic regulations. Some of these factors are predictable but some are not; however, strategic planning must consider both as far as possible.

In broad outline, strategic plans for distribution must allow for future changes, both internally and externally. A plan is an operational model of the distribution system and it can be tested or modified according to results. Such a model will prevent "trial and error" from becoming "trial and disaster." Mathematical models of a system can be manipulated over a wide range of conditions, but expressing them graphically will make them more easily understood.

Strategic planning graphs

The use of graphs in strategic planning for distribution can be illustrated by the decision that faced a pottery manager. He had to choose between two types of warehouse for storing chinaware. The more suitable warehouse for normal conditions, called type A, had lower operating costs for the normal throughput, but its costs increased when the throughput rose or fell. The alternative warehouse, type B, was more expensive to operate under normal conditions, but its operating costs were fairly constant. Plotting operating costs against different throughputs for the two warehouses is shown by the graph in Figure 2:1.

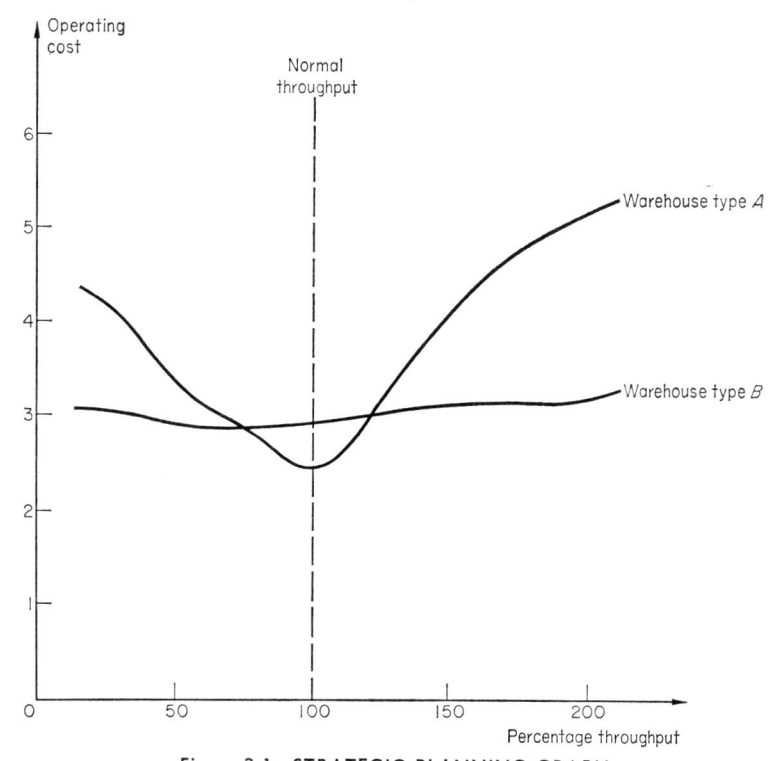

Figure 2:1 STRATEGIC PLANNING GRAPH

Warehouse type A would be the least costly to operate under normal conditions although it could prove to be more costly in the long run if the market fluctuated. The manager would have chosen type A if the market demand for chinaware had been steady; for example, with a contract for a fixed length of time. However, chinaware was sold on the open market and throughputs were influenced by its vagaries. Under these conditions, warehouse type B would be nearly as economic to operate under fluctuatng conditions as with a steady throughput. This was the criterion for effective strategic planning, in this case. With the aid of the strategic planning graph (Figure 2:1), the pottery manager decided in favour of warehouse type B.

When a plan is able to cope with the wide variations in throughput that are typical of most distribution systems, it is called a "robust" one. A suitable test for robustness includes calculating the operating costs for twice the throughput and half the throughput. If the variation in costs for the differing throughputs is marginal, the plan may be regarded as being robust or effective for a dynamic situation.

2:2 SCALE OF PLANNING

An effective strategic plan must have a broad base, because it will be the foundation of future operations. The plan will be the proposal for performing the operations and it must be specific. On the other hand, strategic planning must be general too, because it helps to develop the overall scale of activity.

Naturally, strategic decisions have to be made at a higher level of management than tactical ones. In order to distinguish between strategic and tactical decisions, it is necessary to establish their effects on the framework of the system. The scale of planning is difficult to explain without an illustration, and a suitable one concerning distribution is planning vehicle routes. Strategic decisions will concern the number and sizes of vehicles to be operated, but tactical decisions will concern the selection of drivers or suppliers of fuel. The type of vehicles will form a major branch of the routing framework, but the drivers and fuel suppliers will be minor ones. Consequently, decisions concerning the strategic vehicle policy must come before decisions concerning the tactical operations.

Planning is like the root system of a tree, it keeps the whole structure firmly in the ground at one place, yet it branches out continually to cover a wide area. The terminal roots are very small, but they combine into feeder roots that carry water and nutrients back to the large trunk. Collectively, the roots are an effective system for maintaining the whole tree. In the same way, plans for the tactics used at workplaces evolve from wider operational tactics which are developed successively from implementation strategies, operating strategies and the policies for the complete system. This scale of planning is presented diagrammatically in Figure 2:2.

STRATEGIC PLANNING FOR DISTRIBUTION

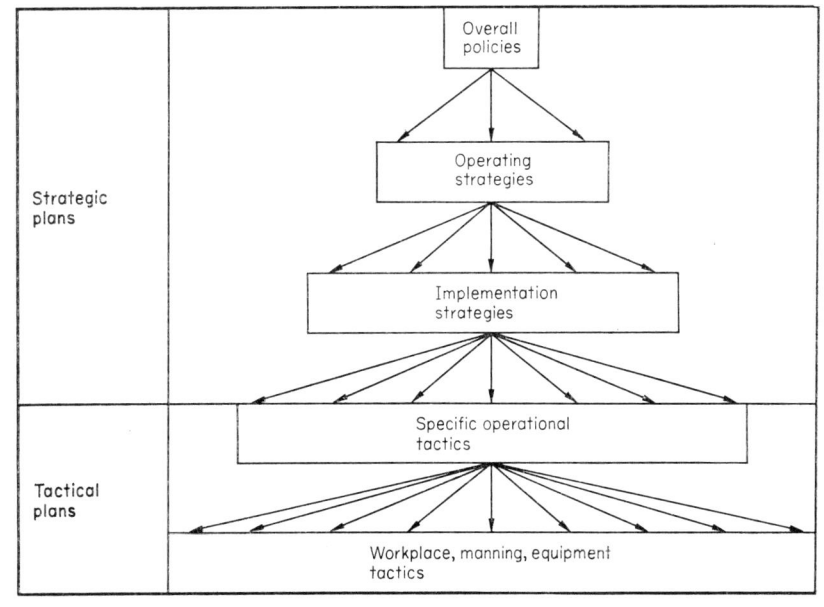

Figure 2:2 SCALE OF PLANNING

2:3 OBJECTIVES OF STRATEGIC PLANNING

Every plan is initiated by the ideas of somebody. Ideas are unique to thinking persons, but shaping them into plans starts with communication, followed by the use of authority for implementing them. Good plans are products of intelligent ideas which commenced as objectives for performing activities.

A plan is imprecise because it is a forecast of the future and its effectiveness cannot be measured in advance with absolute certainty.

Objectives are the yardsticks for measuring success and they will be general for strategies, but specific for tactics. The general objectives for distribution consider the system as a whole, but they will be subdivided as the system is broken down into smaller systems and finally into operations. When this principle is properly understood, managers are in a position to realise the far-reaching effects that their plans will have on individuals. Objectives of strategic planning for distribution are five, fundamentally.

Distribution objectives

1   To provide the service required by customers, of delivering the right number of goods, to the right place, at the right time

STRATEGIC PLANNING FOR DISTRIBUTION

2 To minimise the costs of the complete system while providing the service level desired
3 To comply with the overall policies of the company
4 To make the best use of the resources that are available and to keep investments at a reasonable level
5 To plan for future developments and to control the system so that it provides the maximum service for the minimum cost

2:4 FUTURE OF DISTRIBUTION

The future can be predicted with varying degrees of success depending upon the preciseness of objectives and the probability of events. It is the responsibility of planners to prepare for the future and the success of their efforts will be a measure of the accuracy of their forecasts. Forecasts must be used as a basis for planning. The accuracy of forecasting is improved by discovering the trends that are relevant to the planning period in question.

Statistical methods can be used for processing numerical data in order to extract the meaning and to develop trends. A working knowledge of elementary statistics should be the aim of every manager, because plans will be more effective if they are built up on a predetermined foundation. Statistics try to show the reliability of facts, the order of importance and the validity of forecasts. For the purpose of planning, facts can be expressed as statistical diagrams which are visual aids for presenting information economically and effectively. There can be dangers to using diagrams indiscriminately, because the scale of a graph can cause people to draw the wrong conclusions. Bar chart graphs are specific to activities and their impact can be direct and striking. The most flexible form of graph uses a semi-log scale which illustrates rates of change effectively. A table of numerical facts will be precise for particular conditions, but a graph will give a clearer overall picture by discounting unusual results and smoothing out minor fluctuations.

The usefulness of a bar chart is indicated by Figure 2:4 which represents the throughput of goods at a wholesale warehouse. The graph describes the daily volume for a period of one week and it shows certain trends which are valuable from the planning viewpoint. There are two classes of goods, stock items and luxury items; the daily volume of the former is fairly stable but the luxury items have a peak in mid-week.

Ratios can be useful planning tools and the graph (Figure 2:3) illustrates them too. The ratio of luxury items to stock items will help when planning the resources needed, while the ratio of the end-of-week to mid-week requirements will suggest their weekly distribution. Variations in resource needs can be compared on a daily or weekly basis, also by class of items, with such a bar chart.

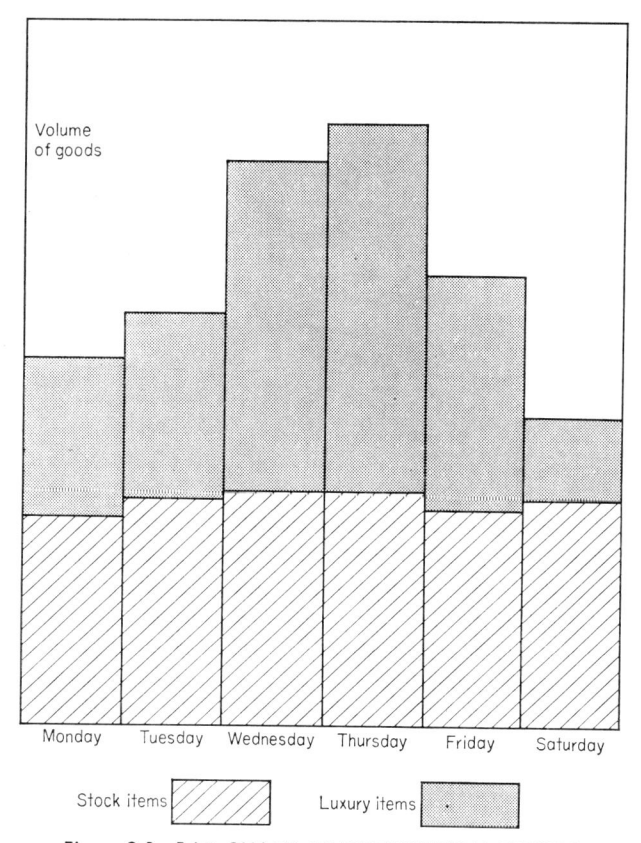

Figure 2:3 BAR CHART OF DISTRIBUTION TRENDS

Strategic plans for distribution. Must take into account both national and international trends, market and economic fluctuations and the latest developments in distribution, marketing and production techniques. The future of distribution depends upon the level of service that will be required and the costs of providing it. Progress in science and technology influence distribution plans and emphasis needs to be placed on standardisation, improved reliability, computerisation, automation and containerisation for a successful system.

Economic factors

Optimal distribution plans are ones that provide the desired service level for the least cost. Distribution costs must be kept as low as possible, because all operations add to the cost of products distributed. In general terms, increasing the number of warehouses or vehicles in a system increases the operating costs; however, the unit cost of items distributed can be reduced by increasing the throughput. Many economic factors affect distribution and it is necessary to balance the costs that rise with increasing throughputs with those that fall. An optimal solution will be the least costly balance that provides the service level desired.

Transport costs

The costs of operating vehicles include standing costs, running costs and overheads. Standing costs are incurred whether a vehicle is delivering goods or not, because they include depreciation, insurance and licences. Running costs vary with the mileage travelled and they are more easily calculated for each vehicle journey; they include fuel, lubricants, tyres, maintenance, wages and sundries. Overheads are incidental to operating vehicles, being such items as the cost of premises, parking areas, supervision and ancillary equipment.

Planning vehicle operations requires factual costs which can be obtained most readily from transport records. Journeys should be measured in monetary terms instead of road distances for economic planning purposes. On long journeys, it is more important to achieve maximum load utilisation than to worry about the least turnround time, while on short journeys, unloading time becomes a larger part of the overall time. Trunking is an example of long journeys, when vehicles should be fully loaded at the start in order to spread the transport costs over a larger number of items. The opposite situation is the case with local deliveries, when it is more important to reduce unloading times than to insist on full loads.

Balancing distribution costs

Fundamentally, the total cost of distribution can be related to warehousing and to delivering, but they are interdependent and the costs of one affect the costs of the other. Usually, increasing the number of warehouses increases the number of vehicles required, but it reduces the vehicle sizes and the average journey length. Optimal solutions must be those that ensure the least overall cost, by balancing the costs of warehousing against the costs of delivering.

Several combinations of warehouses and vehicles are feasible for a distribution system; the simplest combination involves one central warehouse only for delivering directly to customers. Optimally, the central warehouse will be sited at the "centre of demand-cost" for a distribution region. For national distribution in Great Britain the centre of demand will be London in most systems, but it can be found for any system by computing the

STRATEGIC PLANNING FOR DISTRIBUTION

coordinates for customer locations in terms of volume and cost or distance from the supply point.

2:5 COORDINATED CENTRES OF DEMAND

Map coordinates of demand locations can be weighted according to their throughputs in order to find the most strategic site of a supply point for distribution. Ideally, actual transportation costs or distances give a better solution than coordinates, but more work is involved and may be difficult to justify. Generally speaking, for large distribution regions, an approximate site is all that is needed; then studying the local delivery system will help to locate the best supply point more precisely.

Case study

An American manufacturer of automobiles decided that an assembly plant should be set up for distributing automobiles to Western Europe by ship and by rail or road transporters. There was a European distribution network available that comprised twelve distributors, but it was necessary to determine the most strategic site for the assembly plant. Coordinates were used to find the centre of demand-cost for Western Europe, commencing with a scale map of the distribution region (Figure 2:4) that gave the locations of the twelve automobile distributors.

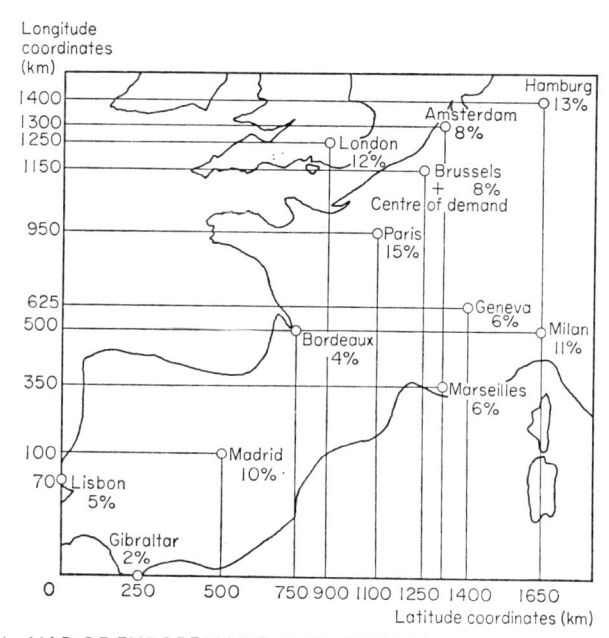

Figure 2:4 MAP OF EUROPEAN DEMAND COORDINATES FOR AUTOMOBILES

STRATEGIC PLANNING FOR DISTRIBUTION

Coordinates at right angles to one another can fix the location of a point when they are measured as the distance from an axis. The map shown in Figure 2:4 has a vertical (or longitudinal) axis passing through a datum point at Lisbon and a horizontal (or latitudinal) axis that passes through Gibraltar. For each demand location, the longitudinal coordinate is measured in kilometres east of the axis through Lisbon and its latitudinal coordinate is measured in kilometres north of the axis through Gibraltar. The demand for automobiles at each location is expressed as a percentage of the total sales forecast for Western Europe.

The next step was to prepare a table of the coordinates (as demand percentage–kilometres) for the distributor locations in order to find the mean distribution coordinate along each axis. The tables in Figures 2:5 and 2:6 give the percentage demand and distance along the axis for each location and the mean distribution coordinates occur at points along the axes that correspond to half the total accumulated percentage–kilometres for each axis.

The accumulated total of latitudinal coordinates was 112 000 percentage–kilometres. The location of the mean point for 56 000 percentage–kilometres was almost on the latitudinal coordinate for Amsterdam, 1300 kilometres east of the vertical axis. In the longitudinal direction, the accumulated total was 75 500 percentage–kilometres which gave a mean value of 37 650 percentage–kilometres. The location of this point was 30 kilometres south of the longitudinal coordinate for Brussels.

Locations	Demand (%)	Latitude coordinates Distance (km)	Latitude coordinates Demand distance	Accumulated total (% km)
Lisbon	5	0	0	0
Gibraltar	2	250	500	500
Madrid	10	500	5 000	5 500
Bordeaux	4	750	3 000	8 500
London	12	900	10 800	19 300
Paris	15	1 100	16 500	35 800
Brussels	8	1 250	10 000	45 800
Amsterdam	8	1 300	10 400	56 200
Marseilles	6	1 300	7 800	64 000
Geneva	6	1 400	8 400	72 400
Hamburg	13	1 650	21 450	93 850
Milan	11	1 650	18 150	112 000

Figure 2:5 TABLE OF LATITUDINAL COORDINATES

STRATEGIC PLANNING FOR DISTRIBUTION

Locations	Demand (%)	Longitude coordinates Distance (km)	Demand distance	Accumulated total (% km)
Gibraltar	2	0	0	0
Lisbon	5	70	350	350
Madrid	10	100	1 000	1 350
Marseilles	6	350	2 100	3 450
Bordeaux	4	500	2 000	5 450
Milan	11	500	5 500	10 950
Geneva	6	625	3 750	14 700
Paris	15	950	14 250	28 950
Brussels	8	1 150	9 200	38 150
London	12	1 250	18 750	46 900
Amsterdam	8	1 300	10 400	57 300
Hamburg	13	1 400	18 200	75 500

Figure 2:6 TABLE OF LONGITUDINAL COORDINATES

The centre of demand-cost for distributing automobiles to Western Europe in this case study was in Belgium, south east of Brussels, in the vicinity of Liege. The search for a site for the assembly plant would take place in this area.

Siting a supply point according to the demand-cost coordinates for a system assumes that transport costs are directly proportional to distances. In practice, this is incorrect and other factors, like road conditions, physical demand locations and methods of delivery, affect the most economical site.

2:6 PLANNING DELIVERIES

Planning procedures for delivering goods to customers must start with factual information relevant to the delivery objectives. The primary objective is a logistical one and it concerns the delivery of the goods ordered to the correct locations according to the customers' instructions. It will be customers who decide the number of goods, the locations and the times for delivery; therefore, data collection should start at the marketing end of distribution.

Basically, the data to be collected will relate to customers, to conditions for delivering the goods ordered and to restrictions in the system. The basic data required for planning deliveries are listed below:

STRATEGIC PLANNING FOR DISTRIBUTION

1 *Customer data required*
 (a) Number of customers
 (b) Locations of customers
 (c) Size and type of orders
 (d) Frequency and seasonality of orders
 (e) Variety of goods ordered
 (f) Lead times for delivering orders
 (g) Customer drop point information
 (h) Invoicing procedures for customers
2 *Delivery data required*
 (a) Size and type of load
 (b) Number of deliveries
 (c) Frequency of deliveries
 (d) Number of drops for each delivery journey
 (e) Unloading times
 (f) Travelling times
 (g) Methods of delivery
 (h) Types of vehicle and selection procedures
 (i) Vehicle operations
3 *Restrictions of the system*
 (a) Times available for delivering
 (b) Conditions of the delivery routes
 (c) Acceptance of goods procedures
 (d) Methods of delivery
 (e) Vehicle capacities
 (f) Availability of vehicles
 (g) Intelligence of personnel
 (h) Terms of orders

Optimising delivery costs:

By and large, transport costs are proportional to route distances and the size of a load has a marginal effect only. Delivery costs are both fixed and variable, but the former are greater although they have less effect on the overall efficiency. Delivering involves two types of transportation:

1 Trunking in bulk from supply points
2 Local deliveries to customers

With trunking, time utilisation is the most important factor when optimising delivery costs, but cost per unit delivered will be smallest for large loads. In the case of local deliveries, distance is the most important factor because it is a realistic measure of delivery costs.

When delivering goods with road vehicles, the greatest efficiency in terms of unit-load cost is obtained with large vehicles and it is always advisable to start by considering the largest size of vehicle that is acceptable.

The unit-load cost increases directly with distance and the size of vehicle; therefore operating efficiencies are greatest when the customer drops are concentrated into small areas. Driving time in relation to the total delivering time is reduced when the size of drops is large. Also tight schedules for local deliveries will reduce delivery costs.

Trunking costs depend upon the delivery distances and the sizes of load. The costs of trunking goods to warehouses must be offset by the savings from manufacturing in quantity. Containerisation plays an important role in strategic planning for distribution, because it allows trunking to be more flexible. Containers can travel by road, rail, air or sea and they can be used as transit depots too.

Local delivery costs are reduced when the density of customers is great, because of the dual advantages of requiring less driving time and providing more frequent delivery service. When the number of vehicles at a depot is large, better maintenance can be provided with more efficient equipment, better supervision and wider technical skills. The number of depots needed for local deliveries will depend upon the lead time for orders related to the delivery time and order size. Frequency of ordering will determine the number and types of vehicle to be operated.

Strategic planning in practice

The best time to save money is before it is spent and strategic planning must aim at providing a good service to the customers as economically as possible. Comparing alternative strategies for this purpose will help to decide the most effective system. There are different strategies for every distribution system and recognising them in order to decide the best is something that can be done only by the people concerned.

Benefits of strategic planning

Strategic planning for distribution will supply the answers to many questions concerning the goods to be distributed, the methods of distributing them, the resources that will be used and the efficiency of the system. The procedure converges and diverges with each question and answer as suggested by the schematic diagram in Figure 2:7.

In ideal circumstances, all customers will receive satisfactory service and promises will be never broken, while factories will operate efficiently and there will be an economic balance between the costs of production/distribution and the incomes from marketing.

STRATEGIC PLANNING FOR DISTRIBUTION

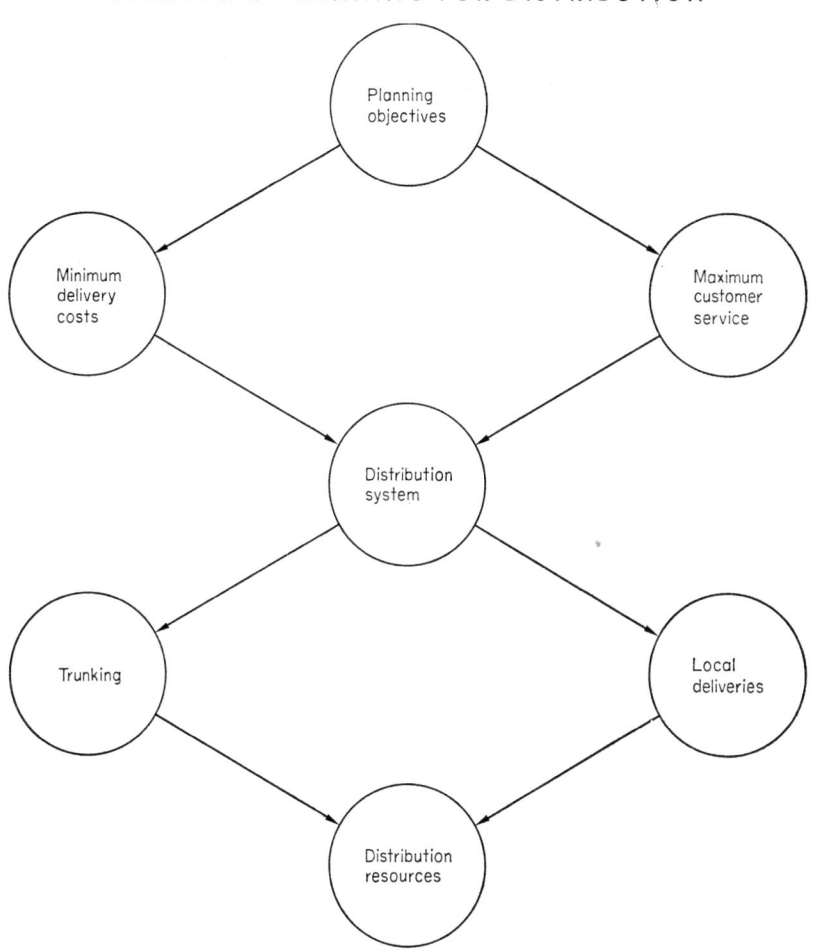

Figure 2:7 STRATEGIC PLANNING FOR DISTRIBUTION

2:7 SYNTHETIC PLANNING STANDARDS

Standard times for planning distribution operations can be prepared synthetically after all the work elements involved have been studied and timed. Every work activity is composed of smaller work elements and if the times for performing them are known, the synthetic time for the whole activity can be obtained by summing the times for all the component elements. In this way, times for doing jobs of work can be estimated quite accurately without the bother of observing them.

Synthetic times are convenient for comparing different activities, methods or systems at the planning stage. The use of synthetic times will be illustrated with an example of handling palletised goods with forklift trucks in a warehouse.

Truck handling times

Three different types of forklift truck were compared in order to choose the most suitable for moving pallet loads from the store and loading them into vehicles. The total time for handling one pallet was built up from the individual times for work elements. The elemental times were obtained from different studies in the warehouse.

Comparing fork-lift trucks. The three trucks for handling goods on wooden pallets were all powered by electric batteries, but their costs differed according to the type of control.

1 *Rider truck.* An expensive, fully automated truck with provision for a riding operator who had foot and hand controls.
2 *Steer truck.* An intermediary type of truck with a pedestrian operator who could stand and ride when a hinged platform was dropped at the rear. Hand controls.
3 *Pallet truck.* A simple, hand-operated truck with a pedestrian operator.

A summary of the movement times for these trucks is presented in Figure

Type of fork-lift truck	Movement in the storage area		Movement from store to vehicle	
	min/pallet	min/yd or m	min/pallet	min/yd or m
1 Rider truck (*RT*)	1.02	0.018	1.35	0.018
2 Steer truck (*ST*)	0.43	0.025	0.77	0.025
3 Pallet truck (*PT*)	0.79	0.027	1.08	0.027

Figure 2:8 TRUCK MOVEMENT AVERAGE TIMES

STRATEGIC PLANNING FOR DISTRIBUTION

2:8. The trucks are compared in terms of the minutes for loading a pallet and minutes for transporting a pallet 1 yard (1m). Elemental times are shown in Figure 2:9 for the complete activity of loading a pallet in the store, transporting it to a vehicle, unloading the pallet into the vehicle and returning empty for another pallet. As expected, the most expensive truck completed the activity most quickly, but economically the intermediary truck proved most suitable for this particular activity.

The total time for transporting a pallet was the sum of the minutes to load a pallet and the distance moved multiplied by the speed. An example of this calculation is collecting a pallet from the store with a rider truck and loading it into a vehicle 50 yards (metres) away.

Minutes per pallet = 1.35
Transport minutes = 0.018 × 50
  = 0.90
Total time per pallet = 2.25 minutes

Description of movement	Operational minutes RT	ST	PT	Remarks
1 Manoeuvre truck to pallet	0.20	0.07	0.27	Working in the storage area. Times affected by layout of the area and truck handling ability
2 Lift pallet load	0.09	0.05		
3 Remove pallet from stack	0.07	0.05	0.17	
4 Prepare to transport	0.15			
5 Take pallet to the vehicle at the loading bay	0.90	1.25	1.35	Transport distance was 50 yd/m
6 Manoeuvre to unload pallet	0.32	0.14	0.17	Unloading the pallet into a vehicle
7 Lower pallet to floor	0.08	0.08	0.20	
8 Withdraw truck forks	0.07	0.06		
9 Prepare to return to store	0.07			
10 Return empty to the stack of pallets in store	0.72	1.11	1.22	Transport distance was 50 yd/m
Total time per pallet	2.67	2.81	3.38	

Figure 2:9 TRUCK HANDLING AND MOVEMENT TIMES

STRATEGIC PLANNING FOR DISTRIBUTION

Pallet handling times. Work operations with the three fork-lift trucks were studied and standard times were established for each element. These times are tabled in Figure 2:9 and they were used for preparing synthetic times for different methods of handling goods in the warehouse. In this way different flow lines, stacking areas and trucks could be compared.

Additional work elements. In addition to the operational times tabulated, time was needed for issuing instructions to the operator, searching for the correct pallet and other minor jobs. These times have been excluded from the truck handling and movement times, but they are summarised in Figure 2:10.

	Work element	Minutes per occurrence	Remarks
1	Await instructions about goods to be moved	0.63	Times depended upon the degree of understanding and teamwork between the forklift truck operator and helper
2	Discuss schedule with helper	0.28	
3	Locate the goods to be moved	0.42	
4	Decide the goods loading sequence	0.24	
5	Wait for pallet to be cleared for loading on truck	0.10	
6	Check contents of pallet load	0.15	
7	Wait while the pallet is secured in the vehicle	0.24	

Figure 2:10 ADDITIONAL HANDLING TIMES

Schematic procedure

Just as work activities can be broken down into elements, a complete process can be broken down into individual activities and operations. When standard times are available for the elements, work contents of different processes can be compiled and compared for planning purposes. A schematic diagram of the warehousing system is presented in Figure 2:11.

Whenever a new method is devised, it should be analysed into activities and elements so that operational times can be developed. According to the

STRATEGIC PLANNING FOR DISTRIBUTION

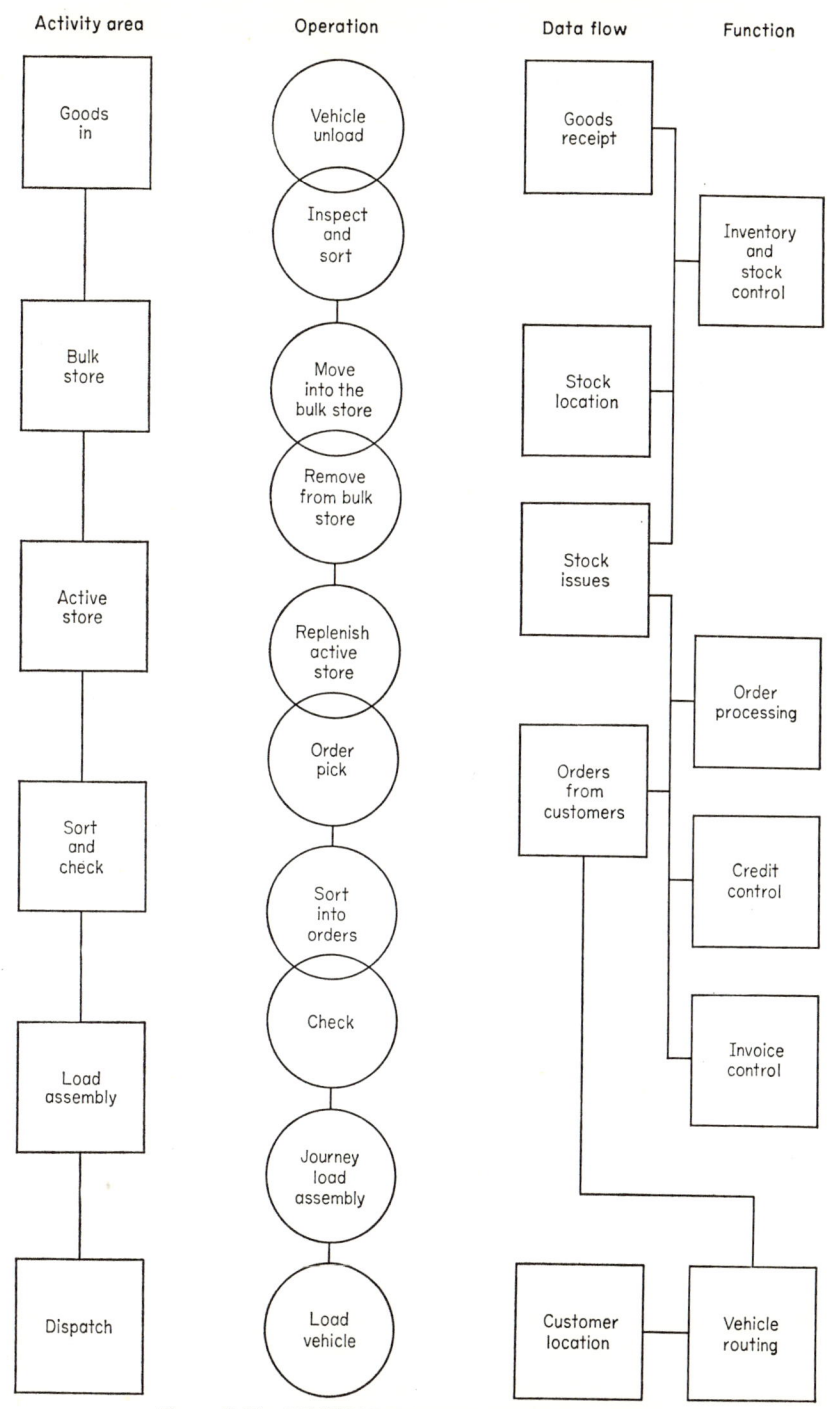

Figure 2:11 SCHEMATIC WAREHOUSING SYSTEM

accuracy of the standard times, the overall work times for a new plan can be synthesised in order to assist decision making.

2:8 BUDGETARY CONTROL IN DISTRIBUTION

Another technique that is suitable for strategic planning is budgetary control. It is very closely associated with standard costing which is similar to standard timing except that it uses costs instead of times. The most effective method of planning is by exercising control over the activities and preparing cost budgets. This combined procedure is called budgetary control which was developed in the United States after the First World War and has become an accepted tool of management all over the world.

A successful plan requires day-to-day control which is a continuing process of measuring the actual results and comparing them with plans.

Preparation of the budget

A budget is an estimation of the expected costs for producing a certain income. Implementing it is rather like spending money before it has been earned. Budgets start with the whole company for a fixed period ahead, usually, a full year. Then budgets can be prepared for individual departments and operations, so that everyone in the company knows how much his job should cost before he starts working on it.

Preparation starts with an analysis of all the cost elements that will be incurred in order to produce the income forecast by the sales department. Company incomes result from sales, but the products have to be made before they can be sold and this needs investment of capital by shareholders.

Sales forecasts can show the expected number of sales over the budgeted period and the income that is expected from them. Preparation of the budget can start when this information has been developed. Estimating production and overhead costs requires sound experience and past records. Trends are useful for estimating future costs and performances and they can be shown by past records or current research. Generally, budgets have to be prepared in working terms; for example, in units of time, volume, weight, sales or cost. In distribution, weight per distance would seem to be a sensible budgetary unit, but few companies consider using it. Nevertheless, some common unit is essential for forecasting and measuring results, so that dissimilar functions can be compared on an equal footing.

Quite often, much useless data is collected without due regard to the total time or cost of preparing budgets. There must be an accepted procedure that prevents time wasting, because budgeting consumes enough time anyway. Budgetary control is a discipline that has to be imposed if it does not develop naturally.

Objectives of budgetary control

Companies continue to exist when they make profits for their owners and an objective of budgetary control is to determine the profits that can be expected over a given period and to see that they are achieved.

Profit is the difference between income and expenditure; therefore, a budget is a profit estimate obtained from the difference of the forecast income and the expected costs. Expected costs include production and the overheads that will be necessary to produce the income. Distribution is an overhead on production.

The distribution manager is responsible for estimating the cost of distributing the number of sales forecast by the marketing department and for controlling the actual costs with those that he forecast. If his cost forecasts were realistic they will have been accepted without change by the general management when they prepared the overall budget.

Controlling budgets requires good cooperation between all staff in a department and this is the responsibility of the manager. He must keep his staff in the picture and solicit their help at all times. Mutual discussions between manager and men lead to successful operations, because everybody feels that they are contributing to the success. This is the essence of teamwork.

A good manager hides nothing from his staff and he gets mutual acceptance whenever changes are necessary. Budgets rarely run their full term without change and it is valuable to compare the actual costs with the budget frequently, in order to reduce the effect of changes. The manager should discuss the budget details with his supervisors and foremen, using tact to exclude any confidential information. Consequently, cooperation has a good chance of developing and the prospect of achieving the budget successfully is bright.

Personal control is the big advantage of budgeting, because the people who helped to forecast the costs for a budget will be responsible for seeing that they are achieved in practice. In this way, the authority attached to a position is related to personal accountability.

3 ANALYSING MARKET DEMAND

A great advantage of analysing market demand from the distribution viewpoint is to discover the levels of service required by customers and to determine the costs of distributing goods to them. Demand analysis aims at searching out and measuring market throughputs, so that management can forecast the volume of sales and distribution needs. Once this is done, the demand can be manipulated according to the resources available.

Forecasting demand
In any company, the demand that is estimated will be the pivot for all planning operations. Successful estimates must be dynamic because they will be tools for guiding decision makers by showing them the probable results from different strategies.

Market research
The basic principles of scientific research are collecting information, analysing it in order to develop strategies and testing these strategies by experimentation. Market research must apply these principles with reference to market demand. A major task of analysing market demand is to find out what the public wants and to determine the value of past service levels in relation to future requirements.

3:1 MARKET DEMAND

The concept of market demand varies with the objectives for analysing it, but here it is being analysed for the purpose of planning a distribution system. The most common marketing factors that determine the demand for a product are its price, its sales promotion and its utility. These factors affect the value of the product and the distribution method. Analysis will improve value, because it is a systematic examination of everything related to a particular objective.

Elasticity of demand
In general, the sensitivity of a market to changes in products or distribution

methods is the elasticity of demand. More precisely, it is the percentage increase or decrease in product demand that results from a marketing change. Conceivably, there may be an expectation elasticity value for each factor that affects the demand for products.

Demand analysis

Demand is a variable factor that is sensitive to the customers, products, costs, times and levels of service in a system. This sensitivity can be measured statistically by correlating the numerical demand for a product with each of these sensitivity factors. The results must be expressed mathematically in order to compare distribution strategies meaningfully.

Correlation analysis. After collecting data concerning the factors that are believed to affect a certain demand, figures for the product sales have to be analysed carefully before and after a particular operational change. The ratio of these figures will be a coefficient of the alteration in demand that results; it will be greater than unity if sales increase after the change, or less than unity if they decrease.

Example of changing demand. A bakery changed the day for delivering prepacked cakes to a seaside resort from Wednesday to Friday and this was believed to be the reason for an increase in demand. Before this change, the mean customer order size was 120 dozens and after it, the mean order size was 150 dozens. The coefficient of demand could be expressed as

$$\frac{150}{120} = 1.25$$

or an increase of 25 per cent in sales due to changing the delivery day.

Similarly, demand coefficients can be calculated for different days of the week or other changes that affect sales, such as type of packing, design of vehicle, or time of the year. Each of these factors will have a coefficient of demand that influences the distribution quantity. An equation can be prepared, for any situation, to include all the factors that affect the demand, in order to plan for the expected sales. The sales expected will be obtained from the original (or normal) quantity multiplied by the demand coefficient for each factor involved successively.

In the bakery example, the normal procedure for distributing to the seaside resort was delivering on Wednesday (coefficient = d), packing the cakes on trays (coefficient = p), using a small general van (coefficient = v) and delivering during the holiday season (coefficient = h). The results from testing alternative procedures are presented as a table in Figure 3:1 and they were used to forecast the expected sales quantity with the aid of correlation analysis.

ANALYSING MARKET DEMAND

Distribution factors that can change	Mean order size (dozens) Pre-change	Mean order size (dozens) Post-change	Coefficient of demand
Delivering on Friday	120	150	$d = 1.25$
Packing in boxes	150	165	$p = 1.10$
Purpose-built van	165	165	$v = 1.00$
Off-season period	165	75	$h = 0.45$

Figure 3:1 TABLE OF DEMAND COEFFICIENTS FOR DISTRIBUTING CAKES

The bakery wanted to know the throughput that could be expected during an off-season period if, the delivery day was Friday, the cakes were packed in cardboard boxes and a purpose-built baker's van was used. The expected throughput (T_E) could be calculated from the correlation equation that included the normal throughput (T_N) and the coefficients (d, p, v and h).

$$\begin{aligned} T_E &= T_N \, (d \times p \times v \times h) \\ &= 120 \, (1.25 \times 1.10 \times 1.00 \times 0.45) \\ &= 120 \times 0.62 \\ &= 75 \text{ dozens} \end{aligned}$$

The throughput to be sold with the new delivery procedure would be 62 per cent that for the normal procedure; it was expected to be 75 dozens of cakes per customer, on average.

Obviously, correlation analysis can be used whenever future trends have to be decided; the expected results from distribution changes will be estimated instead of tested and reliability may suffer slightly as a consequence.

Criteria for good forecasting. There are many ways of guessing future demands, but good forecasts will be most appropriate and effective for given circumstances. An effective forecast must comply with the accuracy desired; it must be feasible so that its achievement can be expected with known certainty; it must be flexible in order to cope with changing conditions; and it must be appropriate to the situation under review.

The value of a good forecast is dependent upon the data available and the method used for preparing it. Value will be improved by comparing

ANALYSING MARKET DEMAND

the actual results with the expected results and there must be a reasonable degree of correlation between them.

Normal demand

The normal demand for a product is the demand that can be expected for a very long time, taking into account all normal circumstances. The difference between the actual and expected results will be a measure of the circumstances. The data used for normal demand calculations must include all known circumstances such as different competitions, changed populations, economic crises or wartime conditions. Normal demand is the most frequent demand that will occur in a market sample, while average demand is the mean for the sample. A little thought will indicate that "normal" is more appropriate than "average," which may be an impractical fraction.

Patterns of demand

The dynamic nature of distribution is reflected by the patterns of demand for products. Patterns refer to the changes in demand with time. Some patterns of demand that can be expected to affect a distribution system are given in Figure 3:2. The slope of a graph will be its coefficient of change; in the trend pattern graph, the mean slope is

$$\frac{800 \text{ tons}}{5 \text{ years}}$$

$= 160$ tons per year rate, of increase, which means that the throughput can be expected to increase annually by 160 tons in this trend. Graphs can be used to show cost patterns as well as demand patterns.

3:2 VALUE ANALYSIS

The value of a distribution system depends upon two conflicting objectives, the quality of service and the cost of operations.

$$\text{Value ratio} = \frac{\text{quality}}{\text{cost}}$$

It is impossible to express quality as a number in order to quantify this ratio; therefore, it must be made equal to unity for comparative purposes by defining it precisely according to the service required. Then the relative value of different distribution systems will be the inverse of their costs and different methods or operations can be compared on equal terms. The value of the distribution function to a company can be improved by increasing the service that it offers or, more usually, by reducing its costs.

Distribution is a fertile field for improving value analytically by examining costs systematically. Changes in value can be compared, relatively, as the inverse of their costs, when quality is unity.

$$\text{value of change} = \frac{\text{new value}}{\text{old value}} = \frac{\text{old cost}}{\text{new cost}}$$

ANALYSING MARKET DEMAND

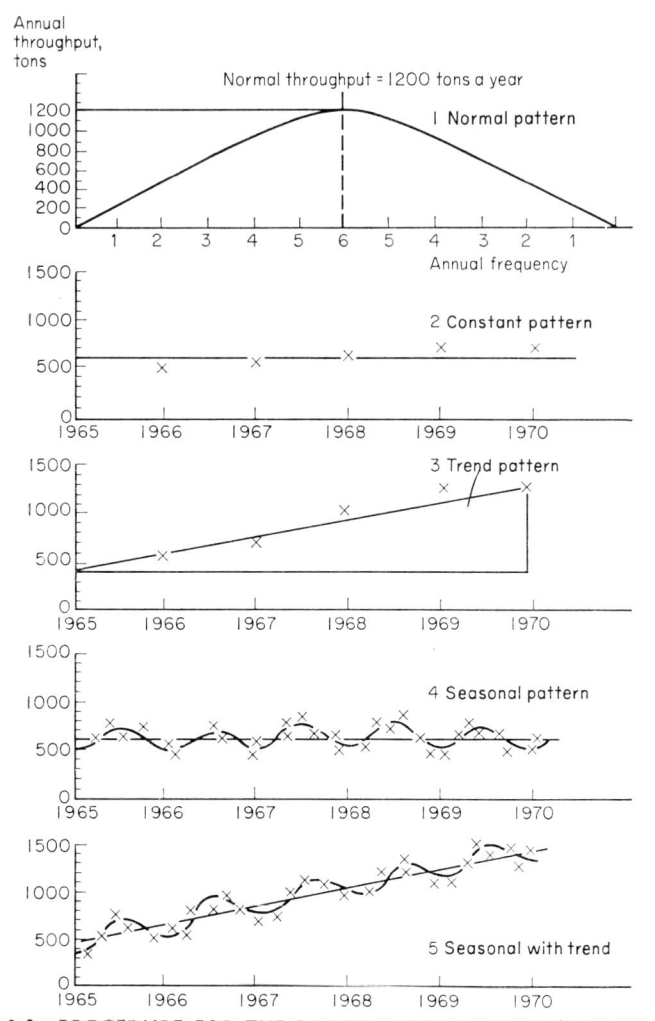

Figure 3:2 PROCEDURE FOR THE DARSIRI METHOD OF VALUE ANALYSIS

This is an age-old concept which will be instinctive to successful distribution managers. Cheap methods can be the best only when they satisfy the service level desired; however, this level must be defined clearly before value can be determined.

Terms of reference for a service quality

In general, a service quality can be defined by five terms of reference and values can be compared only in the same terms:

1 A general description of the service to be given

ANALYSING MARKET DEMAND

2   A detailed specification of the service
3   The functional objective for the service
4   The prestige features of the service
5   The financial worth of the service

In general, these terms of reference can be used in connection with a distribution system, or with any element of the system. They will be illustrated now with reference to a warehouse.

Terms of reference for a warehouse

The value of alternative warehouses can be computed according to their costs only when the service requirements have been clearly defined. The definition, or terms of reference, for a paint storage warehouse may be:

1 *General requirement.* To store paint in cans for distribution to customers
2 *Specific requirements.* To have a storage capacity for 10 000 gallons of paint in 1 pint and 1 gallon cans; to have a floor area of 4000ft^2 on two storeys; to be fitted with racking and to have access lanes for forklift trucks.
3 *Functional requirements.* To accommodate paint in cans on shelves in an organised way that facilitates unloading, effective storage, materials handling and order picking.
4 *Prestige requirement.* The warehouse must be well-lit and ventilated, easy to keep clean and comply with safety regulations.
5 *Financial requirement.* The financial worth of warehousing is negative because it will be a burden on the price of the goods distributed. Financially, the value of this warehouse can be stated as a percentage of the selling price of the paint—that is warehousing costs must not exceed 5 per cent of the selling price of the paint.

Systematic analysis

Performing a systematic analysis of a situation that needs improving, ensures that all the relevant factors will be considered and that the best value will be achieved. The DARSIRI method of value analysis is a systematic method that applies to everything of value. It is based upon method study, correlation analysis and commonsense.

The DARSIRI method has seven stages. When performed in the systematic sequence, the seven stages are certain to improve the value of everything examined. Improvements can be achieved continually until the ultimate in perfection is reached.

Analysing market demand in order to plan a distribution system will improve marketing values by increasing the quality of service given to customers and by decreasing the costs of distribution operations.

The darsiri method of value analysis

The seven logical steps that comprise this method spell the word "darsiri" when they are applied in the correct sequence:

Data collecting will provide facts that can be examined in order to improve value.

Analysing the facts collected will create new ideas for improving value.

Recording these ideas as they are created will be necessary for future references and remembrance.

Speculating on the ideas will suggest different ways for putting them into practice.

Investigating the suggestions will indicate the feasible ones after testing them.

Recommending the best suggestion will be reported to the person with authority for implementation.

Implementing the recommendation with supervision will achieve an improvement in value.

The practice of analysing

It needs commonsense and coordination to put the steps of the DARSIRI method into practice to solve problems. Any analytical project starts by defining the objective, then appointing a team to examine ways of making improvements follows and finally, accepting the responsibility for implementing recommendations will ensure that better value is obtained.

Initiation of a value analysis project requires authority and the person who makes this decision must start by calling a meeting of everybody concerned. The objective of this meeting is to draw up terms of reference and select members for the analysis team. Drawing up the terms of reference involves a great deal of discussion which affords an opportunity of appraising potential team members. The terms of reference must be recorded because they will form the analysis framework.

Choosing the members of an analysis team (or syndicate) is very important; they must be knowledgeable people who are capable of working together and developing good ideas for consideration. In practice, the best size of the team is five people, from different working environments, in order to stimulate one another into new avenues of thinking.

After the initial general meeting, the chosen team must arrange to hold a preliminary meeting of their own. They will need to choose a leader for

ANALYSING MARKET DEMAND

coordinating their efforts and a secretary to record the results. It must be remembered that best results are achieved when all members of the team are treated as equals, no matter what their duties or status in the company. Constructive ideas come from interactions between equal people, but the more their opinions differ the greater the chances of developing universal solutions.

Information is essential for analysis purposes and it must be collected by each team from his own work area in relation to the objective. At the next team meeting, members must analyse the information in order to create new ideas. These ideas must be recorded by the secretary and circulated to members afterwards. Then each member can go away and consider their practical implications so that speculation will be able to develop practical suggestions for improving value.

Each new suggestion must comply with the terms of reference before it can be investigated as a feasible value improver. After investigating all the feasible suggestions, a final meeting of the team will decide which one is the best and it will be recommended for implementation in a report.

The full procedure for the DARSIRI method of value analysis is shown schematically in Figure 3:3.

The DARSIRI method has been applied successfully in most industries and in many parts of the world. It has helped to improve the value of a wide range of products and services by reducing costs or increasing quality. Its success depends upon the intelligence and coordination of the analysis team members, but the very act of putting people together with a common purpose will improve the working atmosphere in any company.

The objective for analysing market demand is to determine the requirements of a distribution system, its functions and its activities. It is a good thing to have a common theme for the purpose of analysis; in the case of distribution it may be the orders from customers. An order is processed through the marketing department in order to prepare manufacturing instructions; then products are made and transferred to the distribution system for delivering to the customers according to their orders. The succession of events and activities is presented in Figure 3:3 as the ordering cycle. Analysis can be used to determine the ordering cycle for a particular distribution system, or it can be used to improve the value of any single element.

3:3 ORDERING CYCLE

Putting the elements of a distribution system into a logical sequence for the ordering cycle will help to decide the areas for making improvements. Data collection starts with orders from customers and analysing develops the

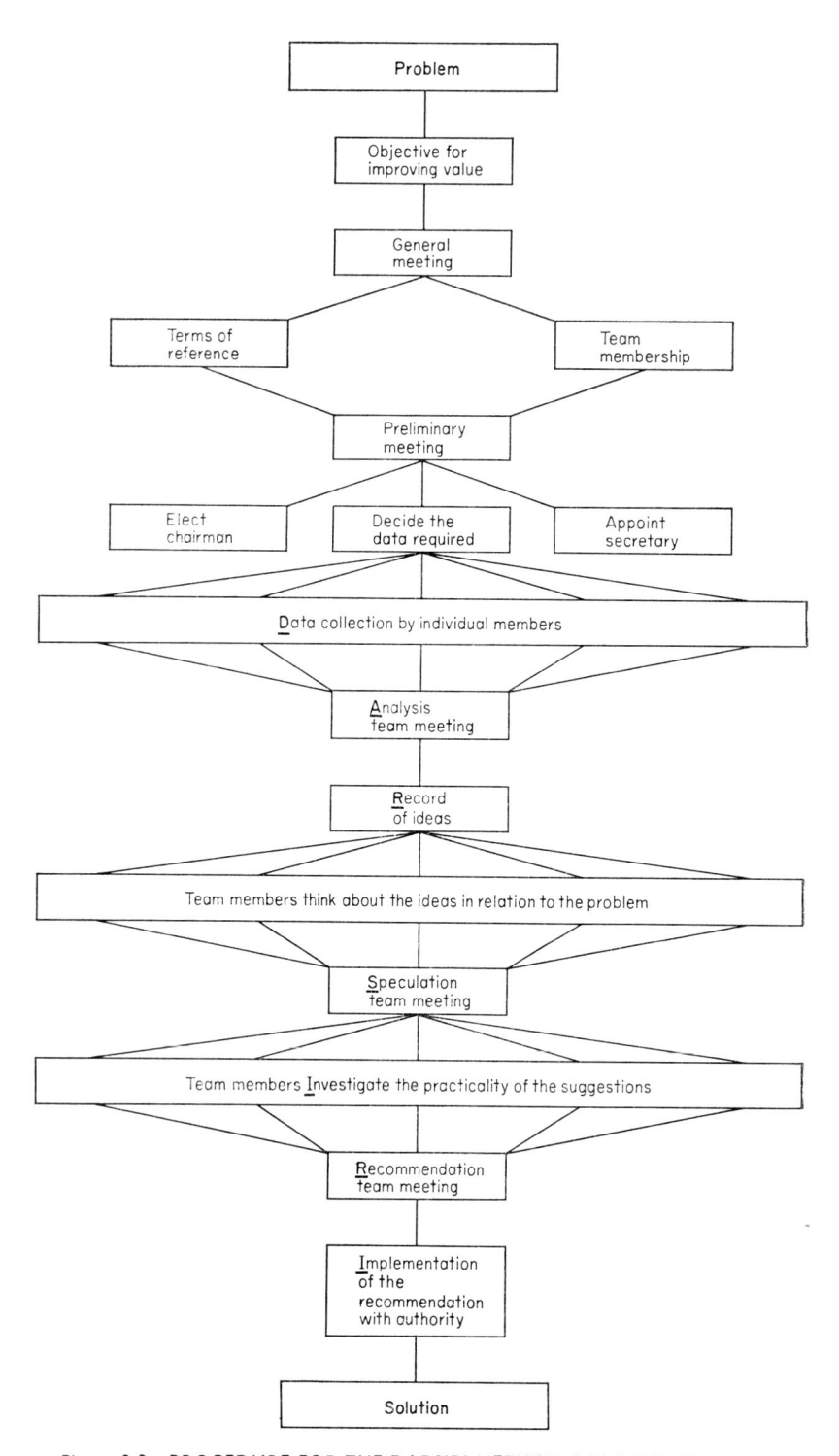

Figure 3:3 PROCEDURE FOR THE DARSIRI METHOD OF VALUE ANALYSIS

ANALYSING MARKET DEMAND

best flow lines for processing them. In this way, a distribution system can be built up functionally by using an order as the common denominator. A cycle of events and activities that is generally applicable has been developed and it is shown in Figure 3:4.

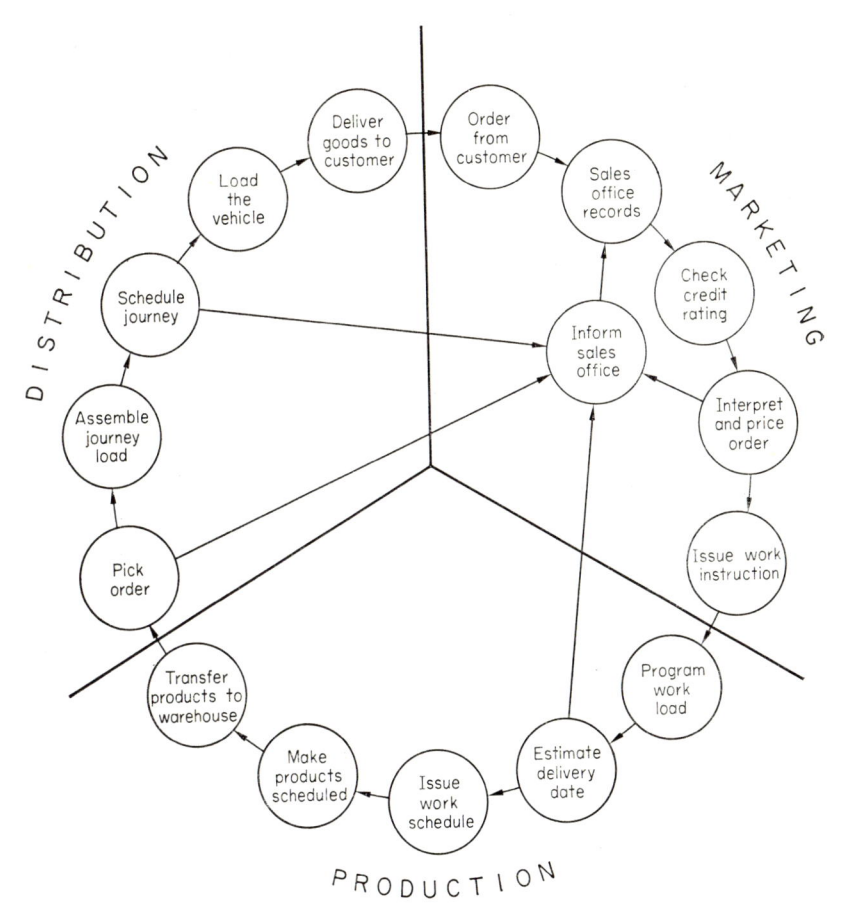

Figure 3:4 ORDERING CYCLE

Elements of the cycle

Each element in the cycle has a value, since it must serve a purpose, and it will cost money. Usually, improvements are made by reducing costs through modifying activities, by eliminating operations or by combining them together. However, the best methods for improving value depend upon circumstances and they can vary from company to company.

It must be realised, from the outset, that reducing the costs of distribution will increase the profit of a company. In an economic balance, costs plus profit must equal the sales income. It is important to believe that profit is really an expenditure.

Income = costs + profit

Actually, profit is the "cost of staying in business." It is divided between dividends to shareholders for providing the capital and reserves for financing future developments of the company. Without profit there will be no investments or developments and no future for the company or its employees.

Order processing

Elements of the ordering cycle follow each other successively, starting with an order being received from a customer. This order determines the goods that are required and the level of service that is expected. The success of a distribution system will depend upon the ability to comply with order requirements while keeping costs down to a budgeted proportion of the income.

The cost of each element in the ordering cycle must be budgeted in order to construct the operating cost framework. When the actual costs are compared with these budgets, it is possible to control a system and measure its success.

Flexibility is a criterion for planning operational budgets because it helps to iron out variations in both customer requirements and operating costs. Performances must be reviewed regularly in the light of results, so that the system can be controlled properly. Control is measured in terms of the differences between actual costs and budgeted costs. It will be implemented by taking corrective action whenever necessary.

Planning a distribution system is a tricky task and planners will have to keep alert to new developments in order to take advantage of opportunities as they arise. Some planning difficulties will arise that concern the modification of long-established relationships, or changing firmly held opinions. Whenever there is a change, new knowledge will be needed and new skills will have to be learned. Unfortunately, it is the nature of people to resist any form of change. On the other hand, changes are a sign of forward progress. Progress makes change incvitable, but people get a great satisfaction from knowing that they are furthering progress with the least disturbance of others.

Changes in a distribution system must be considered carefully, balancing the cost of a new development against the service that will be provided to customers. The service required is a logistic one of delivering goods to customers according to their orders, at the right place, at the right time and in the right quantity.

3:4 DISTRIBUTION LOGISTICS

The costs of distribution depend upon the logistical requirements of the system. In its simplest form, a distribution system comprises a dispatch bay at a factory where customers come to collect the goods that they order. Unfortunately, such a system is extremely rare. When goods have to be held before dispatching to customers, they need to be stored in a warehouse in the meantime. When goods have to be delivered to a customer's premises, there is need for transportation, in the form of vehicles normally. Warehouses and vehicles are the primary resources of a distribution system and planning must try to keep capital investments to a minimum while providing the customers with good service.

Physically, the flow of goods starts at the factory where they are manufactured; then, they are stored in a central warehouse or a number of regional warehouses. Goods are delivered from the factory to the warehouses in bulk, as a rule, by trunking and from the warehouse to customers by local delivery vehicles. The number of warehouses in a system depends upon the nature of ordering and the volume of goods; the value of these factors determines the delivering times and resources needed between factory and customers. The location of warehouses should be near the greatest distribution cost from the viewpoints of marketing, production and finance investments. In this way, deliveries will be kept short and the cost of delivering will be minimised.

National distribution is easiest by post for small items; larger ones can be delivered by public or private carriers. When the volume of goods increases so that these methods are too expensive, a company should consider owning or hiring its delivery vehicles. Owning the delivery fleet is the ultimate in distribution control.

Distribution regions

The distribution of goods to customers can be divided into regions according to demand intensities. The factory warehouse, or central warehouse, will be the only supply point when demand intensities are small. However, increasing intensities will require regional warehouses and, possibly, local depots in different areas of each region.

For local deliveries, each area must be large enough, at least, to justify the full-time employment of a vehicle. When the journey time from warehouse to a delivery area becomes excessive, local depots must be considered for optimising vehicle utilisation. Costs must be compared with service in

ANALYSING MARKET DEMAND

order to decide optimality. It is wise to consider delivering by post or carriers first when optimising the delivery areas.

Factors in distribution

Before a distribution system can be designed it is essential to consider the following factors:

1. The number, size and location of factory units
2. The geographical market locations
3. The number and types of products
4. The frequency of ordering
5. The number and size of orders
6. The need for intermediary warehouses
7. The cost scale of ordering and distributing
8. The budgeted costs for distribution
9. The nature of market demand
10. The method of transportation

Supplying the market

The objective of analysing the market demand is to determine the require-

Key
F = Factors
W = Central warehouse
D = Depot site
C = Customer location

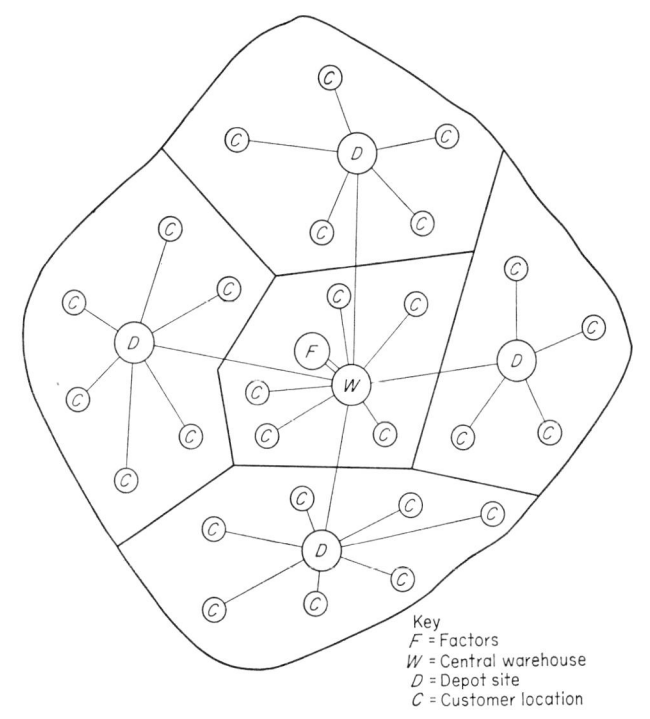

Figure 3:5 DISTRIBUTION NETWORK

ments of a distribution system. Fundamentally, distribution means supplying goods from points of manufacture to locations of demand. In practice, it is usual to have intermediary warehouses and to supply them from factories in bulk as opposed to specific orders to customers. The basic components of planning a distribution system will be siting supply points, routing vehicles, scheduling deliveries and determining the resources required.

Schematically, a distribution network is shown in Figure 3:5. In this diagram, the distribution region is divided into five economic delivery areas, each based on a depot warehouse. The depots are supplied from a central warehouse which is connected directly to the factory. Each distribution system will have its own network and drawing a schematic diagram of it must be an early stage in planning.

Analysis starts with the customer, but designing a distribution system starts at the supply point and works forward to the customers. A first consideration in planning a distribution system, after analysing market demand, will be siting the supply points in relation to customer locations, order lead times and costs of delivering the goods.

3:5 CUSTOMER RATIONALISATION

Just as the rationalisation of production or distribution requires an examination of the costs for performing work operations, customer rationalisation examines the cost of keeping customers. Analysing the value of each customer will help to put orders into perspective. Customers are needed to provide an income for the company, but some provide more income than others, while a few may be costing more than they are contributing.

Cost of keeping customers

The cost of distributing goods to customers is an overhead cost on sales income and each customer is a cost centre regardless of the number or sizes of orders that he places. Keeping a customer on the books involves time for checking records, space for filing information and stocks of goods in case an order is received.

Processing each customer order costs money, no matter what its value is. There are both fixed and variable costs of order processing and an analysis of the process rationally will help to discover relative importances.

Order analysis. A suitable procedure for analysing orders has the following five steps:

1 *List the operations* that are performed on an order, defining the resources and times that are required.

2 *Prepare a diagram* showing the flow of an order through each department, schematically.

ANALYSING MARKET DEMAND

3 *Tabulate the operations*, relating them in groups with the resources and times that are needed.

4 *Obtain costs for the operations*, showing how they vary with throughputs. Marginal costing helps to show the extent that the cost of operations changes as the number of orders changes.

5 *Illustrate graphically* the order processing costs against the number of orders.

Customer service

After analysing the cost of keeping customers, it is important to analyse the service that they are being given. Then, the service can be improved in relation to the value of orders and the cost of these improvements will be in line with income contributions. Comparing the costs of processing orders at each stage will highlight good and bad points, showing where improvements can be made most profitably. A schematic diagram for breaking down elements in the process is given in Figure 3:6.

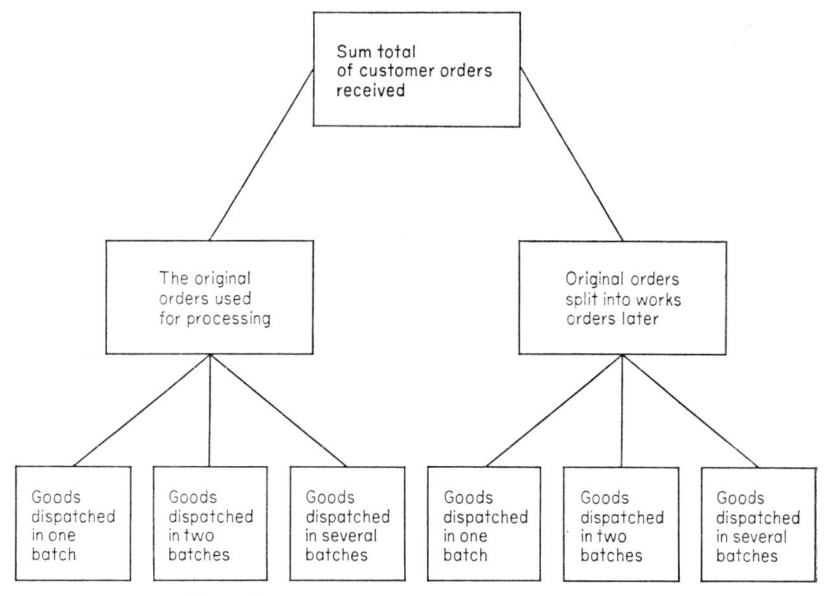

Figure 3:6 ANALYSING ORDER PROCESSING

3:6 PLANNING FOR MARKET DEMAND

Satisfying market demand is an inherent objective of distribution systems and investments of this nature require long-term planning. Another objective is the efficient utilisation of time which is the most precious resource of any system.

ANALYSING MARKET DEMAND

The market has a great influence on planning distribution resource investments and unified planning goes a long way towards successful results. Many problems have to be solved, but most can be prevented by considering interrelationships in the system at the planning stage.

An example to illustrate the need for unified planning concerns an American manufacturer who ran a massive sales promotion campaign a few years ago. Customers were given a large discount for orders requiring twenty-five cases of goods at one time. It had been planned that this discount would be covered by the savings from processing large orders. Unfortunately, the campaign flopped, because distribution costs increased out of proportion. These increases were due to handling in uneconomic batches, because a pallet load of goods comprised twenty-four cases.

This problem was generated by the independent action of the sales department without consulting distribution; however, it could have been the other way round. The moral is that no department in a company can operate successfully in isolation.

Delivery planning

Another example of the need for cooperation between marketing and distributing staff is in the planning of deliveries so that goods can be unloaded directly from the trunking vehicles into local delivery vehicles. This avoids storage costs and multiple handling. Naturally, it needs very good timing, but this can be simplified with cooperation between departments.

A technique known as "drop shipment" is useful in this situation. It involves transporting goods direct to the retail outlet from the supply point, yet invoicing the shipment to the wholesaler or the company head office.

The sales people must be conscious of their primary function of initiating the flow of goods through the complete system. In most economic systems, production adds value, distribution adds cost and marketing adds velocity. If the three functions work together and cooperate, the most efficient flow schedules will be developed. The marketing function has the basic responsibility of providing an outlet for goods that result from the activities of production and distribution.

When marketing dominates distribution patterns, the usual result is increased manufacturing and distributing costs and lower company profits. Thus, plans for satisfying market demand must be balanced in that they consider the effects that they will have on the supporting activities.

3:7 ANALYSING DELIVERY PROBLEMS

The improvement of delivery operations by analysis is especially important in service industries where distribution costs form a large part of pro-

ANALYSING MARKET DEMAND

duct selling prices. The nature of problems that are likely to arise will differ according to the type of product delivered and the market supplied. However, certain principles can be applied to solving most delivery problems. Some of the problems include:

1. What commodities shall be delivered?
2. What costs shall be budgeted?
3. What shall be the extent of the market served?
4. What distribution channels shall be used?
5. What shall be the delivery frequency?
6. What shall be the economic order size?
7. What shall be the levels of service offered?
8. What inventory shall be carried?
9. What goods handling methods shall be implemented?
10. What control measures shall be taken?

The responsibility for solving these problems is shared between the distribution and marketing managers. The relationships between factors that contribute to the causes of these problems make it necessary to analyse selling and delivery operations together. Close coordination at managerial level is the only way of producing workable solutions.

The analysis and investigation is called route engineering sometimes, because it is a standard analytical procedure for building up solutions to delivery problems methodologically. The items to be studied include delivery costs, customer buying patterns, delivery methods, routing techniques, vehicle schedules and manpower utilisation.

Delivery analysis steps

There are four basic steps for analysing delivery operations to be used in conjunction with the dual objective of distribution of improving customer service and reducing operating costs. The steps for improving delivery operations are:

1. Study the existing operations
2. Evaluate their effectiveness meaningfully
3. Determine ways of improving them
4. Develop techniques for controlling service and costs

Following these steps in an orderly manner using a standard procedure, such as the DARSIRI method, can improve delivery operations substantially. Delivery analysis has been able to provide better customer service with cost savings exceeding 20 per cent.

Route engineering

The four steps for analysing delivery problems must be used conscientiously

ANALYSING MARKET DEMAND

and with determination, in order to be successful. The value of any method of improvement depends upon the effort put into applying it. Route engineering is an analytical method that uses the four steps described and it is known to produce improved deliveries by managers who have used it intelligently.

1 *Study and define the existing operations.* This is the first step in route engineering that includes finding the reasons for performing delivery operations. For example, some of the questions that will be asked about local deliveries are:

> What is meant by local delivery?
> What does it do?
> How does it go about it?

In answer, local delivery can be defined as the activity of loading delivery vehicles, driving them to local delivery areas, unloading them at drop points, checking off the goods, obtaining acknowledgement of deliveries and returning empty to the depot.

Analysing the answers must be supplemented by a study of the existing routes and delivery areas. Originally, they would have been designed for different circumstances than those that exist today, in all probability; therefore, they will need updating. Road and traffic conditions change frequently and urban development is a sign of the times. It follows that delivery boundaries have to change too. Studying routes on a suitably scaled map helps to identify daily journeys and develop schedules for longer periods.

All the delivery operations must be studied as part of the whole system. Operations for study include times spent at the depot, handling equipment, vehicle driving times, delays and rest allowances. Vehicle loading will be an important operation and it is often possible to improve load assembly sequences, storage area layouts and methods of handling goods.

Studying the existing operations is the key to the entire delivery analysis, because the existing operations have to be defined before it can be seen if they have been improved successfully.

2 *Evaluate operating effectiveness.* In the second step, measures for evaluating the operations in terms of service and cost need to be developed. Service must be clearly defined in the first step, then the cost of providing it can be measured in order to compare alternative methods.

The total delivery cost includes the costs of loading goods, operating delivery vehicles, making special deliveries, providing handling facilities, supervising operations and paying wages. Some people think that driver and vehicle costs are uncontrollable, because wage rates are established by labour contracts and vehicle costs are fixed by capital investments. While it is true that wage rates are firm, increased driver productivity and improved methods can yield lower unit wage costs, irrespective of hourly rates or bonuses. This is possible since many delivery costs relate to the number of journeys made. The overall efficiency can be improved by operating fewer vehicle hours, driving fewer miles or having vehicles off the road for less time following breakdowns. Once the extent and scope of delivery costs have been determined they can be allocated to operations more rationally. Different deliveries incur different costs and looking at each operation rationally shows where time and money can be saved without impairing the service provided to customers.

Evaluation of operating effectiveness requires a systematic approach that measures the work contents of jobs, the operational times and the costs of delivering goods.

3 *Determine efficient operating methods and procedures.* The third step considers the overall distribution objectives in relation to the existing methods and procedures so that they can be improved or new ones devised.

Improvements can be made by changing delivery days for reducing the driving time, by changing delivery frequencies in order to improve load utilisation and by rearranging the drops along a route for better integration. Labour costs can be reduced by modifying work duties between drivers and mates, or between traffic office and warehouse staff. Sometimes, potential cost savings are brought to light in the areas of materials handling and warehouse design.

Each delivery operation is unique and it needs a custom-built method for adapting it to the complete system effectively. The first steps of route engineering provide the background information that is necessary for changing a delivery system in order to reduce costs, improve service or plan more flexible operations. In the third step, alternative methods and procedures are investigated with a view to making the most apt changes.

4 *Develop techniques for controlling operations.* The fourth step considers the control of delivery operations by comparing their costs with the established level of service required. The use of delivery standards is an aid to controlling operations.

Standards are valuable for planning balanced delivery journeys so that each journey represents a fair work load. Existing delivery schedules must be reviewed in order to find the reasons for delays, the restrictions to efficient deliveries, the values of customer drops or frequencies and the changes in unit load handling policies.

Revising routes and schedules is a regular part of route engineering and

ANALYSING MARKET DEMAND

keeping records up to date will ensure that the aims and objectives are always acceptable.

Reducing delivery time

The four steps for analysing deliveries are illustrated by an example of delivering motor oils to service stations. The original weekly delivery schedule comprised 5 daily journeys, each requiring 8 hours and making a total weekly time of 40 hours.

Studying the delivery operations suggested that the time spent at the depot loading and servicing the vehicle could be halved. Also, the driving time could be reduced by revising the delivery routes. The time spent with customers at service stations was out of the control of drivers and, in any case, it represented part of the service and it should not be reduced. However, investigating the service requirements showed that weekly delivery frequencies were unnecessary in some cases and time could be reduced yet an acceptable level of service still be provided. Analysis enabled some of the delays to be eliminated in order to save more time.

The combined time savings have been tabulated in Figure 3:7 and it can be seen that the weekly operating time has been reduced by just over a quarter. This time saved could be used for other work, for combining journeys or for reducing the number of vehicles on the road at any time.

Delivery procedure	Depot time	Driving time	Drop time	Rest allowance	Delays	Journey total (hours)
1 Original procedure	62	87	254	36	41	8.0
2 Halving the depot time	31	87	254	36	41	7.5
3 Improved routing	31	78	254	36	41	7.3
4 Revised drop frequency	31	52	217	36	41	6.3
5 Reducing delays	31	52	217	36	18	5.9

Mean time (minutes)

Figure 3:7 REDUCING DELIVERY TIME

ANALYSING MARKET DEMAND

Reorganising the journeys from this depot proved that one of the vehicles was redundant; however, one vehicle was due for replacement in the near future. It was recommended that this vehicle should not be replaced and the exercise prevented an unnecessary capital expenditure.

Reducing delivery time is a sure way of reducing costs and a systematic method such as route engineering will go a long way towards improving delivery effectiveness. The qualifications needed are commonsense, a questioning mind and administrative ability, plus a sound knowledge of the deliveries and routes.

4 SITING SUPPLY POINTS

Supply points are the heart of a distribution system and designing the system commences with siting the supply points after the number required by the system has been determined. Normally, products for distribution are manufactured at factories before being stored in warehouses where they enter the distribution system proper.

Analysing the market demand will help to plan the different stages that will be necessary for a distribution system. Initially, planning decisions will be based upon general economic grounds, followed by determining the number of supply points, the warehousing needs and the delivery network. The criteria for deciding the number of stages in a system will be the lead times for orders, the order frequencies, the production quantities and sequences and the delivery times.

Warehouses are supply points for most distribution systems; therefore, it is vital to site them strategically with a view to reducing delivery costs yet providing a good service to customers. The cost of warehousing must be balanced against the savings that accrue from mass production or increased sales which are expected to result from incurring this cost. Balancing costs against savings will help to plan the optimal number and the capacities of warehouses too.

Products in bulk are transferred from factories to warehouses for storage before releasing them to the market according to demand. Each warehouse must supply a predetermined market area which provides the input information for a planning distribution system. There is no scientific method for deciding the number or capacities of warehouses, but commonsense must be applied systematically when considering economies and efficiencies. Variations in distribution procedure make it vital to study each system on its own merits, but a logical approach will always produce a rational system that has a good chance of success.

4:1 LOCATING SUPPLIES FOR DISTRIBUTION

Supplies are the flow medium for a distribution system, being common to all its functions and operations. The location of these supplies must optimise

SITING SUPPLY POINTS

the objectives for planning the distribution system. These overall objectives must compromise the requirements of production and marketing, so that the objectives for warehousing and delivering are compatible.

The best location for the source of supplies differs with each system under consideration, but some factors for investigation are general:

1. Type of distribution system
2. Production requirements
3. Market demand
4. Operating costs
5. Ordering requirements
6. Centre of demand
7. Availability of land or premises
8. Design of warehouses

Industrial specialisation makes it necessary to distribute goods from sources of supply to locations of demand and there are many combinations of sources and locations. The combination chosen finally will determine the functions of a distribution system and the resource requirements.

Functions of distribution

Basically, the functions of distribution are warehousing and delivering. Warehousing is the function of storing the products of manufacture until they are required by a market. Storage is necessary in order to smooth out fluctuations in manufacture and market demand. Delivering is the function of transporting products from sources of supply to location of demand. When these places are some distance apart, transportation is essential. The method of delivering depends upon the nature of products, the available transport and the distribution throughputs.

The warehousing function commences with the receipt of products from a factory; then they are stored safely before being transferred to the delivery function as demanded. The delivery function commences by assembling the products for transportation to the customers; but customers may be intermediary distributors and not the ultimate consumers.

The basic functions of a distribution system are illustrated schematically in Figure 4:1. The system is assumed to start with production and end with customers. Firstly, planning must look at the market demand and analyse it in order to determine the supply resources needed. Later planning reverses this sequence by considering the siting and design of supply points before returning to customers. Planning is made more flexible for distribution purposes when a two way approach is adopted.

Supply sites

The supply sites for a distribution system have to be situated strategically in

SITING SUPPLY POINTS

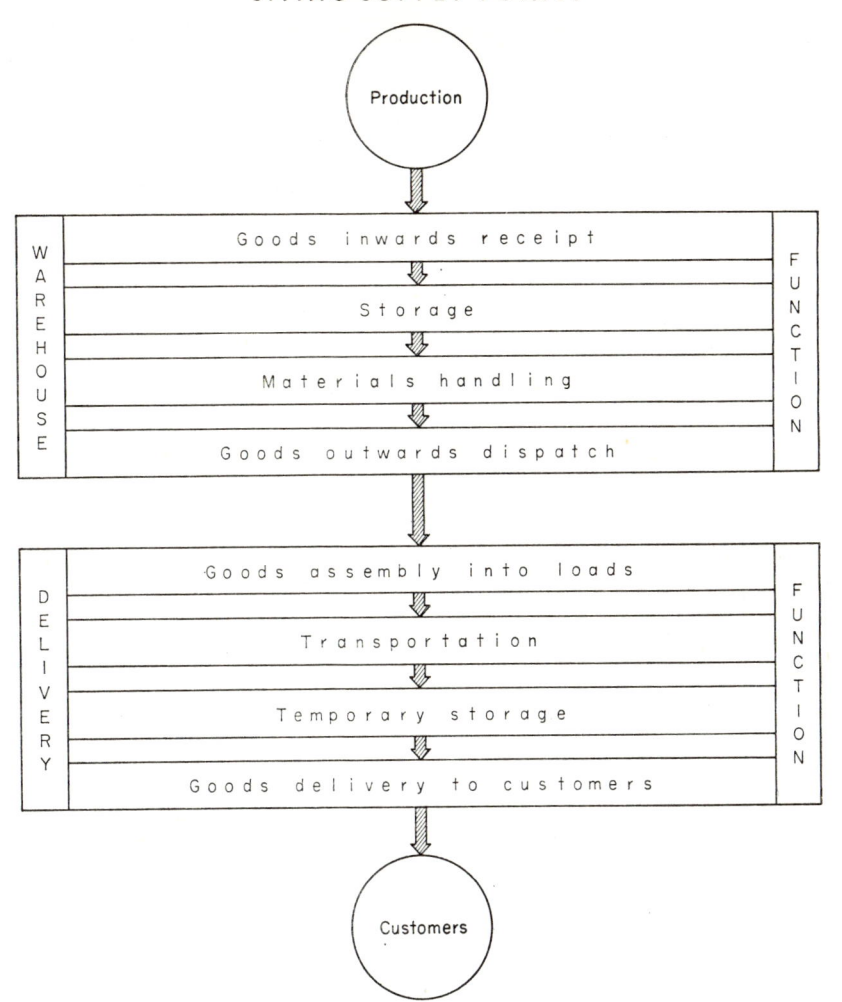

Figure 4:1 DISTRIBUTION SYSTEM

relation to the sources of raw material for production and the locations of market demand. An optimal supply site involves minimal distribution costs.

Costs are reduced when the sources of supply are sited at points where distribution costs are large; for example, costs are large when bulky materials have to be transported to or from remote areas. It is usual to site a source of supply at the location of raw materials for production when they are bulky as in the case of minerals, timber or oil. On the other hand, it is more economic to site the supply point of manufactured goods in the area of greatest market demand.

The rough location of a supply site can be determined with an educated

SITING SUPPLY POINTS

guess based upon past experience and knowledge of distribution methods. It is best to consider distributing to the whole market from one site, at first, and then considering more than one supply point. Economically, the number of supply sites can be found by comparing costs for the same level of service. Experience shows that one central warehouse must carry supplies of all product items, so must two warehouses; but three need carry only half the items each.

Since a distribution system is dynamic, it must be reviewed at regular intervals and plans modified in the light of changes. In this way, costs will be kept as low as possible and the service provided will be as effective as necessary.

The supply points are warehouses, usually, and the focal point for reducing costs of distribution will be their sites. Siting warehouses requires a careful comparison of costs involved before it is possible to decide if the warehousing function shall be centralised or regional. All supply site decisions must result from studying the overall policies and they will be influenced by the following factors:

1. Nature of goods to be distributed
2. Level of service required by customers
3. Individual and total operating costs
4. Methods of warehousing and delivering
5. Planning of resources for the system
6. Effectiveness of controls

Nature of products

Siting supply points will be influenced by the nature of products to be distributed, particularly, perishable goods. When the shelf-life of goods is short, the number of warehouses will be many; however, improved methods of handling and storage help to provide wider market coverage. Seasonal production necessitates complete stock turns within the season and some distributors find that it is easier to maintain inventory control when a single warehouse is operated. Once again, the best solution will require compromise between the variables.

Level of service

In many instances, speedy delivery is essential for providing a level of service that is acceptable. The level of service is most important to the marketing function, because it affects sales. When customers require speedy or variable deliveries, decentralisation of warehouses is preferable, but control of the service level is more effective from a single supply site.

Operating costs

Optimal sites for sources of supply are affected by production costs, marketing costs, labour costs, stockholding costs and delivery costs. One central warehouse requires less capital investment than several regional warehouses, but the cost of delivering goods will be higher. Decentralised warehousing has the advantages of reducing delivery costs, improving customer service and decreasing warehouse capacities. However, these advantages must be balanced against the disadvantages of greater investment in buildings, equipment and labour.

A regional warehouse can be made the central supply point for a market region or a local production plant. This configuration can influence operating costs, but it will provide better control and improve customer service.

Method of warehousing

The size of a warehouse affects the area of a site needed, which may determine its availability at a particular location. The area for a warehouse site must take into account, also, accessibility of receiving and dispatching goods, parking vehicles and constructing roadways. When capital investment in the land and buildings at a supply site is high, one central warehouse will be favoured; however, investment charges can be reduced by selecting a "green field" site away from a town. Regional warehouses are less costly for bulk manufactured goods or for simple construction.

Method of delivering

The geographical locations of supply points have a direct bearing upon transport costs and it is essential to include a study of the delivery methods when investigating a supply site. The method of delivering that is selected will influence the ancillary requirements too; for instance, sea transportation requires access to harbours while air, rail or road transport have their own particular requirements that will affect optimal sites.

Planning of resources

The fewer the supply points in a distribution system, the fewer the resources required and the easier it will be to plan the system. The planning objectives are criteria for siting supply points. Firstly, supply points must be located where they ensure the best service level and, secondly, this service has to be provided for the least transportation, stockholding and controlling cost.

Effectiveness of control

The control network in a system depends upon good communications for effectiveness. Control effectiveness is proportional to the suitability of a communications medium and the number of links in the network; by and large, speed is essential and the fewer the links the better. Centralised control is most direct, but it is least flexible. Normally, a few supply sites are best for the effective control of a distribution system.

Siting considerations

From the production viewpoint, the number of supply sites must maximise production efficiencies and minimise production costs. These conflicting requirements make it necessary to compromise in order to select an optimal site.

Preparing models of a distribution system allows its variables to be manipulated in order to achieve the best compromise without risking capital. The first model to be considered should be a centralised system, and then the number of stages can be increased when the customer service required justifies it.

The central site can be found roughly with coordinates of the demand locations. More precise supply sites require analysing the market demand and distribution costs.

When one or more optimal sites have been determined for a system, a network can be developed which includes delivery routes and schedules. The final stage of planning will be testing the sites proposed experimentally, in order to discover the level of service that can be provided and the operating costs.

4:2 METHODS OF SITING

The objectives for siting supply points must ensure a satisfactory level of service and keep costs down. An optimal site will comply with both requirements, but it will be found only after a systematic search and appraisal of alternative sites.

Exhaustive search method

This method for siting supply points is infallible, because every possible site is considered and compared with the objectives for the system. Delivering costs are the most important variable when controlling a system and the supply site has a great effect on them in the form of delivery distances.

Usually, delivery costs are proportional to distances between the supply site and customer locations, and an exhaustive search investigates all distances involved for different combinations. All possible costs will be collected and examined. Examinations are enhanced by drawing maps that pinpoint delivery costs. Maps that show "iso-cost" contour lines assist planning by

SITING SUPPLY POINTS

defining cost areas. Iso-cost contours are lines drawn through points of similar cost and these are illustrated in Figure 4:2 for delivering goods to the four countries.

Iso-cost contour maps

The distribution costs related to a particular system can be plotted on a map as an aid to planning in order to improve their value. Contour lines can be drawn through all points with the same cost concentrically around the optimal site. The optimal site will be found with cost coordinates. Locating the supply site elsewhere increases the distribution costs, but this may be unavoidable in some instances.

In order to keep unavoidable costs to a minimum, iso-cost contours will define the least cost limits when searching for alternative sites. The optimal supply site in Figure 4:2 is at Antwerp and iso-cost contours encircle it at 10 per cent cost increase intervals.

Figure 4:2 ISO-COST CONTOUR MAP

The centre of least delivery cost is found by cost coordinates at right angles to each other and the search for a supply site must be made in this vicinity first. When no site is available, the cost of supply from neighbouring areas will have to be considered. In the map for the Low Countries, the supply site can be moved 100 kilometres north of Antwerp, to Rotter-

SITING SUPPLY POINTS

dam, before the total cost of distribution increases by 10 per cent; however, it can move only 50 kilometres west, to Ghent, for the same increase.

Systematic search methods

The great volume of calculation and investigation that is involved with the exhaustive search method can be reduced by omitting unusual situations, like very low or high demands. A less complicated method consists of estimating the demand throughputs for market areas and assuming that the best site will be found in the area of greatest demand. A rough search can be performed by dividing the whole region into areas and examining them systematically. These areas may be based, arbitrarily, upon 10 kilometre grid squares and Ordnance Survey maps are useful for this purpose.

Analogue siting methods

Siting problems can be solved mechanically with animated diagrams or models. One simple working model comprises a map pasted on a wooden board or table with holes drilled at each demand location. Then a thin string is passed through each hole and their ends knotted together above the table. The throughput at each demand location is represented by an equivalent weight attached to the end of its string below the table as shown in Figure 4:3. When the appropriate number of weights has been added, the different string tensions will pull on the knot above the table, but the knot will be free to move and it will settle when the tensions are in equilibrium. The optimal supply site is found from the map as the place where the knot settles.

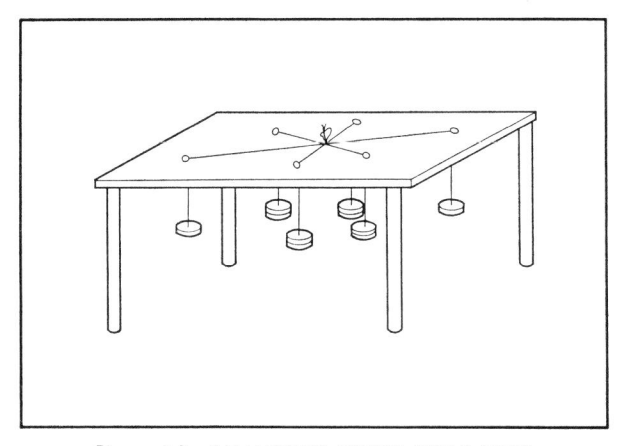

Figure 4:3 ANALOGUE SITING SIMULATOR

SITING SUPPLY POINTS

Natural obstacles like rivers and mountains can be circumnavigated by sticking pins into the map at places of strategic passages that avoid them. Other analogue siting methods make use of electric current and variable resistances, but they are more complex to construct.

4:3 SITING ACCORDING TO DEMAND

Supply points for a distribution system can be sited quite precisely with reference to the demand locations and delivery routes to them. Combining warehousing and delivering costs will allow optimal supply sites to be determined. Warehousing costs can be considered as being fixed, but delivery costs will increase with the distance from the warehouse source of supply. Since the smallest costs will be found close to the supply site, overall costs will be least when that site is in the vicinity of the greatest demand. This condition applies regardless of the number of supply sites required.

It follows that the size of demand is more important than delivery distances, initially. The demand locations can be joined together as a demand network in order to find the area of greatest demand. Distance will become important only when there is more than one area with the greatest demand.

Line theorem

Distribution costs depend upon the throughput of goods and the delivery distances, basically. The throughput affects total costs more than distances, because it is directly related to the market demand. Consequently, it is advisable to consider demand before distance.

The line theorem states that the supply site with the least throughput depends upon the magnitude of individual demands in a system. It assumes that all demands are effective at locations that can be connected together into a line network. The network will be simplified by combining minor branches with major ones until a single main line results. There are a number of procedures for establishing the main line of the system and determining the location of the greatest demand.

The location of the greatest demand along the main line is found by summing the individual demands, starting at one end. The optimal supply point will be the location of greatest demand. When the sum of individual demands equals or just exceeds half the total demand for the system, this location will be a supply point. This point is confirmed by summing the demands from the opposite end of the line. However, if a different location is reached that is equal to half the total demand there will be two equal supply points for the system. They can be reduced to one point only when the respective delivery distances are calculated.

SITING SUPPLY POINTS

First of all, the procedures for finding centres of greatest demand will be considered before studying actual cases where distance is involved.

Two demand locations system. The simplest distribution system comprises just two locations of market demand and the optimal supply point will be at the location with the greater demand. In this case, the least volume of goods will have to be transported to the other location. When each location has the same demand, all points on the line connecting them will be equally optimal. A two demand locations system is shown in Figure 4:4.

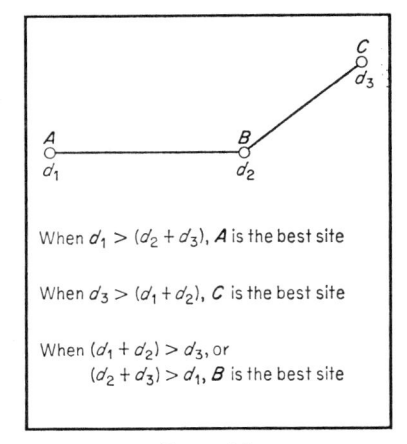

Three demand locations system. When there are three locations of market demand they must be considered on the same supply line, but its length is

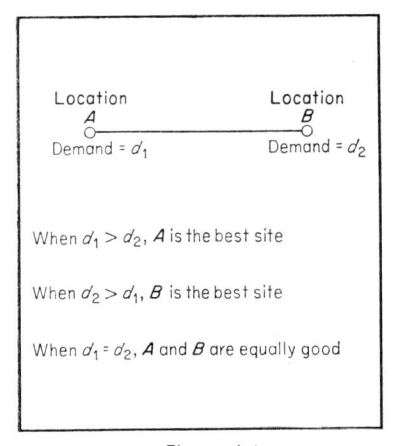

Figure 4:4
TWO DEMAND LOCATIONS SYSTEM

Location A — Demand = d_1
Location B — Demand = d_2

When $d_1 > d_2$, A is the best site

When $d_2 > d_1$, B is the best site

When $d_1 = d_2$, A and B are equally good

Figure 4:5
THREE DEMAND LOCATIONS SYSTEM

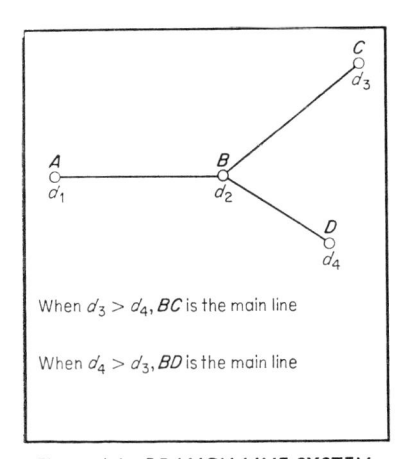

When $d_1 > (d_2 + d_3)$, A is the best site

When $d_3 > (d_1 + d_2)$, C is the best site

When $(d_1 + d_2) > d_3$, or $(d_2 + d_3) > d_1$, B is the best site

Figure 4:6 BRANCH LINE SYSTEM

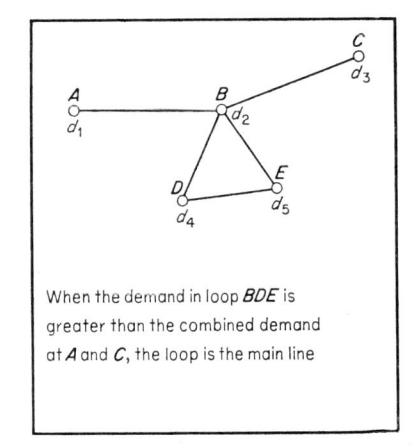

When $d_3 > d_4$, BC is the main line

When $d_4 > d_3$, BD is the main line

Figure 4:7 LOOP LINE SYSTEM

When the demand in loop BDE is greater than the combined demand at A and C, the loop is the main line

SITING SUPPLY POINTS

unimportant. The optimal supply site will be at the location with a larger demand than the other two combined together. When each demand is less than the other two, the central location will be the optimal supply site. The different configurations of a three locations system are shown in Figure 4:5.

Branch line system. A system with a number of branch lines can be reduced to a single main line by eliminating branches with the smallest demands. The system shown in Figure 4:6 has two branches and the branch containing the greater demand will be the main line. The demand in a branch line is considered to affect the main line demand at the junction.

Considering the demand in a system, a line with branches is an extension of a two locations system. Delivering to locations of a branch line, the distance up the branch has to be covered regardless of the supply site and demand is effective at the junction and not at some distance from it.

Loop line system. Sometimes, two or more branch lines are combined into a loop as shown in Figure 4:7. The loop can be regarded as a single branch line and the procedure for finding an optimal site is the same as that for a branch line system. If the total demand in the loop is greater than the demand for the rest of the system, the supply site will be located along the loop line which must be considered as the main line and the rest of the system as a branch of it.

4:4 SOLVING COMPLEX SITING PROBLEMS

Complex siting problems can be solved with the aid of the line theorem after they have been reduced to one of the basic forms described. When it is impossible to find optimal sites by considering only the demand at locations, distribution costs or distances must be included too. Systems with two or more locations of equal demand can be resolved to give a single supply site by comparing the demand-cost vectors at demand locations. A demand-cost vector is the product of the demand and the cost of delivering it from the supply site. Normally, cost is proportional to distance and the demand is expressed as weight or volume. Therefore, the demand-cost vector may be defined in units of distance and weight or volume—for example ton–miles or cubic metre–kilometres.

When two demands are equal, multiplying them by the appropriate supply distance will produce different demand-cost vectors and enable one of them to be differentiated as the better supply site. Figure 4:8 illustrates such a situation.

In the diagram, the best supply site can be either location *C* or location *D*, because their demands are equal. The choice between locations of equal

SITING SUPPLY POINTS

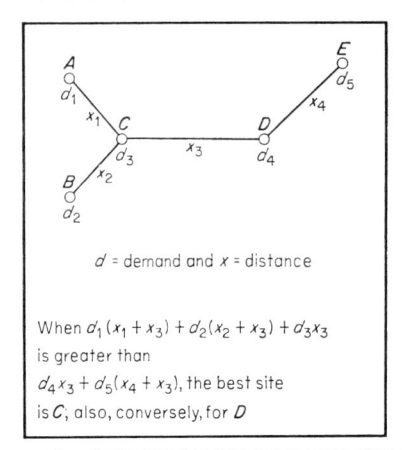

[Figure box contents:]
d = demand and x = distance

When $d_1(x_1 + x_3) + d_2(x_2 + x_3) + d_3 x_3$
is greater than
$d_4 x_3 + d_5(x_4 + x_3)$, the best site
is C, also, conversely, for D

Figure 4:8 COMPLEX DISTRIBUTION SYSTEM

demand is decided by comparing their demand-cost vectors. A vector has both magnitude and direction; in the case of distribution vectors, magnitude is the demand for goods as weight, volume or quantity, while direction is the cost or distance for delivering goods to customers.

The choice between locations C and D for the supply site in Figure 4:8 can be resolved by comparing their demand-cost vectors. The optimal site will be at the location of least demand-cost.

1   The demand cost for supplying D from C is:
$d_4 + d_5 (x_4 + x_3)$

2   The demand cost for supplying C from D is:
$d_3 \times_3 + d (x_1 + x_3) + d_2 (x_2 + x_3)$

When the former is smaller, location C will be the optimal site; conversely, when the latter is smaller, location D will be the optimal site.

Choice with more than two sites

It happens quite often that more than one supply point is needed for a distribution system and the vector comparison procedure will be unsuitable for finding optimal sites. Only the demands and the number of sites required are necessary for siting them optimally.

One site of supply will be at the centre of demand, which is at the location of the mean of the total demand. The line network for a system must be constructed and the demand locations reduced to a single line, then the demand can be cumulated from either end and the optimal site will be at the location where half the demand is reached or just exceeded. Mathematically, the optimal site will occur at the location where the cumulated demand is $D/2n$, when D = total demand and n = number of sites required.

SITING SUPPLY POINTS

Two supply sites will occur at the locations where the cumulated demand is

$$\frac{D}{2n} \text{ and } \frac{3D}{2n}$$

More than two sites will be sited optimally at locations where the total demand and number of sites required comply with the following progression:

$$\frac{D}{2n} \quad \frac{3D}{2n} \quad \frac{5D}{2n} \quad \frac{7D}{2n} \quad \frac{9D}{2n} \quad \frac{(2n-1)\,D}{2n}$$

This progression is suitable for cumulated demand locations of a distribution system that has been reduced to a single line. It is illustrated in Figure 4:9 for a system of seven demand locations located equidistantly. Each location requires one van-load of goods and the total demand is seven van-loads. The locations for one, two, three and four optimal sites can be calculated with the aid of the progression above.

One site $n = 1$ and the optimal site will occur where the cumulated demand reaches

$$\frac{D}{2n} = \frac{7}{2\frac{2}{3}}$$

van-loads. This cumulated demand is reached at location D.

Two sites $n = 2$ and the optimal sites will occur at locations where the cumulated demand reaches

$$\frac{D}{2n} = \frac{7}{4}$$

van-loads and

$$\frac{3D}{2n} = \frac{21}{4}$$

van-loads. The sites will be at locations B and F.

Three sites $n = 3$ and the optimal sites will occur at locations where the cumulated demand reaches

$$\frac{D}{2n} = \frac{7}{6}$$

van-loads

$$\frac{3D}{2n} = \frac{21}{6}$$

van-loads and

$$\frac{5D}{2n} = \frac{35}{6}$$

van-loads. These sites will be at locations B, D and F.

SITING SUPPLY POINTS

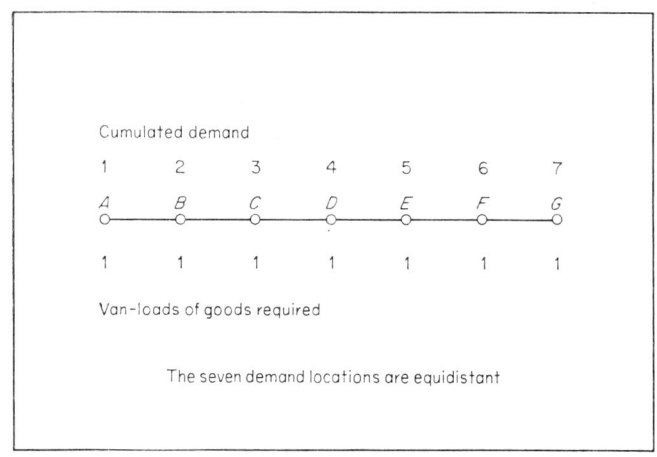

Figure 4:9 MORE THAN TWO SUPPLY SITES

Four sites $n = 4$ and the optimal sites will occur at locations where the cumulated demand reaches

$$\frac{D}{2n} = \frac{7}{8}, \quad \frac{3D}{2n} = \frac{21}{8}, \quad \frac{5D}{2n} = \frac{35}{8}, \text{ and } \frac{7D}{2n} = \frac{49}{8}$$

van-loads. These sites will be at locations A, C, E and G.

Application of the line theorem

Although the different configurations that are explained by the line theorem have been presented in simple terms, practical people find it easier to follow from a practical illustration. In the next chapter, a real life case study is used to illustrate the practical advantages of the line theorem. This case study can be adapted to suit many different situations and it is hoped that distribution managers will find it useful for deciding the best supply sites.

5 DECIDING THE BEST SUPPLY SITES

The best supply sites are ones that satisfy the service level required by customers and keep delivery costs to a minimum. The market area supplied from a supply point depends upon the total demand of the area and the service level required. Normally, service is related to delivery times and the quantity of goods ordered; therefore, order lead time affects the boundaries of supply areas.

5:1 NUMBER OF SUPPLY SITES

The factors that affect the number of supply sites required in a distribution system include the total demand, the customer locations, the warehouse types, the number and sizes of vehicles, the total cost of deliveries and the order lead times available. The number of sites can be found empirically by trial and error, but a systematic approach will help to reduce the number of trials. One of the most important factors in all systems is the order lead time, because it determines the level of service that will be offered to customers.

Order lead time

The difference between the time when a customer places an order and the time that the goods are required is the order lead time. During this time, the following activities have to be performed:

1   Processing the order
2   Assembling the goods specified by the order
3   Delivering the goods to the customer

Each of these activities has a duration that varies with circumstances, but the first two will be fairly stable and the third variable. Therefore, it will be delivery time that most affects the number of supply sites required.

    The furthest economic distance that customers can be located from a supply point will depend upon the delivery time in relation to the order lead time. Deciding the number of sites is rather complex, because of the

DECIDING THE BEST SUPPLY SITES

large number of variables which will be pertinent to particular delivery systems.

As an illustration, the economic delivery distance can increase as the order lead time and the delivery time available increase. When the time that is available for delivering is one day and the transportation method is by road vehicles, the economic distance will be a product of the daily driving time permitted and the average speed of the vehicle. In Britain, the Road Transport Act restricts the driving time of one man to ten hours in twenty four and this determines the distance that can be driven in one day. Any customers located outside a radius equivalent to ten hours' driving time from a supply site cannot receive goods with an order lead time of one day. When this sort of situation prevails, alternative delivery methods must be considered, or the service level must be changed, or the site for another supply point must be investigated.

An additional supply point will be necessary when the extra delivery times required are sufficient to justify additional vehicles. There is no standard procedure for deciding the limits of delivery routes from a supply point and each system must be considered individually. Normally, the time available for deliveries can be converted into distance when the average driving speed is known; then route limits can be fixed fairly accurately on a map.

Total demand

Another criterion for deciding the number of supply sites required is the total demand of a market area. The total demand, divided by the capacity of the largest single transport vehicle that can be operated, will decide the number of vehicles required for maximum efficiency. In practice, it is impossible to operate fully-laden vehicles all the time, due to variable customer requirements. The size of vehicle that should be operated must be the largest possible in order to obtain maximum economy.

Number of vehicles

The conditions for the maximum efficiency and economy of operating vehicles are conflicting and the optimal number must be a compromise. By and large, the available delivery time will determine the number of journeys required and the total demand will determine the number of vehicles. However, there must be an acceptable balance between the numbers of journeys and vehicles for the best performance.

Supply areas

It has been shown that order lead times affect operational times; thus, delivery times will be instrumental in deciding the size of a market area

DECIDING THE BEST SUPPLY SITES

that can be supplied from a warehouse. Converting the available times into distances will decide the maximum lengths of routes, and then a map can be drawn to show the boundary of each supply area with the customer locations that can be supplied along each feasible route.

Delivery ratios

The factors involved in deciding the best supply sites can be summarised as a set of ratios:

1 *Daily journeys:*
$$\text{Number of journeys} = \frac{\text{total full load delivery distances}}{\text{daily delivery distance}}$$

2 *Vehicles required:*
$$\text{Number of vehicles} = \frac{\text{total demand for the order period}}{\text{standard vehicle capacity}}$$

3 *Order cycle:*
$$\text{Number of days} = \frac{\text{number of daily journeys required}}{\text{number of vehicles required}}$$

When the order cycle is longer than the order lead time, more vehicles will be required in order to reduce the number of days.

Number of journeys

It is advisable to prepare a network for customer locations within the permissible limits of each supply area. The customer drop points can be allocated to routes by starting from the end of each line nearest the boundary. The demand is cumulated at each location, working in towards the supply point, until a full load is obtained. A certain amount of "give and take" is necessary when compiling loads but each full load must be sufficient for one vehicle journey. Continuing inwards until all customer demands are satisfied determines the total number of journeys required for the area. Scheduling deliveries will include the durations of journeys too.

The order cycle ratio of journeys to number of vehicles gives the number of delivering days that will be required in order to supply all the customer orders in the area. At the end of each cycle period, the cycle must be repeated as more orders are placed.

5:2 THE NUMBER OF SITES AND DISTRIBUTION COSTS

Analysing cannot solve siting problems alone, but it offers a basis for making sound decisions and helps to optimise the number of sites and their costs. An understanding of how distribution costs vary with warehouse numbers provides guide lines for deciding the best combination of site number and costs. The chart in Figure 5:1 presents, in a simplified manner, the general

DECIDING THE BEST SUPPLY SITES

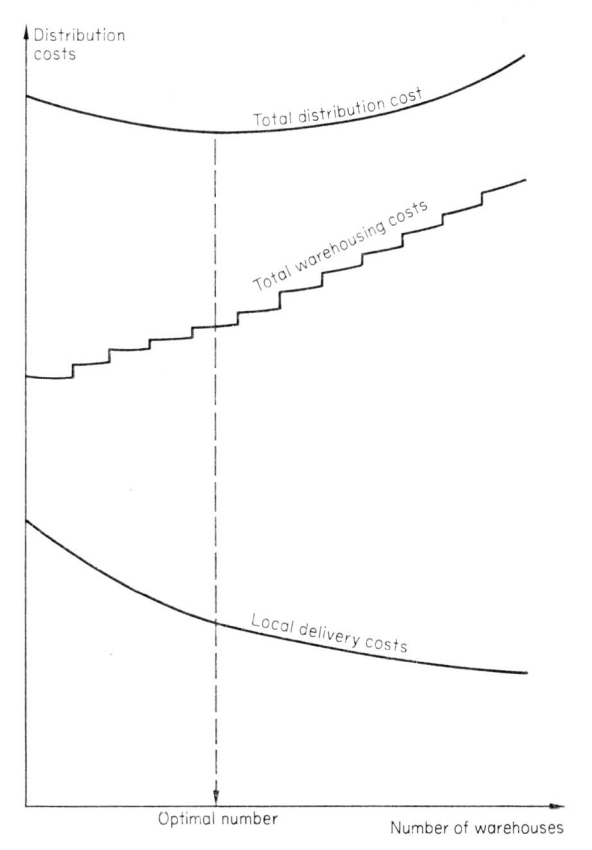

Figure 5:1 COST VARIATIONS AND THE NUMBER OF WAREHOUSES

variations of delivery, warehousing and inventory carrying costs with an increasing number of warehouses.

Cost variations

The costs of trunking from factory to warehouse, warehouse operations and inventory increase in steps as the number of warehouses increases, but the costs of local deliveries decrease quite sharply before levelling out under the same conditions. In combination, it is seen that the total distribution cost decreases before rising again when the number of sites increases.

Mathematical analysis

The relationships between warehouse number and distribution costs can be clarified by analysing the cost data mathematically. The basic information will be fairly simple, but the large number of combinations that can occur

DECIDING THE BEST SUPPLY SITES

will make calculating the least overall cost a lengthy operation. Repetitive calculations can be reduced when results are expressed graphically, while time can be saved by computerisation.

Cost optimisation example

The distribution costs of an Australian garden tools manufacturer were getting out of hand and it was decided to review them by mathematical analysis. The annual total distribution cost exceeded the combined asset values of the twelve company-owned depots and the first suggestion considered was to close down some of the depots.

Mathematical analysis of the distribution system by industrial engineering consultants produced a more satisfactory solution. The analysis started by collecting data on depot investment costs, stockholding costs, labour costs and vehicle operating costs. These costs were tabulated for comparative purposes and a summary table of delivery costs is shown in Figure 5:2

Delivery factors	Size of vehicles		
	8-ton	10-ton	20-ton
Journeys per month	85	72	38
Working days per month needed	340	290	150
Total time needed (hours/month)	3 400	2 900	1 500
Number of vehicles needed	15	12	7
Running costs (cents/mile)	6.0	7.0	8.5
Mileage per month	68 000	57 000	30 000
Standing cost ($A per month)	1 500	1 600	1 400
Total cost ($A per month)	15 500	14 200	9 000
Cost per ton carried ($A)	20	18	12

Figure 5:2 DELIVERY COSTS DATA

Analysing the data collected included costing the vehicle journeys, allocating the demand to depots, revising the depot sites and studying past sales records. The country was divided into supply areas for depots, according to demands, and each proposed depot was sited at a major market town. The number of annual deliveries needed for each area was estimated

DECIDING THE BEST SUPPLY SITES

from sales records, then the number of orders was related to delivery lead times.

Routes were studied with a large scale map; pins and pieces of cotton were used to test route feasibility. Altogether, the minimum number of journeys that were required came to 450, using 20-ton trucks and each journey was costed in relation to its route distance. Different sizes of vehicles were investigated and 20-ton models proved to be most economic for the orders and delivery frequencies involved.

Similar data was developed for areas where carriers could be employed and all the figures were processed by a computer in order to find the least costly combination for the whole distribution system. The most economic system computed saved nearly one quarter of the current annual distribution cost. In this optimal system, goods would be trunked from the factory direct to depots with company-owned vehicles, the necessary number of depots would be reduced to seven and the supplies to local dealers would be delivered by hired vans or public carriers in different areas.

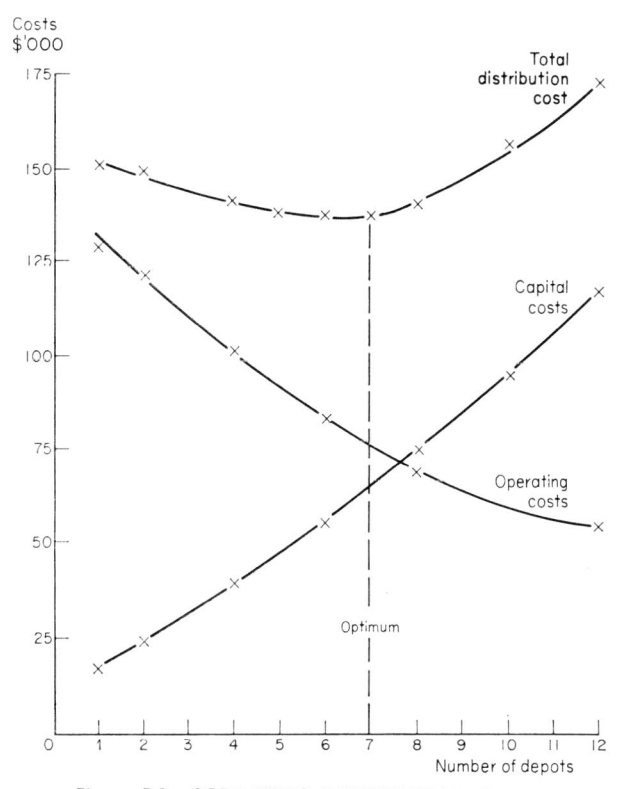

Figure 5:3 OPTIMISING DISTRIBUTION COSTS

DECIDING THE BEST SUPPLY SITES

Later, additional savings were obtained by streamlining particular routes, incorporating sales offices with the depots and establishing vehicle maintenance facilities at strategic points.

A chart showing the distribution costs for different numbers of depots is shown in Figure 5:3.

The capital investment costs in buildings and vehicles rose steadily as the number of depots increased, but operating costs decreased relatively. Combining these costs showed that the optimum, or least total cost, was equivalent to seven depots.

Distribution costs and lead time

The delivery lead time available after an order is placed affects the cost of distribution directly. The longer the lead time available the greater the inventory of goods that has to be held in stock; consequently, distribution costs will rise. Sometimes, a longer lead allows better utilisation of the production time which can reduce production costs. But these savings can be wiped out by the cost of carrying extra stock due to the reduced accuracy of forecasting over the longer period.

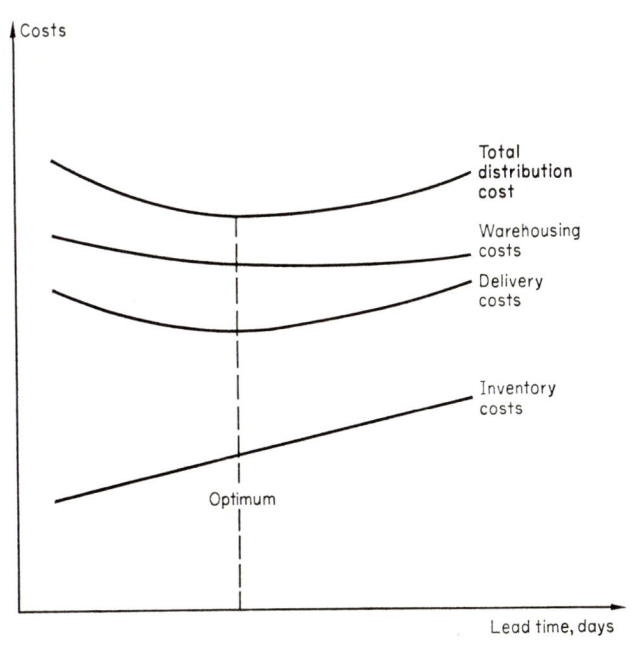

Figure 5:4 RELATIONSHIPS BETWEEN COSTS AND LEAD TIME

The relationships between costs and delivery lead time are shown in Figure 5:4. For a particular system, there is an optimal lead time when the

DECIDING THE BEST SUPPLY SITES

combined delivery costs, warehouse operating costs and inventory costs are minimal. The optimum varies according to the conditions.

An important factor that is often overlooked is the need for good stock control when trying to reduce distribution costs; it should be realised that stock control can be a tool for controlling distribution costs.

5:3 VARIABLE FACTORS OF SITING

Until now, the factors of siting have been related to market demand and distribution costs. Both play important parts in deciding the best supply sites, but the best sites may be unavailable or inconvenient and it will become necessary to examine other factors too. These factors vary from system to system and from site to site. For example, the supply source may be a factory or a regional warehouse, the vehicle types available may differ or the throughput of goods may fluctuate from time to time.

Effect of plant size on factory siting

The size of a site affects the design of a factory. When a factory is built it has to be designed for a standard production throughput which sets a limit to the volume of goods that will be stored and the delivery frequency that can be offered. As with other planning aspects, the production potential and the market demand must be balanced in order to optimise the distribution system.

Siting problems

Solutions to problems of siting warehouses can be developed by starting with an appraisal of the requirements of the distribution system and a statement of its objectives. The variable factors that affect the system must be examined at the supply points siting stage. A system may need only one supply point when siting it at the centre of demand for the whole system will be optimal. Regardless of the number of supply points needed, one of them at the centre of total demand will be necessary always.

When more than one site is needed, distance becomes a prime factor and dividing the distribution region into compact areas with a central supply point will help to keep down costs. Often, it is convenient to make these areas hexagonal in shape and siting the supply point should be in a town that is both central and well served by roads.

Site location

The location of a supply site will be a focal point when considering changes in marketing policies, new delivery outlets, different transportation routes and other methods of distribution. Correctly sited, an efficient warehouse can improve the overall profitability of a company.

DECIDING THE BEST SUPPLY SITES

There are five variable factors that carry weight when deciding whether to centralise or decentralise the warehousing function:

1. The type of goods to be handled
2. The level of service required
3. The total distribution cost
4. The method of transportation selected
5. The degree of control necessary

Other factors will have to be taken into account, also, when deciding the best supply site location and the availability of labour will be quite important in most cases. Different systems or methods should be compared as models, in order to assess the effect of different locations on the efficiency and economy of the complete distribution network.

Variations in demand

It is necessary to hold stocks in order to prevent delivery delays when market demand fluctuates. The first buffer stocks will be held at retail outlets as a safeguard against immediate demand variations and another stock will be necessary at the production end of the system. A third stock must be held near the centre of the system as a buffer against differences that will occur between the market demands and production outputs. These variations will affect the operating efficiency of a distribution system, but not the actual siting of factories and warehouses.

Variations in demand may occur between different distribution areas as a result of factors like sales promotion, customer preferences, product popularity or transport efficiencies. These are minor variations and the important general ones will be discussed now in more detail.

Variation in overhead costs

Overhead costs are incurred regardless of throughputs, operating efficiencies or distribution procedures, and siting has a major effect upon them. The site of a supply source involves overhead cost factors such as rates, rent, building investments and development charges. These overheads are necessary for satisfying production requirements; consequently, they will increase as the number of production sites increases. On the other hand, unit overhead costs can be reduced by increasing the production throughput which will require more storage facilities. Once again, the optimal solution will be a compromise between the production overheads that increase with the number of sites and the distribution overheads that decrease as a result. The optimum will be the least total cost which is shown in Figure 5:5 for a varying number of sites.

Obviously, where production overhead costs are high in relation to distribution, such as for precision machinery, increasing the distribution through-

DECIDING THE BEST SUPPLY SITES

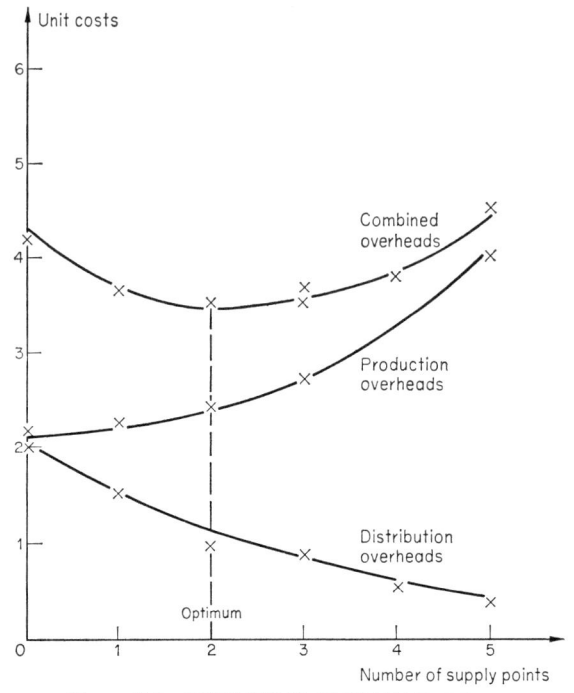

Figure 5:5 OPTIMISING OVERHEAD COSTS

put has little effect on total overhead costs. The reverse is the case when distribution costs are relatively high, for example with frozen foods; then the throughput will be critical. The correct siting of supply points is vital, because the total distribution cost is an overhead on products which can amount to 40 per cent of the price or more.

Variation in transport requirements

The road and rail transport for delivering goods is of two kinds, trunking and local deliveries. The former influences optimal production sites and the latter influences depot siting. The requirements of trunking include facilities for loading and parking articulated vehicles, containerisation and fully mechanised materials handling at warehouses. Spare trailers enable trunking to be operated independently of local deliveries.

Local deliveries need vans, usually, and the depot sites have to be designed for operating them. Goods are delivered from depots directly to customer locations.

A simple transit depot consists of a hard standing for parking the vehicles, a covered area for transferring the goods from trailers to vans, a small office and a warehouse for storing goods. As the number of vehicles required in-

DECIDING THE BEST SUPPLY SITES

creases, it becomes more economic to provide facilities for their maintenance, bulk storage of goods, rest rooms for drivers and the like.

Transport variations can be optimised by balancing costs against savings. More depot sites mean that fewer vans will be required, but more bulk-carrying vehicles. It can be shown graphically that the best general balance is obtained with one central supply site and about ten regional depots. Below ten depots, costs rise quite sharply and above this number the costs rise only slowly.

Variation in production outputs

Distribution throughputs are specific to production outputs; therefore, the throughput of a distribution system must be planned to suit particular production requirements. Unfortunately, production outputs are uncontrollable in some industries. Minimising distribution costs according to variations in production outputs requires the combination of several cost/throughput graphs which may become complicated at times. An example of varying production outputs that affect a distribution system is presented in Chapter 10 with reference to the motor industry.

5:4 DEPOT SITING

A distribution system must be planned as an integrated whole, so that each function is related to the others and there are no duplications. In this way, the best utilisation of time and equipment is ensured. The siting of depots, the routing of vehicles and the scheduling of deliveries all contribute to the price of goods. These costs are indirect to either production or marketing, but they affect financial profitability directly.

Depots are warehouses for local deliveries, basically, and there are a number of questions which must be considered before selecting the site for a depot:

1. How many depots are required for providing the service level necessary?
2. Where will they be sited, strategically, in relation to land values, labour resources and distribution costs?
3. What is the range of goods that will be stocked at each depot for supplying to its distribution area?
4. What must be the size of the depot and how much land is needed for the site?
5. What will be the depot requirements in the future and can the system be modified if necessary?

Deciding depot sites

The best method for deciding the number and locations of depot sites is

DECIDING THE BEST SUPPLY SITES

to start from the position of having no depots at all. Then it is comparatively simple to site one depot at the centre of demand with the aid of coordinates; the value of each coordinate will be equated in terms of its costs and service level. Then two depots can be sited optimally, assuming that each will be responsible for approximately half the demand. This process of siting continues for the estimated total number of depot sites. The overall cost and service level of each site must be evaluated and then they can be compared in order to find the best. The site with the least total cost for providing the service level desired will be the one chosen.

When the approximate location for a depot has been decided, its practical implications must be examined. The cost of land may be important in a built-up area, or the optimal site may apply to a fairly wide area. In addition to differences in land prices, there is the interest on capital to be considered as well as the availability of labour. However, these variations are small when compared with overall warehousing and delivering costs.

The service level offered to customers may be a measure of the goods ordered or the time for delivery, and both are incorporated in the order lead time. Multiplying order quantity by delivery time or distance has the effect of giving greatest importance to large orders.

The steps that must be followed in order to optimise the siting of a depot are shown in Figure 5:6; additionally, they can be followed for formulating the structure of any distribution system. The schematic diagram is a general concept that becomes specific when operational data is included. It is very useful for showing the factors that have to be considered when deciding the best sites for depots, because it develops an understanding of the interplay between the different variable factors that make distribution a dynamic function.

5:5 THE BEST SITE FOR A SUPPLY POINT

In order to illustrate the procedures siting a supply point, the example of the Florida Ice Company and the problem of siting their refrigeration plant optimally will be studied in detail.

The company delivered blocks of ice to different customers in the American state of Florida and all the ice was supplied from one refrigeration plant. Siting the plant had a marked effect on the total cost of distribution and the service level provided to customers. The capital investment in a refrigeration plant was considerable and it was uneconomic to operate more than one plant for supplying the total demand in this example.

The problem of deciding the optimal site for the refrigeration plant has

DECIDING THE BEST SUPPLY SITES

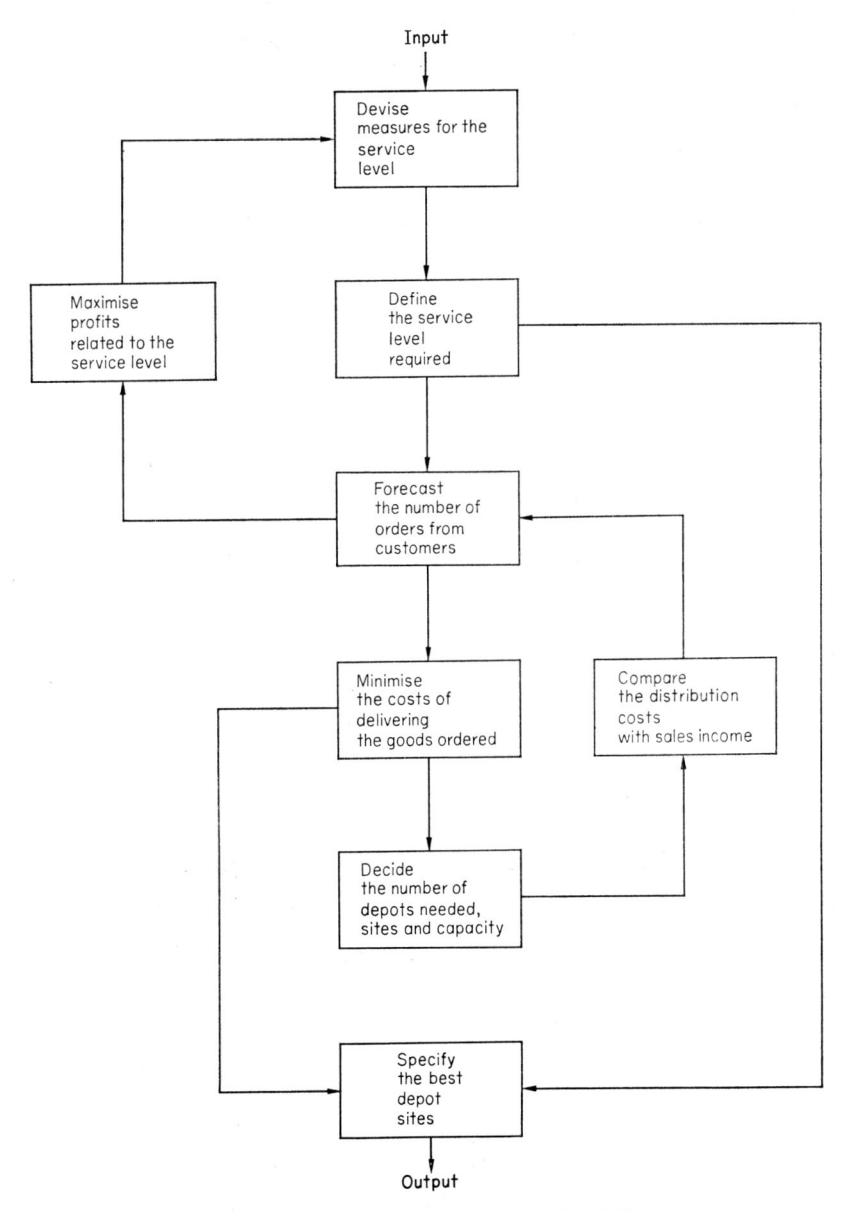

```
                    Input
                      ↓
              ┌───────────────┐
        ┌────→│ Devise        │
        │     │ measures for  │
        │     │ the service   │
        │     │ level         │
        │     └───────┬───────┘
        │             ↓
┌───────┴──────┐  ┌───────────────┐
│ Maximise     │  │ Define        │
│ profits      │  │ the service   │←──────────────┐
│ related to   │  │ level         │               │
│ the service  │  │ required      │               │
│ level        │  └───────┬───────┘               │
└──────────────┘          ↓                       │
        │        ┌───────────────┐                │
        └───────→│ Forecast      │←───────────┐   │
                 │ the number of │            │   │
                 │ orders from   │            │   │
                 │ customers     │            │   │
                 └───────┬───────┘            │   │
                         ↓                    │   │
                 ┌───────────────┐   ┌────────┴───┴──┐
                 │ Minimise      │   │ Compare       │
                 │ the costs of  │   │ the distribu- │
                 │ delivering    │   │ tion costs    │
                 │ the goods     │   │ with sales    │
                 │ ordered       │   │ income        │
                 └───────┬───────┘   └───────┬───────┘
                         ↓                   │
                 ┌───────────────┐           │
                 │ Decide        │           │
                 │ the number of │───────────┘
                 │ depots needed,│
                 │ sites and     │
                 │ capacity      │
                 └───────┬───────┘
                         ↓
                 ┌───────────────┐
                 │ Specify       │
                 │ the best      │←──────────
                 │ depot         │
                 │ sites         │
                 └───────┬───────┘
                         ↓
                      Output
```

Figure 5:6 DEPOT SITING PROCEDURE

DECIDING THE BEST SUPPLY SITES

been expanded in order to illustrate the different procedures that have been described already for solving general siting problems (see Chapter 4).

Two demand locations system

Originally, the Florida Ice Company was formed by the amalgamation of two smaller companies, one in Miami and one in Jacksonville. The joint management decided that ice demands in these two cities should be supplied from a single refrigeration plant. The demands at the two locations and the rail distance between them are shown in Figure 5:7. The demands are expressed as tons of ice required per week.

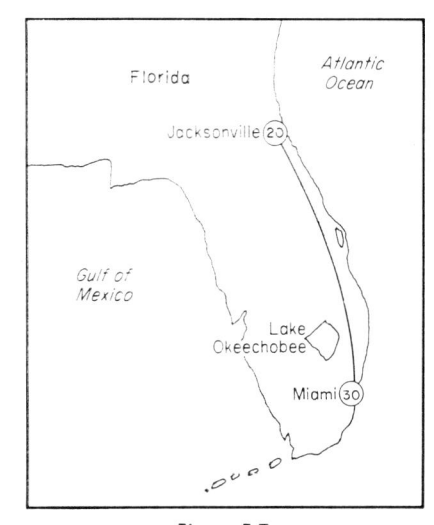

Figure 5:7
FLORIDA ICE COMPANY:
FIRST SYSTEM

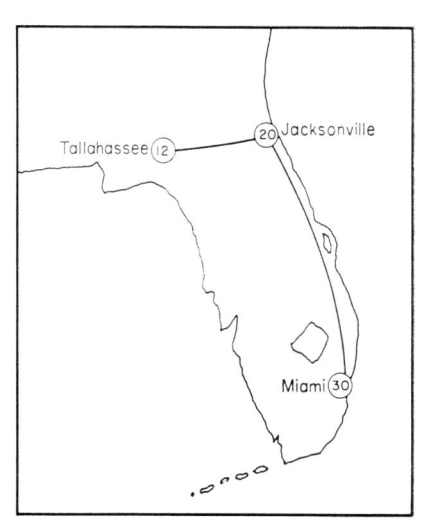

Figure 5:8
FLORIDA ICE COMPANY:
SECOND SYSTEM

Solution. Since the greatest demand was at Miami, the plant should be sited there optimally.

Three demand locations system

Planning the distribution system for the Florida Ice Company should investigate future market demands for ice. Demands were likely to develop in other areas of the state and supplying them would have to be considered when planning the system strategically.

In the near future, a demand in Tallahassee should be considered, when the distribution system would comprise one supply site and three demand locations. This second system is shown in Figure 5:8.

Solution. Referring to the three demand locations system in Section 4:3,

DECIDING THE BEST SUPPLY SITES

the best site would be at Jacksonville, because the sum of the demands at Tallahassee and Jacksonville was greater than the demand at Miami.

Branch line system

A development of the previous system could produce a branch line in order to supply demand in Tampa. The four demands are shown in Figure 5:9 along with the mileages between locations.

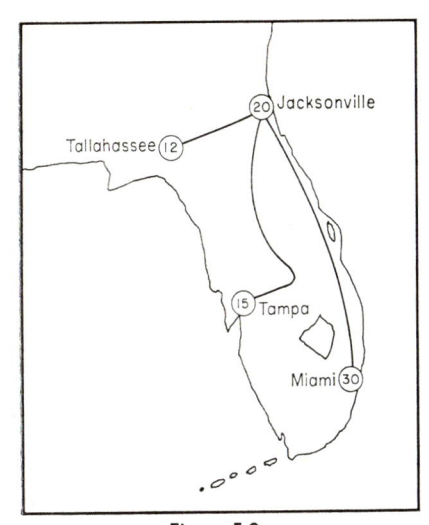

Figure 5:9
FLORIDA ICE COMPANY:
THIRD SYSTEM

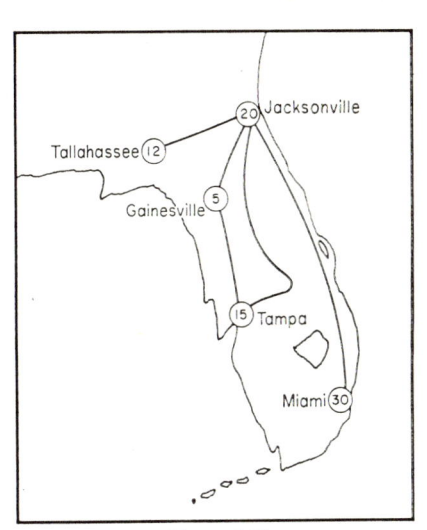

Figure 5:10
FLORIDA ICE COMPANY:
FOURTH SYSTEM

When dealing with the best supply site for a branch line system the line between the two greatest demands is considered to be part of the main line. In this example, the main line would run from Miami to Jacksonville, and then both Tallahassee and Tampa would be at the end of branch lines, initially. The Tampa branch had the greater demand of the two branches; therefore, it would form the rest of the main line.

Solution. The best supply site would lie on the main line from Miami to Tampa through Jacksonville which was equivalent to a three locations system. Consulting the rules given in Figure 4:5 showed that Jacksonville was still the best location for the refrigeration plant in this system.

Loop line system

While optimising the site of the refrigeration plant for the Florida Ice Company, strategic planning should include the possibility of supplying a demand

DECIDING THE BEST SUPPLY SITES

at Gainesville which was on a minor route from Jacksonville to Tampa. In this case, there would be a loop line system as shown in Figure 5:10.

The loop comprised demand locations at Jacksonville, Tampa and Gainesville with a total demand of 40 tons of ice per week. The loop demand was greater than half the total demand for the whole system. Therefore, it could be regarded as the main line and it would include the best supply site for the whole system.

Solution. Taking the loop as the main line it could be assumed that Tallahassee and Miami were on branch lines and their demands should be added to Jacksonville, because they would have to be delivered from there. This made the greatest demand for the system to be located at Jacksonville, so that it would be the best supply site still.

Complex system

Finally, the possibility of the Florida Ice Company supplying other main towns in the state was considered. A complex network for delivering ice to these towns was prepared (see Figure 5:11) and the demands were forecast by marketing experts. The planners were now faced with the problem of deciding the best site for a large refrigeration plant that would supply the whole system satisfactorily for the least distribution cost. Once again, the delivery costs were taken to be proportional to route mileages.

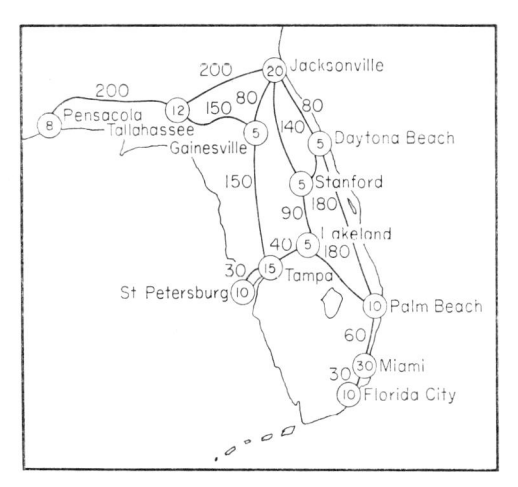

Figure 5:11 FLORIDA ICE COMPANY: COMPLEX SYSTEM

Basically, the complex system comprised one loop line and three branch lines. Jacksonville could be included with three of the lines and it was

DECIDING THE BEST SUPPLY SITES

thought that it might be the best site, until the demand-distances were resolved for the whole system. Initially, Jacksonville was included with the Pensacola branch line only, for the sake of convenience and illustration.

The four lines with their demand locations and tonnages of ice required each week are presented below.

1. *Loop/line system*
   Gainesville (5 tons)+Tampa (15 tons)+St Petersburg (10 tons)+Lakeland (5 tons)+Stanford (5 tons)   = 40 tons

2. *Branch line system*
   Pensacola (8 tons)+Tallahassee (12 tons)+Jacksonville (20 tons)   = 40 tons

3. *Branch line system*
   Florida City (10 tons)+Miami (30 tons)   = 40 tons

4. *Branch line system*
   Daytona Beach (5 tons)+Palm Beach (10 tons)   = 15 tons

   Total demand = 135 tons

According to the line theorem, the best supply site should be located in the line system with the greatest demand, but three lines had the same demand in this example; only the last one could be discounted. These line systems of equal demand were differentiated from one another by calculating their demand-cost vectors. Cost was proportional to delivery distance and the best supply site would be decided by calculating the total demand-distance vector for each system.

Solution. Supply points for the three line systems of equal demand would be at Tampa, Jacksonville and Miami; therefore, the best supply point for the complete system would be located at one of these cities.

Comparing the demand-distance vectors (as ton-miles) for the three locations was performed in tabular form and the basic figures are shown in Figure 5:12. The ton-mile cost vectors were converted into financial terms by multiplying them with the appropriate delivery costs per ton-mile. The mileages were based upon rail trunking distances and local delivery distances were excluded.

The total distribution cost vectors, in ton-miles, for the three feasible sites proved that supplying from Tampa would involve the least cost; therefore, it would be the best site for the refrigeration plant in the complex system.

DECIDING THE BEST SUPPLY SITES

Line system index	Demand locations	Demand (tons)	Tampa Distance miles	Tampa Vector ton-miles	Jacksonville Distance miles	Jacksonville Vector ton-miles	Miami Distance miles	Miami Vector ton-miles
1	Gainesville	5	150	750	80	400	430	2 150
	Tampa	15	0	0	230	3 450	280	4 200
	St Petersburg	10	30	300	260	2 600	310	3 100
	Lakeland	5	40	200	230	1 150	240	1 200
	Stanford	5	130	650	140	700	330	1 650
	Total	40	—	1 900	—	8 300	—	12 300
2	Pensacola	8	500	4 000	400	3 200	720	5 760
	Tallahassee	12	300	3 600	200	2 400	520	6 240
	Jacksonville	20	230	4 600	0	0	320	6 400
	Total	40	—	12 200	—	5 600	—	18 400
3	Florida City	10	310	3 100	350	3 500	30	300
	Miami	30	280	8 400	320	9 600	0	0
	Total	40	—	11 500	—	13 100	—	300
4	Daytona Beach	5	200	1 000	80	400	240	1 200
	Palm Beach	10	220	2 200	260	2 600	60	600
	Total	15	—	3 200	—	3 000	—	1 800
	Total demand costs			28 800		30 000		32 800

Figure 5:12 TABLE OF DISTRIBUTION COST VECTORS

1 Supplying from Tampa   28 800 ton-miles
2 Supplying from Jacksonville 30 000 ton-miles
3 Supplying from Miami   32 800 ton-miles

More than one supply site

The locations for more than one refrigeration plant site, in the example for the Florida Ice Company, would be found with the aid of the progression described in Section 4:4.

$$\frac{D}{2n} \quad \frac{3D}{2n} \quad \frac{5D}{2n} \quad \frac{7D}{2n} \quad \frac{9D}{2n} \quad \frac{(2n-1)D}{2n}.$$

Solution. The system could be reduced to a single line from Tampa to

DECIDING THE BEST SUPPLY SITES

Miami via Jacksonville. The Daytona Beach demand could be supplied from Jacksonville and the Palm Beach demand from Miami.

		Cumulated total
Tampa total demand	= 40 tons	40 tons
Jacksonville total demand	= 45 tons	85 tons
Miami total demand	= 50 tons	135 tons

Total system demand (D) = 135 tons

The sites for more than one supply source can be obtained from the progression above.

Two refrigeration plant sites

Two plant sites should be located where the cumulated demand from one end of the main line equalled

$$\frac{D}{2n} \text{ and } \frac{3D}{2n} \text{ tons}$$

when $n = 2$ sites and $D =$ total demand.

First site: $\dfrac{D}{2n} = \dfrac{135}{4} = 34$ tons at Tampa

Second site: $\dfrac{3D}{2n} = \dfrac{405}{4} = 101$ tons at Miami

Three refrigeration plant sites

For obvious reasons, the sites for three refrigeration plants would be at Tampa, Jacksonville and Miami, should they be required at a later date.

Solution. This example of a practical distribution system illustrates the fact that the final decision when siting the best supply points rests upon the least overall distribution cost of providing the desired service level. Also, the best supply site differs with the conditions of a system, which makes it essential to define the objectives before planning commences. It is safe to play around with a system at the planning stage, but investing resources without a full understanding of the factors involved is folly.

The logical sequence for planning a distribution system starts with defining the objectives, followed by developing the overall requirements, deciding the best supply points, routing the transport, scheduling the deliveries and planning the resources. Following this systematic procedure has the best chance of producing a successful distribution system.

6 ROUTING DELIVERY VEHICLES

After the best supply sites for a distribution system have been decided, the next stage of planning is to develop the routes for supplying goods to customers. There are many different methods available for delivering goods: by mail, by public carriers, by air, by water. by rail or by road. Only the last method is within the direct control of suppliers when their own vehicles are used; therefore, delivering goods by road is the most important from their viewpoint when planning a distribution system.

When planning, each of the different methods available for delivering goods must be considered and public transport should come first. When public transport has been proved unsuitable, hiring or owning the vehicles can be considered. The main drawback to using public transport is the reduced control, particularly delivery times to customers, which may affect the service level that can be offered. Despite this disadvantage, the merits of public transport may include cost savings and they should be investigated fully before a company acquires its own vehicles. The most successful decisions result from the analysis of every possibility.

Routing vehicles for delivering goods can start as soon as the best supply sites have been decided and established. Initially, it is advisable to prepare a map of the distribution system in order to show the supply points and customer locations. The first routes to be examined will be straight lines between points, because they will give an overall impression of the complete network.

Starting diagrammatically and proceeding step by step is the surest way of discovering the best routes for vehicles. Many years of experience can provide good solutions more quickly, but there will be a certain amount of luck involved in most cases. The future of a company may depend upon a good distribution network and it is too big a risk to gamble on guesswork. However, good guesswork is enhanced by systematic planning which can turn an experienced person into an expert.

A scientific approach is essential for reducing the considerable effort that is involved for planning vehicle routes. Science has three successive stages; firstly, getting the facts relating to a particular objective; secondly, examining them and developing theories that can explain their causes; thirdly, testing the theories in order to see if they are acceptable in practice.

The value of the scientific approach for routing vehicles is illustrated by the simple example of delivering goods to three locations, A, B and C. The first route investigated could be delivering to A, then to B and, finally, to C. Writing down all the combinations that are possible for routing vehicles to these three points produces six altogether.

The total number of combinations is a factorial of the locations involved. A factorial is the product of all the whole numbers involved. For example, the factorial number of routes for delivering to three locations is $3 \times 2 \times 1 = 6$. For four locations, it is $4 \times 3 \times 2 \times 1 = 24$ and so on.

It needs very little thought to realise that the number of alternative routes that can be developed for large distribution systems is colossal. Reducing this number is where the scientific use of commonsense is valuable. For instance, if there is a big mountain between points A and B in the three locations example given earlier, the route combinations ABC, BAC, CAB and CBA can be ignored because they are impractical. This is scientific thinking and it has eliminated four of the six possible routes straight away. Routing problems are never as simple as this, but a scientific approach is certain to reduce the effort of considering every possible route.

6:1 SCIENTIFIC ROUTING

Scientific procedures start with getting the facts and the facts for scientific routing include details of the supply sites, customer locations, delivery vehicles and operating conditions.

Getting routing facts

The source of supply may be a warehouse, a railway truck, a sandpit or any one of a number of alternatives. Details of the supply site will be the first facts to be collected when routing vehicles scientifically.

Facts about customer locations include the map references for drop points, details of the goods ordered, order frequencies and lead times, accessibility at drop points, working hours and other relevant information. Collecting facts about supply sites and customer locations reduces the number of possibilities that need to be considered when selecting the vehicles and routes.

The goods ordered will determine the type and size of vehicles that are suitable for different routes. The accessibility at drop points will limit the wheelbase or height of vehicles that can be used. It has been stated already that large vehicles are the most economic to operate when fully laden; therefore, the largest size of vehicle that can be fully loaded should be considered first when routing delivery vehicles. Often, this restricts the number of routes that can be used and the speeds of travel.

The capacity of a vehicle may be limited by its laden weight or volume, the financial value of its load or the time needed to deliver a load. Delivery times will be affected by average speeds, road conditions and unloading times.

Operating conditions vary with different distribution systems, but some conditions that must be considered in most cases include the maximum driving time permitted, the fuel consumption, the road congestion, the speed limits, the road restrictions, gradients and obstacles, the human element, the types of road and the working hours.

Examining the facts

Every examination must have a standard for exercising judgement, since decisions are based upon choosing between alternatives for achieving objectives. It follows that examining routes involves inspecting the facts and judging them against the objectives. When planning delivery routes, the facts collected must be examined in relation to the objectives for routing the vehicles between supply sites and customer locations.

The standard for judging the alternatives may be just a mental picture or it may be a complex mathematical equation. The former is suitable for judging a beauty competition, but the latter will be more suitable for designing a torsional suspension unit for a truck. Routing standards are rarely as specific as these examples, because they have to be flexible or adaptable.

The first feasible route developed for a delivery journey will provide the standard for judging the best of several alternatives. Every route that is developed must be compared with the objectives in order to see if it is feasible. At this stage, the best route will be hypothetical although it may appear to be quite feasible.

Testing the theories

A feasible route that has been developed in the mind, on a piece of paper, or as a working model, must be tested in practice before it can be incorporated in a practical distribution system. In practice, vehicle routes must ensure that the greatest customer service and the most economical vehicle operation are provided.

Optimal routes

The conditions for optimality when routing vehicles are the least operating costs and the quickest delivery times. The least cost is essential from the company's point of view and the quickest time is an appropriate measure of customer service level.

Costs can be reduced by investing money in only the bare essentials that are necessary for providing the service desired. Delivery times can be reduced by planning for the fastest vehicle speeds. Delivery speeds are increased by selecting the shortest routes, the fastest vehicles and the quickest turnrounds.

Fundamentally, the efficient routing of vehicles for distributing goods depends upon selecting optimal depot sites. Conversely, an optimal depot site depends upon efficient routing. This is paradoxical because there is no such thing as one optimal route when many delivery vehicles are involved.

6:2 FACTORS THAT AFFECT VEHICLE ROUTING

In some cases, the theoretical solution to a routing problem will be illogical because it may recommend an inexact number of vehicles. Consequently, it will be necessary to round up the number of vehicles to the next whole number and reduce the overall efficiency slightly; however, minor adjustments between adjacent delivery areas can produce some cost savings. In general, it may be possible to save up to half the number of vehicles required for several delivery areas when small adjustments are made to vehicle routes and schedules.

The best solution results from analysing the whole distribution system before allocating vehicles to specific delivery areas and routes.

Effect of area boundaries

Looking at the broad picture of a distribution system helps to determine the boundaries for delivery areas because the routes and depot sites are considered together. A change in one area may start a wave of changes throughout the whole system; on the other hand, another vehicle in one area may have an insignificant effect on the whole system.

Reviewing vehicle routes

Distribution systems are continually changing; therefore, the best system applies for a short time only. Each system needs reviewing regularly, but the frequency of rerouting vehicles will vary according to the nature of the products distributed and their markets.

It is advisable to allow a little "slack time" when routing vehicles, but each vehicle must start on its journey fully laden. Regular delivery times and frequencies are a measure of goods customer service, but they restrict the optimisation of vehicle routes.

Variable routing factors

When routing delivery vehicles, there are four basic conditions that affect vehicle operating costs and times:

1   Fully loaded: up to the first call

2   Partly loaded: between calls
3   Unloading: at drop points
4   Empty: returning to the supply point

Speed restrictions

The speed of a vehicle varies with its load, with the congestion of the roads and with other minor restrictions. British law restricts goods vehicles to 40 m.p.h. (65km/hr) on open roads, while Trade Union agreements set the upper speed limits for vehicles weighing under 5 tons. These limits are averages of 22 m.p.h. (35km/hr) in restricted zones and 28 m.p.h. (45km/hr) in de-restricted zones. Also, the length of time that one driver may drive a vehicle in any day is ten hours maximum.

Distance restrictions

These speed restrictions make it unlawful in Britain to exceed 280 miles a day on open roads with one driver, or 220 miles per day in restricted zones. Then, it follows that the overall length of a delivery route for any one day must be less than 220 or 280 miles according to the zones encountered.

Time restrictions

Other restrictions arise from such factors as the time spent at drop points, the length of time for loading and unloading and the delays that occur on the journey or at drop points. In order to allow for delays, certain contingency allowances must be included in the delivery schedules.

Capacity restrictions

Variations in the load capacities of vehicles are caused by restrictions to the permissible size or type of vehicle. Normally, large deliveries will incur the smallest handling charges, but compromises will have to be made between order sizes, vehicle capacities and similar scheduling factors before it is possible to determine optimal routes.

The capacity of a vehicle affects the number and type of calls that it can make on any particular route. Also, it restricts the size of orders, the nature of routes and calls, the distances between drop points and the times for unloading.

6:3 DEVELOPING VEHICLE ROUTES

Efficient routing means finding the shortest distance and time between a number of points in combination. The least number of vehicles that will provide customers with a desirable level of service will keep down operating costs. Transport costs are related directly to distances in most cases.

ROUTING DELIVERY VEHICLES

The number of vehicles for a delivery network depends upon the restrictions outlined already, but the number has to be decided before it is possible to develop routes. Then, the next step is to check the feasibilities for a predetermined minimum number of vehicles. Sometimes, the number of vehicles will have to be altered, because of interrelationships with other variables in the system. Complex systems contain many alternatives which have to be compared before it is possible to develop the best combinations. The use of a computer may be advisable when developing routing networks. Usually, it is easiest to develop a network by "rule of thumb," because many of the restrictions will be uncertain until the system has been tested. The least disastrous tests are made with models.

Pin and string method

Basically, this method is a model that comprises a map of the area mounted upon a board with a pin inserted at each customer drop point. Then, a string or cotton is cut to a length representing the delivery time available and one end is pinned to the supply site. One string is cut for the time available for each vehicle, for example, the driving time per day per vehicle. A feasible route will be found by passing each string around a set of pins and back to the depot. Any surplus string after returning to the depot indicates that time is available for other work, since the string length represents the working time available. Delay at a drop point can be represented by winding the string around the pin until a length equivalent to the expected unloading time has been expended. Iteration, or "trial and error," will be necessary in order to find the best routes for each vehicle. Although "trial and error" can be time consuming, this method is easily understood by ordinary people and it produces satisfactory routes.

The pin and string method is suitable for developing long-term trunking routes but a different method has to be used for routing short-term journeys.

Sub-area group method

This is a simple model suitable for planning daily routes and local deliveries. The local delivery area which can be served from a depot supply point is divided into a number of sub-areas. Map coordinates can be used for this purpose, but it has been found that GPO post code areas are very good, particularly when orders are received or invoices dispatched by mail. It is advisable to equate the orders and vehicle loads in units of the goods to be delivered; for example, as cases, drums or pallet-loads. The order units are totalled and divided by the capacity of one vehicle in order to calculate the number of vehicles that will be required for each sub-area.

In this routing method, the number of vehicle loads for each sub-area are grouped in clusters, starting at the outer edge of the sub-area and working inwards towards the depot. It is assumed that vehicles assigned to the outer edge of the sub-area will set out first and a route is planned for dropping each load. Then, delivery times can be calculated and adjustments made by iteration until optimal routes are obtained. A combination of the sub-area group and pin and string methods will solve most routing problems in an understandable manner.

Long routes

When there is little demand in an area, it may be advisable to extend routes over two or more days rather than operate vehicles underloaded and return to the depot each day. When the distance is too great for a round trip to be completed in one day with one driver, there are a number of alternatives that can be investigated.

Staging points. Two or more drivers can be assigned to each vehicle; the first drives to a staging point where the vehicle is transferred to a second driver. The second driver can be based at the staging point, can travel to it by train or can travel with the vehicle. Very long journeys will need more than one staging point. When a staging point can be located mid-way along a route which involves one day's driving on either side, two drivers and two vehicles can be utilised in order to prevent drivers spending nights away from home. The depot based driver drives loaded vehicles to the staging point and drives empty ones back, while the second driver delivers locally to customers.

Overnight stops. When the route for delivering a full vehicle load requires more than one day's driving, the driver must stop somewhere overnight.

Transfer depots. It may be worth while to set up transfer depots for serving remote areas. These small depots will be sited strategically at distances equivalent to one day's return trip from the supply site.

Delivering to remote areas. The costs of delivering goods to remote customers must be calculated for all the methods available in order to find the most economical. Whatever the method chosen, the extra costs of delivering to remote areas has to be included in the total cost of the distribution system. Usually, carriers can offer more favourable delivery terms, because their vehicles make up full loads with different types of goods.

A simple solution for problems concerning the delivery of goods to remote areas can be obtained by combining trunking and transit depots. Each container trailer becomes the transit store for supplying local delivery vans.

6:4 COMPUTERISED ROUTING

When the objectives for a distribution system can be expressed in numerical terms, equations can be developed for describing the operations; then, it is possible to perform iteration with a computer in order to obtain an optimal routing solution. Computers perform repetitive calculations rapidly and accurately provided that they are programmed correctly. A program can be an equation for the routing objective and it will have to be fed into the computer along with relevant data. The computer compares the data with the objective electronically and discovers the combination of facts that best complies with the system requirements.

Developing a program which tells the computer how to arrive at an optimal solution by "trial and error" may be the limiting factor. Programs for standard distribution problems are available and some are suitable for adopting to include different restrictions or variables.

Savings theory

A useful program for computerised routing is the savings theory which compares the costs of alternative routes from a supply source by iteration. The first feasible solution accumulates the total costs of delivery to each customer separately. Combining customer journeys together reduces the total number of journeys required so that savings will be obtained. The more customer drops that can be combined to form a single vehicle journey, the less costly the total distribution cost will be.

An optimal route will be one with the least delivery cost or distance and it will occur when no further savings can be made by combining customer drops. Several computer programs are based upon this concept, but it is important to use one that is appropriate to the system under consideration.

Measuring delivery costs

Records for delivery operations provide the facts for determining operating costs. These costs must be expressed in terms of route distances or volumes in order to make them meaningful for the purpose of measuring delivery costs. The most appropriate term is cost per unit of distance—for example, pence per mile or cents per kilometre. Subsequently, route costs can be compared by their distances multiplied by the cost per distance unit.

Computers can be programmed to measure distances between distribution points and calculate route costs. Distances are measured relatively by a computer if a reference map is divided into grid squares. The distance of a journey route that is to be measured will be defined by map co-ordinates of the change points along the route. The straight line distance between the coordinates of two points is the hypoteneuse of the right-angled triangle that is defined by the coordinates. This distance becomes more accurate as the size of the triangles used for computing distances gets smaller.

Distances computed in this way will be fair estimates of true route distances when multiplied by contingency factors. Contingency factors will be ratios of the actual route distance and the computed distance. Different route conditions will give different factors. A factor of 1.1 is applicable to most urban road routes and 1.2 is suitable for rural road routes where the choice of alternative roads is restricted.

6:5 ESTIMATING ROUTE DISTANCES

When comparing routes, the delivery costs can be estimated by calculating route distances. Naturally, the most accurate method of measuring distance is to travel the route with a vehicle and observe the odometer readings. However, this can be involved and time consuming; therefore, approximations are more acceptable in practice.

Distances can be estimated readily with the aid of scale maps and grid coordinates. The use of coordinates and simple geometry produces route distances quickly and they are sufficiently accurate for vehicle route planning.

The use of coordinates will be illustrated by estimating the alternative distances between distribution points in order to optimise the costs of routing newspaper delivery vehicles.

Route optimisation example

A local distributor of newspapers wished to optimise the delivery route from Alba to Birni and Cosmo as shown in Figure 6:1. Two alternative routes could be used to avoid the lake; the direct route that involved travelling from Alba to Cosmo and supplying Birni from Dudu; or the circuitous route via Ende.

Coordinates for the locations were drawn on a map in order to obtain horizontal and vertical distances between locations (see Figure 6:1). Distances could be estimated with the aid of Pythagoras' Theorem.

1 *Direct route*: In the triangle ACM, the distance *AC* was the square root of *CM* squared plus *AM* squared and the distance for supplying *B* which was twice *DB*.

$AC = \sqrt{4^2+7^2} = \sqrt{65} = $ 8.1km
$2DB = 2\times3 \qquad\qquad = $ 6.0km
Total distance $\qquad\qquad = $ 14.1km

ROUTING DELIVERY VEHICLES

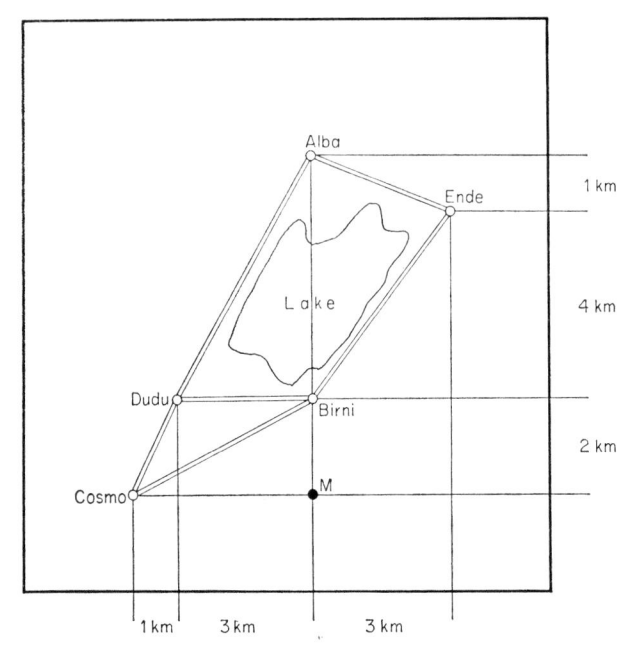

Figure 6:1 ROUTE OPTIMISATION WITH COORDINATES

2 *Circuitous route*: The continuous route for supply Alba, Birni and Cosmo was *AEBC*. Once again, coordinates and simple geometry were used to estimate the total distance.

$AE = \sqrt{1^2+3^2} = \sqrt{10} = 3.2$km
$EB = \sqrt{4^2+3^2} = \sqrt{25} = 5.0$km
$BC = \sqrt{2^2+4^2} = \sqrt{20} = \underline{4.5\text{km}}$
Total distance $= 12.7$km

Solution. Distributing newspapers by the circuitous route would be 1.4km shorter than the direct route with backtracking to Birni; therefore, it was optimal.

The contingency factor for this example could be calculated after the optimal route had been measured. It was found to be 13.9 km in fact.

Contingency factor $= \dfrac{13.9}{12.7} = 1.1$

In future estimates for this distribution area multiplying the estimated distances by 1.1 would produce acceptable delivery distances.

6:6 JOURNEY PLANNING

Journey planning can be described as a technique for breaking down distribution areas into routes which ensure that the largest vehicles are operated, the route distances are minimal and the service provided is maximal for the least total operating cost.

Distribution areas

The size of a distribution area affects the length and duration of delivery journeys. The shorter a journey the quicker the goods can be delivered to customers, but long journeys have the ability of absorbing delays along the route. Effective vehicle utilisation depends upon the loading and unloading times with short journeys and upon the loadability with long journeys.

Service level

Journey planning has the objective of optimising routes in terms of delivery times which determine the customer service level that can be provided. The length of a journey affects the delivery time to customers, but return journeys must be taken into account too. Other factors that affect the journey times include loading and unloading, and good load organisation is an advantage.

Journey effectiveness

When an effective journey has been developed, all ineffective times such as delays, slow driving, faulty loading and stoppages will be minimised. Delivery operations must be speeded up whenever possible; for example, mechanical handling can cut the time for loading goods to one-fifth the time required for manual loading. The value of this reduction can be appreciated when it is realised that the shorter the time spent loading a vehicle the longer the time it can be on the road.

Increased journeys example

When the average distance for delivering a load of goods is 30 miles (50km), a vehicle can be expected to deliver ten loads in a week if it is loaded manually. Under similar conditions, mechanised loading can increase the number of journeys to eighteen.

The value of mechanical handling can be determined by estimating the savings that it affords and comparing them with the costs of buying the equipment. In this example, the vehicle fleet required would be halved with

ROUTING DELIVERY VEHICLES

mechanised loading which could cover the extra cost of buying forklift trucks and conveyors.

Mechanical handling

The main advantages of using mechanical handling equipment at warehouses are reduced time and effort, faster throughputs and less storage space. The handling of goods individually can be eliminated by using bulk vehicles, palletisation, containers or vehicles with removable bodies.

Time is reduced when loads can be assembled in quantity, on pallets for example, and loading and unloading will be made easier. Operational times can be controlled more accurately with mechanised equipment, because work durations are more predictable.

Analysing routes

The analytical methods for routing delivery vehicles that have been described in this chapter are suitable for solving most static routing problems. Difficulties arise when trying to plan a number of different routes with a variety of vehicles that have different delivery times.

Complex problems are the result of conflicts between variables and they can be solved satisfactorily only after defining each objective clearly. Then restrictions to the achievement of each objective can be determined and steps can be taken to overcome them. In practice, changes always occur with the passage of time and new problems will arise continually; therefore, routes must be reviewed and revised regularly.

6:7 ASSIGNING VEHICLES TO ROUTES

Distribution systems are rarely consistent; routes differ, loads differ and vehicles differ. Practical problems of assigning different vehicles to different routes can be solved with linear programming by intelligent distribution managers. An appropriate technique that uses iteration can be performed on pieces of squared paper with simple arithmetic, step by step systematically.

The problem that confronted the distribution supervisor of a bakery will be used to illustrate the technique of linear programming related to the assignment of vehicles to routes.

Assignment problem

A bakery with a small fleet of delivery vehicles wanted to provide an efficient service to customers in its locality without hiring additional vehicles. The distribution supervisor obtained a list of the retail outlets and their daily requirements of bread which was needed before twelve o'clock. The delivery vans started out at six each morning. This information was related to the

ROUTING DELIVERY VEHICLES

capacities of the available vans and the daily delivery routes so that a table could be produced for showing the work times involved.

The assignment method of linear programming was used to find the best solution for assigning the bread delivery vans to routes. It was an appropriate method that was quick and easy to use manually.

Basically, the method uses a matrix, or table, of the variables and manipulates them mathematically without altering the overall objective. In this case, the variables were different delivery vans and different customer locations, while the objective was to deliver all the orders before noon. The units to be compared were delivery times which varied with the van capacities and the route distances.

Each van was given a letter for identifying it and each delivery route was defined by its main town. The delivery time for each combination of van and town was expressed in hours. Iteration proceeded according to five recognised steps, starting with the preparation of a square matrix which is shown in Figure 6:2.

Step 1. Prepare a time matrix of the times required for delivering bread to the different towns with the different vans. Delivery time was really a measure of cost and the first matrix is called a cost matrix, normally (see Figure 6:2).

Routes \ Vans	A	B	C	D	E	F
Kington	4	2	8	4	5	4
Lenham	6	8	7	5	7	5
Milton	3	6	3	5	5	3
Norton	3	6	2	3	7	8
Otford	7	6	3	8	4	3
Purley	7	4	5	4	5	3

Figure 6:2
TIME MATRIX

Routes \ Vans	A	B	C	D	E	F
Kington	2	0	6	2	3	2
Lenham	1	3	2	0	2	0
Milton	0	3	0	2	2	0
Norton	1	4	0	1	5	6
Otford	4	3	0	5	1	0
Purley	4	1	2	1	2	0

Figure 6:3
FIRST REVISED TIME MATRIX

Step 2. Perform zero computation along the rows of the matrix. This meant finding the optimal van for each route and making its delivery time equal to zero. In the case of Kington, delivering with van B required the least time of 2 hours and it was made zero by subtracting 2 hours from every delivery time in the row.

ROUTING DELIVERY VEHICLES

The time matrix was revised (see Figure 6:3) in order to show the optimal van for each route—that is, the least time for delivering to each town. The solution was impractical at this stage, because different routes at times required the same van while there would be no work at all for van E.

Step 3. Repeat zero computation down the columns. This meant finding the optimal route for each van and making its delivery time equal to zero in the same way as for the previous step. It is perfectly legitimate to perform zero computation, because the overall relationships between the times are not altered.

The second revised time matrix is shown in Figure 6:4. It was realised

Vans / Routes	A	B	C	D	E	F
Kington	2	0	6	2	2	2
Lenham	1	3	2	0	1	0
Milton	0	3	0	2	1	0
Norton	1	4	0	1	4	6
Otford	4	3	0	5	0	0
Purley	4	1	2	1	1	0

Figure 6:4
SECOND REVISED TIME MATRIX

Vans / Routes	A	B	C	D	E	F
Kington	2	[0]	6	2	2	2
Lenham	1	3	2	0	1	⦻
Milton	0	3	⦻	2	1	⦻
Norton	1	4	[0]	1	4	6
Otford	4	3	⦻	5	0	⦻
Purley	4	1	2	1	1	[0]

Figure 6:5
THIRD REVISED TIME MATRIX

that the same route could be delivered optimally by more than one van in three instances, to Lenham, Milton and Otford. However, there were optimal options for each row and column row.

Step 4. Examine each row systematically in order to have only one option in each row. When there was only one zero in a route row, that van would be optimal and it should not be assigned to any other route. Consequently, any other zeros in the same column as the single zero in a row had to be crossed out. The optimal van for each route row was denoted by outlining its zero with a square as shown in Figure 6:5.

In this step, rows K, N and P had single zeros and they were outlined, while additional zeros in their columns were crossed out. At the end of this step, vans had been assigned to three of the routes optimally.

Step 5. Examine each column systematically in order to make one route

ROUTING DELIVERY VEHICLES

optimal for each van. The same procedure for outlining zeros and crossing out others in the same rows was used as in the fourth step.

The final matrix, which is presented in Figure 6:6, had an optimal combination for each row and column. Therefore, it was an optimal solution for this assignment problem.

Routes \ Vans	A	B	C	D	E	F
Kington	2	[0]	6	2	2	2
Lenham	1	3	2	[0]	1	✗
Milton	[0]	3	✗	2	1	✗
Norton	1	4	[0]	1	4	6
Otford	4	3	✗	5	[0]	✗
Purley	4	1	2	1	1	[0]

Figure 6:6 FINAL TIME MATRIX

Sometimes, problems are not solved completely at this stage, because more than one zero remains in certain rows or columns. In order to optimise them, steps four and five must be repeated continually until only one zero remains in each column, then the solution will be optimal.

Solution. The most effective assignment of bakery vans to routes is shown by the outlined zeros in Figure 6:6. It represented the least overall delivery time for both vans and routes; therefore, it had to be an optimal solution.

Optimal solution

1   Assign van A to Milton for 3 hours' work
2   Assign van B to Kington for 2 hours' work
3   Assign van C to Norton for 2 hours' work
4   Assign van D to Lenham for 5 hours' work
5   Assign van E to Otford for 4 hours' work
6   Assign van F to Purley for 3 hours' work

In five simple steps, a complete assignment solution had been obtained in which all the delivery work involved less than five hours' duration—that is completed by noon. The same solution could have been obtained with pure mathematics, but it would have required 6×6 = 36 calculations and comparing every result in order to find the least time.

This example shows that the use of logic in conjunction with a scientific procedure can solve routing problems with operations research without resorting to the expense of a computer.

Delivery schedules

It has been shown that the time taken for delivering goods to customers affects the cost of deliveries and the service level provided. Routes are static, but they become dynamic when delivery times are incorporated; then they are known as "schedules." Routing and scheduling have to be considered together in order to make them compatible.

A schedule gives the time sequence for making deliveries to customers and the process of scheduling cannot commence until the vehicles have been routed.

7 SCHEDULING DELIVERIES

The scheduling of deliveries to customers involves the planning of vehicle journeys so that orders are delivered on the right days and the vehicles are utilised efficiently. In scheduling problems, the variable factors are time and sequence. Time is the more critical factor in most distribution systems because it determines the customer service level, the size of inventory that has to be carried, the number of warehouses and vehicles, the personnel employed and the throughput of goods. Sequence is an extension of the time factor, because it determines the order in time for performing the operations.

Scheduling problems occur when there are conflicts between different sequences and an important factor in solving them is defining the scale of importance. Naturally, performing the most important operations first produces the best overall efficiency by reducing the cost of delays.

The overall objective of scheduling deliveries is to sequence orders and loads so that costs and delays are minimised. There are three general forms of scheduling problem that apply to delivering goods.

1 *Vehicle interference problems.* Conflicts of this nature concern several vehicles routed from the same supply depot. Journeys may be regular or random according to the routes and the customers visited. The sequence of journeys for a vehicle or the sequence of calls along a route, must be planned in order to minimise utilisation, yet minimise the cost of delivering goods.
2 *Route balancing problems.* In this case deliveries must be grouped along routes so that each vehicle is fully utilised and the work load is balanced out throughout periods of time and between vehicles.
3 *Journey planning problems.* Solving problems of this type means optimising the route sequence between different customer locations with a view to obtaining the greatest effectiveness and the least cost.

Iteration can be used to find the best schedule of events when the objective is to deliver, according to a time sequence. The sequence can be developed geographically with the aid of network analysis. Several methods of net-

SCHEDULING DELIVERIES

work analysis are available including critical path scheduling, the critical path method and PERT. All of these methods are more appropriate to production sequences than delivery schedules because the activities only have duration and cost. Deliveries have to be planned according to route directions in addition to duration and cost; consequently, systematic planning by iteration has a better value.

7:1 SCHEDULING DELIVERY VEHICLES

There is a close relationship between the routing of vehicles and the scheduling of deliveries and each will influence the other. The objectives of routing will be dependent upon the delivery schedules that will be used and the objectives of scheduling must include details of the routes to be followed. Routing is based upon static locations of supply and demand, while scheduling involves dynamic sequences for delivering goods. Goods scheduling is achieved by paying attention to detail, because small errors in timing can be expensive and are irretrievable.

Objectives for scheduling

Goods schedules are both feasible and practical to operate. The following factors must be included in the objectives for scheduling deliveries:

1. Operating times for incorporating in schedules must have been tested in practice
2. Schedules must have been tested by simulation for at least one complete cycle before being accepted as operational
3. Vehicles must be utilised efficiently and economically
4. All orders must be delivered to the customers on time or sooner
5. The effect of delays must be reduced and the inventory of stocks held at warehouses must be kept to a minimum

Scheduling bulk delivery vehicles

Transporting goods in bulk requires large and expensive vehicles, but their operating costs are reduced by using articulated vehicles, because each prime mover (tractor) is independent of the trailers. A tractor can transport one loaded trailer to a depot and return with a different one empty. In this way, coordinating tractors with a greater number of trailers will reduce the total scheduling time.

7:2 METHODS OF SCHEDULING DELIVERY VEHICLES

After siting the depots for a distribution system and routing the delivery

SCHEDULING DELIVERIES

vehicles according to the customer locations, the journeys have to be scheduled. Scheduling is an intuitive process that can be performed successfully by "trial and error" or iteration. The objective of iteration will be to develop effective vehicle schedules in terms of the capacities available and utilised. Straightforward scheduling problems can be solved repetitively with a computer, but when foresight is needed for investigating alternative possibilities the human brain is more effective.

Scheduling charts

There are limits to the complexity of a scheduling problem which can be handled by any brain; in the case of a human brain, it is believed that fourteen is the greatest number of different colours that can be visualised on a two dimensional scheduling chart.

A typical scheduling chart shows capacity as one coordinate against different variables, such as time, vehicle utilisation or drop point locations. Other charts plot these variables against one another, or a multi-coloured chart can show all four variables simultaneously against the number and load capacities of vehicles.

Symbols can be used on the charts for clarity of expression, and may represent the location of vehicles, the direction of travel, the nature of goods for delivery or drop points.

Planning deliveries

When making plans for scheduling delivery vehicles, it is essential to commence by collecting every item of information that is available and relevant. Then, the information must be studied so that different strategies for the deliveries become apparent. An analysis of scheduling methods will highlight important operations and elements, that is analysing delivery data, preparing summary sheets, making tentative schedules and deciding vehicle requirements. Records should be filed for future reference. The output of the planning stage provides a basis for later implementation and control.

Journey planning calculations

When planning journeys for delivery vehicles, it is useful to collect all the data that is available into tables which will help to make scheduling more meaningful. Much important information that is necessary for calculating journey schedules can be obtained from drivers' records or customers' records. Some useful pieces of information are listed below:

1. Delivery area references
2. Major towns delivery areas
3. Number and addresses of customers
4. Size of deliveries and frequencies

5 Number of drops for each route
6 Unloading times
7 Driving times
8 Combined journey times
9 Capacity and dimensions of vehicles
10 Number of journeys related to vehicle capacities
11 Duration of journeys related to routes
12 Restrictions to journey times

Planning standards

In many cases, it is possible to standardise the repetitive elements of vehicle schedules, either by synthetic methods after performing work measurement or by analysing similar elements and operations. Some examples are:

1 Drop times are proportional to the size of orders
2 Unloading constants
3 Journey constants, that is confirming the route before starting, meal breaks, refuelling and completing vehicle records

7:3 VARIABLE FACTORS OF SCHEDULING

Factors that affect scheduling differ according to the load capacities of vehicles and the geographical locations of customers, but every variable must be considered in relation to its time duration when delivering from warehouses. After determining feasible routes for each journey, it is important to analyse the time factors, either directly or synthetically.

Summary of variable factors

1 *Geographical factors.* The physical nature of a distribution area affects the journey routes and times, but all distances have to be converted into times when planning schedules.
2 *Remote areas.* Deciding how to deliver goods to remote areas must be based upon economic considerations.
3 *Peaking factors.* When trade is seasonal, the locations of customers differ, the size of orders may vary or the nature of orders may change. An incidental peaking factor that must be considered is traffic congestion, either during the day, week, month or year. Peaking factors can be analysed geographically.
4 *Delivery frequencies.* The minimum size of orders is a factor that affects the frequency of deliveries to customers.
5 *Delivery by contracted carriers.* It is advisable to allocate a journey to a carrier when the time for driving to and from an area is so great that it

SCHEDULING DELIVERIES

restricts the number of deliveries that can be made or it causes a journey to be uneconomic.

Inaccuracies in planning standards

A standard is valid as long as the factors that were used to develop it remain valid; when there is a factorial change, the standard must be revised. The factors that are likely to affect delivery schedules invariably include unloading times, traffic congestion, road works, different order sizes and variable numbers of drops.

7:4 VEHICLES REQUIRED FOR DELIVERIES

There are many types of vehicle, both different types of chassis and types of body; consequently, it is necessary to relate the type of vehicle to the type of delivery, journey and route before the number of vehicles required can be determined. When there are delivery peaks, it may be feasible to consider two different types of vehicle, one for the basic fleet and one for supplementing it during the peak periods.

Basic vehicles required

The requirements for a basic fleet of vehicles will depend upon the long-term delivery factors, because the vehicles will be operated economically only when they deliver regularly throughout the year. Other factors affecting the operation of a basic fleet arise from average delivery situations—that is, mean loads, drop distances, times and journeys.

Supplementary vehicles required

The capacities of the vehicles required for a distribution system will depend upon the size and number of orders, the accessibility at drop points, the normal traffic congestion and the routes and distances involved. Final decisions are influenced by delivery costs, both capital and running costs; in certain instances, savings in running costs will be offset by increases in capital investment. The standardisation of vehicles has many advantages, planning will be simplified, maintenance procedures will be similar and stocks of vehicle spares will be minimal.

Vehicle utilisation

Achieving the best utilisation of vehicles is of prime importance when scheduling deliveries. Very often it outweighs the value of economies made by increasing load capacities. Small discounts have relatively little effect on overall operating cost, whereas larger loads or more deliveries can have a greater effect.

SCHEDULING DELIVERIES

It is foolish to generalise when setting cost standards for utilising vehicles effectively, but it is wise to compare the costs of alternative methods for delivering goods in order to obtain a utilisation yardstick. It is unlikely that a load utilisation efficiency below 50 per cent will appeal to any transport operators.

Operating vehicles efficiently. The effort of assessing efficiency of vehicle operations can be just as valuable and often more instructive than the result itself, because awareness of difficulties that can arise helps to solve many problems. It is important to allow sufficient time when considering vehicle efficiencies and to bear in mind that the advantages of specialisation are greatest when the vehicles are fully employed. Any measure of efficiency must be based upon factual evidence which has been obtained from a range of operations that were observed over a representative length of time.

Delivery capacity. When deciding the best types of vehicle to be operated, at least five questions must be taken into account:

1. Are the deliveries more suitable for rigid or articulated vehicles?
2. Which is the best type of body: flat deck, van or a special design?
3. Are the axle ratios, wheel loadings and engine power adequate?
4. Have all transport regulations been considered, particularly regarding brakes, tyres, loading and weight distribution?
5. What are the different methods of loading and unloading the vehicle?

7:5 REQUIREMENTS OF GOOD SCHEDULING

Good scheduling and routing of distribution vehicles increase their capacities and reduce their operating cost. A schematic presentation is given in Figure 7:1 which will assist managers to produce good vehicle schedules. Whereas routing can be planned with string diagrams, they are unsuitable for scheduling, because it is dynamic; consequently, a planning must be able to show relationships between the variables on a time scale.

There are three basic requirements for any planning procedure, namely the input of information, developing plans and the output to be implemented. In the case of vehicle scheduling, the relevant planning inputs, developments and outputs are shown in Figure 7:5; it is necessary to store

SCHEDULING DELIVERIES

Input	Developments
Geographic information Depot sites and customer locations Delivery data and routes Customer service levels Vehicle types and capacities Operating costs Operational times and duties Vehicle hire and carriers Loading procedures Work measurement data Personnel available Investment required Competition and limits Operating restrictions Distribution records Planning standards	Distribution areas Work loads by areas Revision of area boundaries Scheduling charts Journey planning Daily delivery procedures Loading efficiencies Route efficiencies Delivery frequencies Seasonal fluctuations Contracted services Delivery schedules Vehicle requirements Vehicle selection Scheduling efficiencies Sensitivity analysis

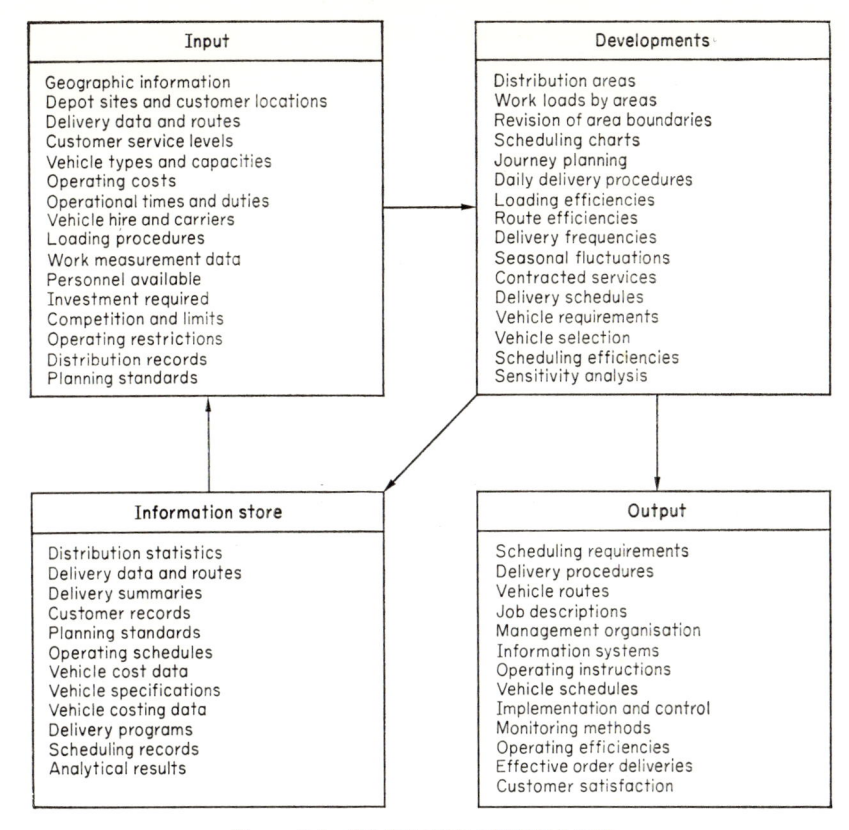

Information store	Output
Distribution statistics Delivery data and routes Delivery summaries Customer records Planning standards Operating schedules Vehicle cost data Vehicle specifications Vehicle costing data Delivery programs Scheduling records Analytical results	Scheduling requirements Delivery procedures Vehicle routes Job descriptions Management organisation Information systems Operating instructions Vehicle schedules Implementation and control Monitoring methods Operating efficiencies Effective order deliveries Customer satisfaction

Figure 7:1 SCHEMATIC SCHEDULING

the material used for developing the plans so that it will provide reference information when reviewing the system or planning a new one.

Other considerations

The best vehicle schedules are based upon past experience and they are unlikely to be prepared very frequently. Schedules can be improved by revising them according to operational results. When the basic distribution policies and past records have been studied, the task of scheduling should be performed by someone with personal experience of vehicle operations. In most instances, the implementation of a vehicle schedule is entirely within the control of drivers and they will know the pertinent improvements covering short cuts, route and vehicle characteristics, customers' temperaments and performance limits. It is possible to calculate optimal vehicle loads and schedules in the office but the final criteria of success rests with the operators.

Owing to the large number of variations that have to be considered when

SCHEDULING DELIVERIES

scheduling vehicles, it is difficult to program a computer realistically and programs tend to be impractical. Some distributors have abandoned computerised scheduling programs for this reason; for example, schedules have been known to route 10-ton vehicles over a bridge with a 5-ton load limit and to schedule all-night transport via a ferry that closed down at 21 00 hours. Obviously, these silly solutions resulted from inadequate input information, but they do illustrate the importance of collecting as much factual data as possible, right at the start of scheduling.

7:6 JOURNEY SCHEDULING

Planning the journeys for delivering goods has intrigued mathematicians for many years and theories have been published on this subject regularly. Both the routing and scheduling of vehicles is involved in journey planning and a method for solving this kind of problem is called "The travelling salesman method." This title is appropriate because a salesman must minimise the total distance that he travels when calling on customers within the time available.

The method involves much repetitive iteration and computer programs have been produced for performing it rapidly. Unfortunately, these programs are useless without the relevant data that makes them meaningful. Keeping records of deliveries is essential for planning journeys, whether by computer or manually.

Manual journey planning

Information for planning journeys can be recorded by the dispatch section of a distribution department, because this is where the goods ordered are loaded on to the vehicles. If orders are accumulated throughout the day and, at a certain time, they can be used to plan journey loads for the next day.

It is common practice to group the orders geographically and to work through them in some sequence when journey planning, either the large or important customer first, the nearest or farthest customers first or just loading vehicles as they become available. Each person will have his own planning methods, but a logical method is to load the largest vehicles first and to assign them to distant customers. Another method is to balance vehicle capacities and orders so that splitting orders into different vehicles is avoided. Generally, depots are sited at main towns where the largest customers are to be found; therefore, it may be advisable to assign the largest vehicles to the nearest routes in many cases.

Obviously, there will be anomalies and conflicts whatever the method

SCHEDULING DELIVERIES

that is used for journey planning and it is necessary to weigh up all the factors in order to find the best solutions. A survey of the deliveries according to orders, areas and vehicles is the only way of determining the true requirements for scheduling. Without doubt, preparing a simple set of rules for journey planning which is illustrated by clear descriptions, diagrams and charts for checking performance, will achieve worthwhile savings for any company. Little extra cost will be involved but the control of deliveries scheduling will be greatly improved.

Using an experienced ex-driver for journey planning has its advantages. He will know the best performance of different vehicles and drivers, the best ways of dealing with different loads, routes and customers and, especially, he will have the ability to handle unexpected situations. Included among unexpected situations are vehicle breakdowns, driver absences and road diversions due to road works, obstructions, floods or similar restrictions. He will have experienced these difficulties before, which will make manual journey planning more relevant and adaptable.

Usually, the clerks in a dispatch office need to refer to maps when compiling the orders into loads and it is necessary to provide them with good maps that show route distances. In many instances, it is advisable to send junior staff out with vehicles in order to experience the problems of journey planning for themselves. First hand experience is worth more than book knowledge or instructions from a senior, yet it costs less to acquire, as a rule. Manual journey planning allows orders to be held over or advanced to cope with day-to-day fluctuations; this is vital for controlling and organising effectively.

People are more flexible than computers, because they can exercise initiative or discretion for overcoming immediate difficulties and they can give instructions that allow for individual interpretation. Finally, the unusual is fairly common in delivery scheduling, because certain orders may be undelivered or last minute changes have to be made; consequently, personal experience and authority are necessary for alleviating probems.

Graphical journey planning

Schedules for deliveries can be planned graphically when there is a specific sequence of events to be followed. Linear programming methods are available and the transportation method is suitable for some situations. However, it can be time consuming and the use of other graphical methods may appear to be more operational. Graphical timetables are used by airlines for scheduling flights and they may be applicable for scheduling deliveries when vehicles arrive and depart continually.

Scheduling charts have been developed in some companies which express the routes as networks for evaluating the distances between all customers

SCHEDULING DELIVERIES

and depots. The distance matrix, as it is called, is similar to the tables that appear in the back of motoring handbooks for the distances between towns. Additional charts can be prepared for each vehicle that show the times for individual deliveries instead of distances.

Linear programming expresses different combinations in the form of a matrix that incorporates measures of optimality in terms of cost or profit. Distribution is a cost on all companies and minimising costs is the objective for linear programs that deal with scheduling.

7:7 OPERATIONAL PROGRAMMING

Optimal scheduling implies performing various operations in a sequence that maximises effectiveness or minimises cost. Mathematically, an optimal solution is obtained by calculating the outcome of every possible combination of events in the correct sequence. Operationally, logic can be employed usefully for programming sequences; feasible sequences must be produced and examined, on a time basis, step by step.

The optimal schedule is the combination of events that complies with requirements for the least time or cost. A chart can be used for examining the feasible sequences on a time scale, while the sequence that is required for feasibility can be shown in a table that allows comparisons to be made. The procedure for using logical iteration will be demonstrated with the aid of a problem that concerned the scheduling of journey load assembly at a textile warehouse.

Operational scheduling problem

Orders for wool and cotton cloths were processed by the dispatch office of the textile warehouse and this problem concerned the best sequence for assembling cloth for four orders. The cloth was used for clothing manufacture and it was essential for the vehicles to be loaded in sequences that complied with customers' factory requirements. In order to obtain the best utilisation of the materials handling time, it was necessary to prepare an operational schedule for assembling the orders.

The four orders were from green, black, brown, and grey; although each customer required all four types of cloth, called A, B, C and D, the sequences for loading them differed. For convenience, a standard time of 10 minutes was taken for assembling each item of cloth ordered. Each order represented a full vehicle load, and each type of cloth in rolls was removed from the warehouse by its own fork-lift truck operator. The sequences for assembling the items into loads according to the order requirements were compiled into a sequence matrix (see Figure 7:2).

SCHEDULING DELIVERIES

Customers	Sequence of items			
Green	A	B	C	D
Black	A	C	B	D
Brown	B	C	D	A
Grey	B	C	D	A

Figure 7:2 SEQUENCE MATRIX

Each item had to be assembled individually and it could be seen from the sequence matrix that, initially, two orders required item *A* to be assembled first and two required item *B* first. This meant that the assembly of two orders could commence immediately and the operators who handled items *C* and *D* would be idle for the first ten-minute period. In order to reduce the total idle time, an operational schedule was prepared for showing successive steps.

Step 1. A basic time chart was prepared for the process of developing the operational time sequences for assembling customer orders. The basic time chart that was employed is shown in Figure 7:3. Customer orders, by name, were extended vertically on the left and the available time (eighty minutes) was shown horizontally at ten-minute intervals.

Step 2. The objective for the optimal sequence was defined as the assembly of as many items at one time as possible in order to reduce the idle time to a minimum.

Initially, only items *A* and *B* could be assembled in the first ten-minute period of time and they were entered on the time chart against the orders for green and brown (see Figure 7:3).

Step 3. The assembly of items for the orders continued, gathering as many items at a time as possible. The sequence matrix was consulted (see Figure 7:2) to find that three items could be assembled in the second time period.

SCHEDULING DELIVERIES

Customer orders	Operational time available (Minutes)							
	10	20	30	40	50	60	70	80
Green	A							
Black								
Brown	B							
Grey								

Figure 7:3 BASIC TIME CHART

Item *B* was assembled with the green order, item *A* with the black order and item *C* with the brown order. The grey order was still waiting to commence assembly.

Step 4. In the third period of time, three more items could be assembled in order to comply with the sequence matrix (see Figure 7:2). The operator who handled item *A* would be idle this time.

Item *C* was required for both the green order and the black order and the choice was made in favour of green because this order was the more

Customer orders	Operational times available (Minutes)							
	10	20	30	40	50	60	70	80
Green	A	B	C	D				
Black		A		C	B		D	
Brown	B	C	D	A				
Grey			B		C	D	A	

Figure 7:4 PARTIALLY COMPLETED TIME CHART

SCHEDULING DELIVERIES

urgent of the two. In this period, the assembly of the grey order could commence with the availability of item *B*.

Step 5. The orders for green and brown were completed in the fourth period of time and the grey had to wait again.

The state of affairs after assembling loads for forty minutes is shown on Figure 7:4 when the first two completed orders were ready for loading into vehicles.

Step 6. Only the orders for black and grey remained to be assembled and items *B* and *C* were gathered in the fifth period of time.

Step 7. In the sixth time period, item *D* was required for both of the remaining orders. It could be assembled with the black order in order to complete it, but this would mean that the grey order could not be completed until the last available period. However, assembling item *D* with the grey order would reduce the overall time required by ten minutes and this was done.

Step 8. The remaining two orders for black and grey were completed by gathering items *A* and *D*. The final schedule was checked with the sequence matrix in order to confirm sequences. Figure 7:5 shows the final time chart.

Customer orders	Operational times available (Minutes)							
	10	20	30	40	50	60	70	80
Green	A	B	C	D				
Black		A		C				
Brown	B	C	D	A				
Grey				B				

Figure 7:5 FINAL TIME CHART

Solution. An optimal sequence of operations was achieved, in this example, after eight steps using logical iteration. The total elapsed time was seventy minutes which was within the objective time limit and each operator was

SCHEDULING DELIVERIES

idle for thirty minutes only. In specific cases, the idle time can be utilised by performing other work, but this example was used to illustrate a method of scheduling operations that others can put into practice according to their individual needs.

8 PREPARING DISTRIBUTION PLANS

Distribution plans must be prepared in advance of delivering the goods in order to make the system flexible. A systematic approach prevents important factors from being overlooked, and it must commence by deciding the distribution objectives and analysing the relevant information starting with the market. The correct method of delivering must be established for each consignment of goods so that an efficient service will be given to all customers. The skill of preparing good distribution plans lies in the ability to select the best methods that ensure speedy, economic and organised deliveries. Often, different methods have to be used in combination in order to provide an efficient service at the least cost.

8:1 PLANNING ECONOMIC DELIVERIES

Transport delivery costs can be reduced by operating the largest size of vehicle possible, by carrying the biggest loads, by operating the vehicle as quickly as permitted and by controlling the utilisation of time and money. Of course, achieving these objectives produces the ideal solution, but they can be yardsticks for preparing practical delivery plans nevertheless. Vehicle standing charges are among the biggest transport costs and they are incurred whether the vehicles are on the road or not. In fact, over half total vehicle operating cost is contributed by standing charges. Their effect upon unit delivery costs can be reduced by utilising the vehicles better in terms of time and loads. However, there must be a balance between payloads and time utilisation that ensures the greatest service for the least cost.

Time utilisation is improved by speedy turnrounds with the aid of swopbodies on vehicles, or containers and trailers for preloading purposes. Other advantages of adaptable vehicles include the use of different bodies on the same chassis, the ability to service or repair containers and tractor units independently of each other and the spread of fixed costs over a large number of deliveries.

Planning routes

Route planning is an integral part of preparing distribution plans, because

PREPARING DISTRIBUTION PLANS

each vehicle must be routed on journeys according to a planned schedule for good time utilisation. Sending out vehicles without knowing when they will return is a costly mistake that must be avoided. The manager and drivers must realise that good working relationships improve operational efficiencies. Productivity agreements help to prevent time wasting and time is money. A vehicle stationary at the side of the road costs money and when the reasons for this are properly understood, the distribution system will be planned on a sound footing. Reducing the operating costs is essential for keeping operators in jobs and for keeping companies in business.

Some recent discussions have centred around the use of computers for preparing routing plans and operating costs have been reduced by some large companies with complex distribution systems. For other distributors, the use of practical knowledge and special experience can be more important and less expensive. Drivers should be encouraged to operate the quickest and most direct routes without wasting time unduly and this is sure to produce cost savings. Other operating advantages can be gained by speeding up deliveries so that the vehicles will be available as soon as possible for servicing, for refuelling and for checking, as well as for reloading.

Good vehicle utilisation entails running the vehicles fully laden as much as possible, which is the key to reducing costs. This is possible only when the distribution system is well controlled. Good control means knowing the whereabouts, the loaded state and availability of each vehicle in a fleet.

Distribution cost savings

The cost of distributing goods can be reduced in many ways. Production staff can help by making the right goods at the right prices; warehousing staff can help by keeping the correct stock levels and properly organising the storage of goods; delivery staff can help by maintaining the vehicles in good condition and operating efficient schedules that ensure the speedy movement of goods; while marketing staff can see that orders comply with the needs of distributing them.

All these people are responsible for operating the distribution system economically, because they form its only live resource. The attitudes of operators and managers create the working atmosphere that determines the overall effectiveness of a system.

Distribution rationalisation

The process of rationalising distribution starts by setting the objectives and organising the resources. Then plans can be prepared for siting the supply points, for routing the vehicles, for scheduling the deliveries and for controlling the system and its operations.

Preparing plans should follow a systematic pattern, commencing with a

PREPARING DISTRIBUTION PLANS

list of all the elements and activities that contribute to the cost of distribution. Some of the important elements are given in the following list:

1. The number of locations of supply points
2. The costs of operating depots and warehouses
3. The methods of handling goods
4. Breakages and spoilt packages when handling goods
5. The number and types of vehicle
6. Vehicle operating costs
7. The methods of delivering goods to customers
8. Route planning, utilisation and dispatch frequencies
9. The cost of employing personnel
10. The overhead costs on land, buildings and equipment
11. The number of journeys and sizes of loads
12. The proportion of return loads
13. Loading and unloading costs
14. Delivery times and turnround frequencies
15. The paperwork necessary for controlling operations
16. The cost of success

All these items and others should be listed, even though it takes a long time to do it thoroughly. Naturally, there will be duplications and some overlapping, but they will be sorted out by grouping the elements listed according to related items. Examining these groups will suggest the details that need to be selected for specific investigation with a view to saving costs and improving performances. The three stages for rationalising distribution are shown schematically in Figure 8:1.

The preparation of rational distribution plans is enhanced by the co-operation of everyone involved. Discussions smooth out difficulties and the plans will be most effective when the people who operate them help to prepare them too. In operation, the implemented plans need to be reviewed continually in order to observe strengths and weaknesses and to update operating costs and times.

Combined routing and scheduling plans

When the sites for supply points have been decided, routing and scheduling the vehicles should be performed together in order to make the best overall plans. Basically, the optimisation of supply sites and vehicle routes is concerned with maximising customer service and minimising distribution costs. Transport costs are assumed to be proportional to the distances travelled when delivering goods to customers. The sites for supply points are determined by analysing market demand and the area boundaries are established by considering the break-even costs for delivering from each site.

PREPARING DISTRIBUTION PLANS

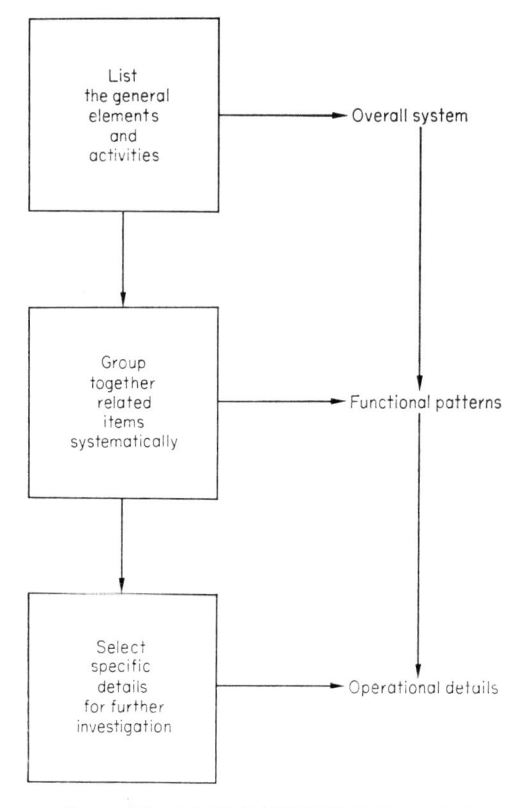

Figure 8:1 RATIONALISATION PROCESS

A simple method for delineating area boundaries involves drawing grid lines on a map and entering the weight and number of customer drops in each grid square. Then, delivering the quantity of goods in each square from neighbouring depots can be costed. Boundaries will be fixed by allocating squares to depots where the delivery costs are least.

Geographical boundaries that are optimal as far as supply sites are concerned may need to be changed in the light of transport delivery costs. Factors that have to be considered vary with the types of delivery—that is, trunking, or bulk delivering, and local deliveries. Planning these two types of delivery will be illustrated with the aid of practical case studies.

8:2 PLANNING TRUNKING DELIVERIES

A wholesale groceries distributor in northern France supplied provisions to supermarkets from two depots, one at Reims and one at Lille. The objec-

PREPARING DISTRIBUTION PLANS

tive for trunking deliveries was to supply the depots with bulk goods so that local deliveries could be made with vans.

Preparing the overall plan commenced with an analysis of the market demand in order to calculate the volume of goods to be handled. Firstly, the number of vans required at depots had to be determined in order to plan the schedule for supplying them.

Number of vans

An examination of the demands showed that a minimum of twenty-one van journeys per week would be needed from the Reims depot and twenty-nine from Lille. Each journey required a full van-load of goods and it would take a whole day to deliver it. A five-day week was worked at the depots.

The ideal number of vans needed for local deliveries was calculated by dividing the number of journeys per week by the five days per working week. This number would provide full time operation of the vans.

Reims depot: 21 journeys per week ÷ 5 = 4.2 vans per week
Lille depot: 29 journeys per week ÷ 5 = 5.8 vans per week

These numbers of vans were impractical and they had to be rounded up to five and six with corresponding reductions in the time utilisation.

Routing the vans

Improving the van time utilisation was possible if the routes were rearranged and the allocation of retail outlets to depots was altered slightly. Reallocating 0.2 of a van per week from Reims to Lille reduced the number of vans needed from eleven to ten—that is, four at Reims and six at Lille.

Trunking to the depots

Local delivery costs were reduced by optimising the number of vans needed and trunking costs could be kept down by operating the smallest feasible number of container vehicles. Each container vehicle comprised a tractor unit and a trailer. Consequently, a tractor could operate independently of a number of different trailers.

Conditions for making trunking deliveries were summarised and incorporated in the distribution objectives.

Trunking conditions

1. One tractor unit will be allocated to each depot
2. The minimum number of trailers will be independent of the two tractors
3. One trailer only can be loaded at a time in the central warehouse
4. Tractor drivers must be at their base depot for weekends

PREPARING DISTRIBUTION PLANS

5   One container can hold sufficient goods for fifteen van-loads
6   There will be two depots with ten local delivery vans between them
7   All deliveries must be made within a five-day working week
8   One delivery van-load will be equivalent to one journey-day
9   Local delivery vans will set out early each morning
10 Each van will deliver standard loads each week to customers along fixed routes

Scheduling bulk deliveries

The articulated container vehicles had to operate with a minimum number of trailers which would be determined by preparing a scheduling chart. One tractor unit was assigned to each depot and the information that was needed for scheduling them included the containers to be supplied to depots, vehicle movements, the daily deliveries of goods by vans and the stock in hand at each depot. The scheduling chart used is shown in Figure 8:2.

Each scheduling chart should cover one complete trunking supply cycle which could be found by relating the volume of goods supplied to the depots that delivered them locally:

Depot	Factors	Initial resources	Week one					Week two					Week three				
			M	T	W	Th	F	M	T	W	Th	F	M	T	W	Th	F
REIMS	Trailers	(15)		(0)	(15)	(0)	(15)			(0)	(15)				(0)	(15)
REIMS	Deliveries	4 vans	4	8	12	16	20	24	28	32	36	40	44	48	52	56	60
REIMS	Stock	15	11	7	18	14	25	21	17	13	9	20	16	12	8	4	15
LILLE	Trailers	(15)	(0)	(15)	(0)	(15)		(0)	(15)	(0)	(15)		(0)	(15)	(0)	(15)	
LILLE	Deliveries	6 vans	6	12	18	24	30	36	42	48	54	60	66	72	78	84	90
LILLE	Stock	15	9	18	12	21	15	9	18	12	21	15	9	18	12	21	15
Number of trailers needed			3	4	4	4	4	4	4	4	4	4	4	4	4	4	2
Loaded trailers in transit				1	1	1	1		1		1	1		1		1	

(15) = Trailer arriving with a loaded container
(0) = Trailer going to central warehouse with an empty container

Figure 8:2 SCHEDULING CHART

PREPARING DISTRIBUTION PLANS

Trunking supplies = local deliveries
Trunking supplies = container loads per week×container capacity (van-loads)
Local deliveries = length of cycle (weeks)×weekly deliveries (van-loads)

The relationship between supplies and deliveries could be expressed as a simple mathematical equation:

$$15T = WV$$

where: 15 = container capacity as van-loads
T = number of trailers required
W = number of weeks for a complete cycle
V = volume of weekly deliveries as van-loads

In addition to the container capacity of fifteen van-loads, the volume of weekly deliveries at each depot was known in advance. The number of trailers required and the length of the trunking cycle could be found by converting the equation into a ratio.

$$\text{Delivery ratio} = \frac{T}{W} = \frac{\text{van-loads delivered per week}}{15}$$

Inserting the number of van-loads to be delivered from each depot allowed the ratio to show the number of containers that would be needed for the cycle duration.

Cycle duration. The number of van journeys at Reims was twenty, with thirty at Lille, after adjusting the delivery areas for maximum time utilisation.

At *Reims*: $\frac{T}{W} = \frac{20}{15} = \frac{4}{3}$ i.e. four container loads every 3 weeks

At *Lille*: $\frac{T}{W} = \frac{30}{15} = \frac{2}{1}$ i.e. two container loads every week

The length of the trunking cycle for both depots together would be three weeks in which time four container loads would be supplied to Reims depot and six to Lille. Before installing the cycle, one container load would be needed at each depot in order to provide initial stocks.

Scheduling chart. Three factors were scheduled on the chart for each depot, namely, the movement of trailers, the cumulated deliveries and the stock on hand at the end of each day. The final stock on hand should be the same as it was at the beginning of the cycle.

The scheduling chart was useful for controlling the deliveries, but a set of rules was necessary in order to keep the operations in line with the trunking conditions.

PREPARING DISTRIBUTION PLANS

Scheduling rules

1   The number of van-loads delivered would be cumulated day by day throughout the full cycle
2   The stock on hand would be calculated by subtracting the number of van-loads delivered each day and adding the number supplied in containers
3   Whenever the stock level fell below the number of van-loads needed for 2 days' work, the tractor would have to take a trailer and an empty container to the central warehouse for a new supply of goods
4   An empty container could not be loaded at the warehouse if one was already loading there, and the schedule would have to be advanced or retarded in order to correct this situation
5   The stock on hand at a depot at the end of a cycle had to be the same as the stock at the beginning
6   The number of trailers needed each day would be shown at the bottom of the chart, along with the number of trailer containers supplied to the depots
7   The stock on hand at a depot could not exceed one container load, because the containers were used as transit warehouses

Solution. In order to comply with the trunking conditions for the system, the optimal number of vans was ten and the number of container trailers was four. These numbers were determined with the aid of a scheduling chart. There would be two trailers with containers and one tractor unit at each depot. In this way, goods could be supplied to the four vans at Reims and the six at Lille for making local deliveries.

The scheduling rules ensured that the resources needed were minimal and the time utilisation was maximal.

8:3   LOCAL DELIVERY RESOURCES PLANNING

The second type of delivering found in a distribution system are local deliveries from depots to customers. The quantities of goods required by customers are specific and orders differ from time to time; consequently, planning local deliveries must place greater emphasis on the service level than the cost of delivering. Keeping down costs is important, but customers' orders are the lifeblood of a distribution system.

Planning local deliveries follows siting the depots and planning the bulk deliveries to them. Then it is necessary to prepare plans for the local delivery

PREPARING DISTRIBUTION PLANS

resources, for the number and sizes of vehicles required, the delivery routes and the drops per vehicle journey.

Example of distributing cased goods

A British distribution company operates with five depots that were sited strategically around the country, but the resources in each region for making local deliveries to customers had to be planned economically and efficiently. The depot at Birmingham for distributing cased goods in the Midlands region of England was being reorganised. The cases varied in size and volume; therefore, deliveries had to be standardised by loading the cases onto pallets and installing mechanical handling equipment. Most orders were large, usually full pallet-loads, but some were small and local deliveries had to be planned so that all orders were delivered efficiently.

Objective. The distribution planning objective was to calculate the number of vehicles and their load carrying capacities that would be required for delivering cased goods locally from the Birmingham depot.

Developing strategies for deliveries. The number of vehicles would depend upon the number, the frequency and the size of the drops, because these factors would determine the routes, the number of journeys and the capacities of vehicles. Initial strategies would be vague until more information had been collected. However, there were three basic alternatives:

1   To own and operate a fleet of vehicles
2   To hire vehicles on contract
3   To employ carriers to deliver the goods

Firstly, owning the vehicles was suitable when there were concentrated delivery areas that ensured full employment; secondly, the vehicles could be hired if capital for purchasing them was not available; and thirdly, carriers would be employed most economically in remote areas. The choice of the strategy for making the deliveries would depend upon the information that was collected with respect to the driving times and distances involved, the drop sizes and frequencies and their different costs.

Planning deliveries

Information was collected in the form of delivery records and it soon became obvious that there was a peak period for deliveries in November when retailers stocked up for Christmas. Vehicle requirements had to be based upon two types of deliveries, in the peak period and during the rest of the year.

Delivery areas. It was decided to divide the Birmingham distribution region in 12 areas using GPO post codes, as the majority of orders were received

PREPARING DISTRIBUTION PLANS

by mail. The customer drop points were grouped according to geographical delivery areas and the orders were classified according to size and frequency; consequently, the number of deliveries required per drop point per month could be calculated.

Delivery frequency. The frequency of deliveries to the different drop points affected the planning of routes and schedules which were based upon planning standard times. Calculations assumed that the average delay between order receipt and order delivery should be 1 day. The delivery frequency for different areas determined the type of vehicles that would be required and the minimum delivery frequency to an area depended upon the maximum number of deliveries required by any one customer each month.

Delivery distances and times. The total distance driven along any journey route comprised the distance to and from the delivery area and the distance driven within the area while delivering to customers.

The straight line distance in crow-miles to an area boundary and back was taken as being double the distance from the depot to the nearest point on its boundary. The driving speed varied according to road conditions and average speed, as follows:

(a) Central urban roads (12 mph)
(b) Urban roads (16 mph)
(c) Country roads (26 mph)
(d) Motorways (45 mph)

In order to convert distances into times when preparing the planning standards, estimated distances in crow-miles were expressed as minutes.

Planning standard minutes =
$$\frac{\text{road distance (crow-miles)} \times 600 \text{ min (daily working time)}}{\text{average speed (mph)}}$$

The average driving time between drop points inside a delivery area was calculated from the estimated mileage, the road conditions and the average speed. Empirically, the planning standard minutes (PSM) between drop points could be obtained with the following formula for the time:

Internal delivery time (PSM) = Average crow-miles per drop × average minutes per mile for the road conditions × number of drop points

$$= 1.2 \left(\frac{\text{delivery area, square miles}}{\text{number of drops}} \right) \times \left(\frac{60 \text{ min}}{\text{average speed, mph}} \right) \times \text{number of drop points}$$

Note that 1.2 is the factor needed to convert crow-miles into road miles.

PREPARING DISTRIBUTION PLANS

Delivery routes. Some routes were restricted in length by the time available and others by the capacity of vehicles. The maximum time legally available per day including overtime was 600 minutes and for half a day, a journey time limit of 270 minutes was assumed. A five-day week comprised 50 hours or 3000 minutes and it was recommended that the vehicles should start from the depot by 0730 so that deliveries could be made during customers' working hours.

Unloading time. The time for offloading the cases at stop points varied with the number of cases to be delivered and they were classified into numerical groups so that standard times could be allocated according to the work study analysis (Figure 8:3). The total unloading time for all the orders to be delivered in an area at one time could be calculated in this way, or the average unloading time per order could be obtained by dividing the total time by the total number of orders.

Vehicle capacities. The capacities of different vehicles were expressed in terms of cases and they were used as planning standards. The types of

Group	Unloading method	Order size (cases)	PSM
1	By hand	0—12	4.2 min
2	By hand	12—24	6.2 min
3	By hand	25—50	11.2 min
4	By hand	51—300	25.0 min
5	Pallet loads	51—300	22.5 min
6	Pallet loads	over 300	36.0 min

Figure 8:3 STANDARD OFFLOADING TIMES

PREPARING DISTRIBUTION PLANS

vehicle were designated by their weight capacities, but converting capacities into volumes enabled them to be expressed in cases (see Figure 8:4).

Vehicle capacity	30-cwt	8-ton	12-ton	16-ton
Average number of cases	80	260	400	1000

Figure 8:4 CAPACITIES OF VEHICLES

On several routes the maximum vehicle weight was restricted to 8 tons by bridge load limits and the vehicle size was limited by the turning radius required at drop points. The maximum capacity of a delivery vehicle was 8 tons and the number needed had to be determined for each area.

Vehicles required. In order to illustrate the procedure for planning the number of vehicles required for local deliveries, three different adjoining areas will be considered. However, it is wrong to think of an area on its own in practice, because efficiency and economy can be improved by combining areas or routes. Only vehicles with a capacity of 8 tons or less were considered in this case.

Procedure for planning local delivery resources

In order to obtain an effective solution, the objective had to be defined clearly; then planning the strategies could proceed after collecting the basic information. The first step was to investigate the distribution system as a whole and then to consider each depot in turn. This particular problem concerned the Birmingham regional depot only, which distributed cased goods to the Midlands; the region was divided into delivery areas according to the Post Office postcodes (see Figure 8:5).

Delivery areas. The Midlands region was divided into areas approximately 400 square miles in size, each based upon a postcode which was a convenient form of classification. Basically, there were twelve delivery areas with varying trade intensities; the greatest intensity being in the centre around the Birmingham depot site. The areas were designated by their Post Office postcodes and are shown as a schematic map of the region in Figure 8:5.

Collecting information

In order to calculate the number and size of vehicles to be operated, it was necessary to collect information about the current deliveries in the region

PREPARING DISTRIBUTION PLANS

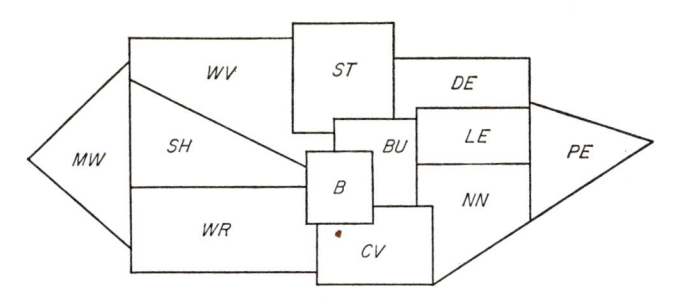

Figure 8:5 CODED DELIVERY AREAS IN THE MIDLANDS

and also about expected trends. Sources of information were vehicle and customer records and sales forecasts. The number of cases delivered throughout the year varied little except for a peak in the month of November. Distribution volumes were fairly constant during the off-peak months but the volume nearly trebled in the peak period. The annual volume of cases for delivery could be estimated mathematically:

Annual volume (cases) = peak month (cases) + 11 × off-peak month (cases)

If the cases ratio for peak month/off-peak month was P and the number of cases delivered in an off-peak month was Q, an estimate of the annual volume would be $11Q+PQ$ cases, that is annual volume = $Q(11+P)$ cases.

The expected numbers of cases to be delivered in the twelve Midlands areas were tabulated and they are shown for off-peak and peak months of 1970 in Figure 8:6.

The equation for estimating the annual volume in cases delivered was tested with these figures for 1969:

$$P = \frac{\text{peak month cases}}{\text{off-peak month cases}}$$
$$= \frac{31\,790}{12\,480}$$
$$= 2.55$$

The actual volume delivered in January 1970 was 12 310 cases; therefore, the annual volume could be estimated.

Estimated annual volume = $Q(11+B)$ cases
= 12 310 × 13.55
= 166 700 cases

137

PREPARING DISTRIBUTION PLANS

An error of less than 2 per cent was achieved by this estimate when compared with the actual volume at the end of 1970.

The 1971 sales forecasts for the delivery areas were used in connection with the planning standards for calculating future vehicle requirements; the estimates are tabulated in Figure 8:7.

AREA		NUMBER OF CASES		
Postcode	Main town	Off-peak month	Peak month	Annual volume
B	Birmingham	1 480	4 950	21 230
BU	Burton-on-Trent	1 120	3 180	15 500
CV	Coventry	1 240	4 200	17 840
WR	Worcester	870	1 840	11 410
SH	Shrewsbury	830	1 650	10 560
WV	Wolverhampton	1 220	3 690	17 110
MW	Welshpool	200	740	2 940
ST	Stafford	1 050	2 210	13 760
DE	Derby	1 190	2 400	15 490
LE	Leicester	1 070	2 350	14 120
NN	Northampton	1 280	2 560	16 640
PE	Peterborough	930	2 020	12 250
Whole region		12 480	31 790	168 850

Figure 8:6 CASES DELIVERED TO THE REGION IN 1970

Planning standards

Were used for calculating the number and sizes of vehicles required in each delivery area. In this way, standardisation helped to simplify the work involved. The planning standards had been tested in practice and were acceptable. They were expressed as elements of vehicle operations according to the elapsed time expressed in minutes. The planning standards for vehicle

PREPARING DISTRIBUTION PLANS

AREA	NUMBER OF CASES		
Postcode	Off-peak month	Peak month	Annual volume
B	1 520	5 030	21 750
BU	1 130	3 220	15 650
CV	1 250	4 270	18 020
WR	870	1 860	11 430
SH	830	1 680	10 810
WV	1 240	3 720	17 360
MW	210	750	3 060
ST	1 070	2 250	14 020
DE	1 210	2 460	15 770
LE	1 100	2 390	14 490
NN	1 320	2 610	17 130
PE	950	2 080	12 530
Region	12 700	32 320	172 020

Figure 8:7 ESTIMATED CASES FOR DELIVERY IN 1971

operations when delivering cased goods are tabulated in Figure 8:8. PSM indicates a planning standard minute.

A preliminary examination of the road conditions in the region showed that it was impossible to operate standard vehicles in excess of 8-tons capacity due to road restrictions. Since the vehicles had to be covered in order to protect the cased goods, vans were selected and the alternative capacities considered were 30-cwt, 5-tons and 8-tons.

The accuracy of time estimates based upon planning standards would be affected by the variations that occurred when unloading the vehicles; therefore, mean times were used for calculating the delivery standard times.

PREPARING DISTRIBUTION PLANS

Location of customers in the delivery areas, were defined by sticking pins into a map of the region according to the locations of drop points.

Methods of planning deliveries for different customers will be shown with reference to one delivery area only. However, all deliveries can be calculated in the same way and the total vehicle requirements used to optimise the system. The area chosen for illustrating the calculations is coded SH and has Shrewsbury as its main town (see Figure 8:9).

Customer order sizes varied only slightly from month to month in the off-peak period and it was decided to cater for the maximum off-peak monthly requirement. The estimated monthly requirement of cases in 1971 is represented as a table for the eight customer locations in the SH area in Figure 8:10.

Planning standard	Minutes		
1 Variable unloading time	Varies from 4 to 36 min according to the number of cases dropped Mean drop time = 10 min		
2 Variable journey time	In towns: 6.0 min per crow-mile Urban roads: 4.5 min per crow-mile Rural roads: 2.75 min per crow-mile Motorways: 1.6 min per crow-mile		
Vehicle capacity	30-cwt	5-tons	8-tons
3 Variable loading time	15 min	10 min	15 min
4 Constant unloading time	4 min	5 min	5 min

5 Constant journey time:
  (i) Pre-delivery check
  (ii) In-transit allowance
  (iii) Post-delivery check
	
	10 min
	5%
	15 min
		
		12 min
		5%
		15 min
			
			12 min
			5%
			15 min

6 Load capacity (cases)	80	260	400

Figure 8:8 DELIVERY PLANNING STANDARDS

PREPARING DISTRIBUTION PLANS

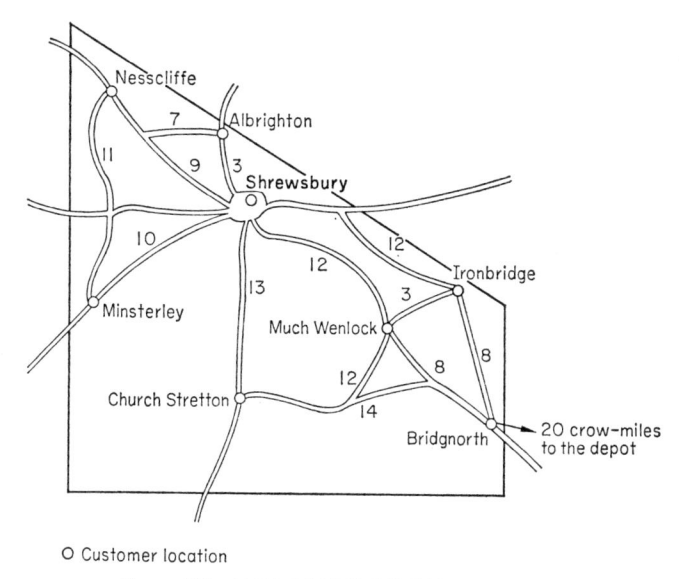

Figure 8:9 MAP OF THE DELIVERY AREA *SH*

Customer order frequencies depended upon storage facilities at the drop points. The maximum order frequency in the off-peak period was twice a month and, in the peak period, four times per month. These were used as the minimum delivery frequencies for this area.

Load capacities of vehicles were determined in terms of the average number of cases for each of the vehicle sizes. Considering the monthly customer requirements and the case capacity of the largest vehicle (8 tons), there had to be slightly more than two trips in an off-peak month and four in the peak month. This complied with the order frequencies and it was used as a basis for the vehicle journey calculations.

Vehicle journey calculations

The number of journeys depended upon the number of vehicles required, the customer order sizes and frequencies, the vehicle capacities and the delivery routes.

The Midlands region was about 10 000 square miles in area and it was sub-divided into 12 areas according to their postcodes. Customers' orders were grouped into the areas according to:

1   Drop point location
2   Number of cases ordered

PREPARING DISTRIBUTION PLANS

3   Delivery frequency
4   Average size of drops delivered (cases)
5   Total number of cases delivered each month

Elements of vehicle operations were expressed as times which were used as planning standards. The largest size of vehicle had an average capacity of 400 cases. The average number of journeys per month in each area depended upon the number and sizes of orders divided by the vehicle capacity:

Off-peak monthly journey frequency $= \dfrac{830}{400} = 2.1$

Peak monthly journey frequency $= \dfrac{1680}{400} = 4.2$

Journey times

Each journey comprised the travelling time to and from the delivery area, travelling within the area, plus the non-driving time. The planning standards

Customer location	Order size (as cases per month)	
	Off-peak	Peak
Bridgnorth	160	300
Ironbridge	80	150
Much Wenlock	50	100
Church Stretton	80	160
Shrewsbury	220	450
Albrighton	100	210
Nesscliffe	60	120
Minsterley	80	190
Delivery area total	830	1680

Figure 8:10   ESTIMATED MONTHLY REQUIREMENTS

PREPARING DISTRIBUTION PLANS

are presented in Figure 8:8 and they were used for calculating the total journey time.

1. Driving time to and from the area $= \dfrac{2(60 \times \text{crow-miles}) \text{ min}}{\text{average miles per hour}}$

2. Journey constants applied to all the delivery areas and they comprised:
   (a) Time at depot for loading a vehicle
   (b) Time for performing pre-delivery checks
   (c) In-transit time allowances
   (d) Time for performing post-delivery checks

3. Driving time within an area depended upon the average road speed, the number of drop points and the distances between them

   A simple equation was developed for the planning standard total time within an area after measuring its area in crow-miles

   $$\text{PSM} = \text{number of drops} \times 1.2 \sqrt{\dfrac{\text{area}}{\text{number of drops}}} \times \text{average speed}$$

   $$= 1.2 \sqrt{\text{number of drops} \times \text{area}} \times \text{average speed (minutes per crow-mile)}$$

4. Unloading times at drop points varied with the number of cases offloaded, but it was found that a mean time of 10 minutes per drop was acceptable overall

5. The maximum time that was available for each daily journey was obtained by deduction
   Total working time per day = 600 min
   Less driving time to and from the area
   Less journey constants
   Less internal driving time
   Less unloading times

When planning the delivery schedule, the variable times to be considered were the internal driving and unloading times. A composite equation was evolved for calculating these times:

Time available = 600 minutes—time to and from area—constant times
$= $ internal driving time + unloading time
$= (1.2\sqrt{\text{number of drops} \times \text{area}} \times \text{average speed} + (15 \times \text{number of drops}))$

Therefore, the feasible number of drops per day (N) was given by the following equation:

$$N = \left(\dfrac{M}{12\,R\sqrt{A}}\right)^{\frac{2}{3}}$$

PREPARING DISTRIBUTION PLANS

where N = number of drops per day
M = time available in minutes
R = average road speed in minutes per crow-mile
A = area in square crow-miles

The number of journeys per month in the area could be obtained by dividing the number of drop points by the monthly journey frequency (F).

$$\text{Journeys per month } (J) = \sum \frac{\text{drop points} \times F}{N}$$

The capacity of a vehicle was decided by dividing the monthly total number of cases by journeys per month (J).

$$\text{Vehicle capacity per journey} = \frac{\Sigma \text{ cases per month}}{J}$$

Summary of vehicle journey calculations
1. Determine load capacities of vehicles
2. Determine the planning standard times
3. Calculate the period journey frequency
4. Calculate the journey times
5. Determine the number of drops per day
6. Determine the number of journeys required
7. Decide the vehicle capacities

Applying the vehicle journey calculations to the problem
1 *Vehicle load capacities*
30-cwt van = 80 cases
5-ton van = 260 cases
8-ton van = 400 cases

2 *Planning standard times for 8-ton van*
Variable loading time	15 min per journey
Constant unloading time	5 min per drop
Average unloading time	10 min per drop
Average road speed	3.5 min per crow-mile for mixed urban and country roads

Constant journey times per day:
Pre-delivery checks	12 min
In-transit allowance	30 min
Post-delivery checks	15 min

3 *Monthly journey frequencies*
Off-peak	2.1 journeys
Peak	4.2 journeys

PREPARING DISTRIBUTION PLANS

4 *Journey times*

Driving time to and from the area	$= \dfrac{2(60 \text{ min} \times 20 \text{ crow-miles})}{21 \text{ mile/hr}}$
	$= 115$ min
Constant journey times	$= 12+30+15 = 57$ min
Loading time (8-ton van)	$= 15$ min
Time available for deliveries	$= 60-115-57-15$
	$= 413$ min
Time required for deliveries	$=$ internal driving time + unloading time
Number of drop points	$= 8$
Internal driving time	$= 1.2 \sqrt{\text{number of drops} \times \text{area} \times \text{average speed}}$
	$= 1.2 \times \sqrt{8 \times 400 \times 3.5}$
	$= 238$ min
Unloading time	$=$ number of drops $\times 15$ min $= 8 \times 15$
	$= 120$ min
Total time required	$= 238+120$ min
	$= 358$ min
Time available for deliveries	$= 413$ min
Surplus time per day	$= 55$ min

Vehicle requirements

The daily journey time utilised by one 8-ton van was $600-55 = 545$ minutes for the eight drop points; therefore, 1 day would be required for delivering to all customers in the SH area. The time frequency for daily journeys to the area could be expressed as 1.0 and it was calculated that the load frequency for an off-peak month was 2.1 for one 8-ton vehicle. Therefore, the combined journey frequencies were $1.0 \times 2.1 = 2.1$ journey days with an 8-ton load.

Journey frequencies for 8-ton vans were converted into round numbers by considering smaller vans with a fractional capacity of an 8-ton van for the surplus amounts. That is:

8-ton van $= 1.00$ journey-load
5-ton van $= 0.65$ journey-load
30-cwt van $= 0.20$ journey-load

It followed that the requirement for area SH in an off-peak month was 2.1 8-ton van-days or 2 8-ton van-days and 1 30-cwt van-day.

PREPARING DISTRIBUTION PLANS

Equation for estimating 8-ton van-days required

Monthly 8-ton van-days = journey frequency×8-ton van-load frequency

Where: 1 5-ton van-day = 0.65×8-ton van-day
and: 1 30-cwt van-day = 0.2×8-ton van-day

also: 1 30-cwt van-day = 0.325×5-ton van-day

Examination of the delivery area SH showed that there would be half a day's work in an off-peak month for the 30-cwt van if it delivered goods to the Much Wenlock customer only. As a result the planning times were corrected for this revision and they are given in Figure 8:11.

Vehicle requirements for the areas

When considering the three areas SH, WV and MW together, the theoretical number of journeys could be reduced by combining journeys in practice. In an off-peak month 5 van-days were required anyway, but the additional deliveries could be made in 1 day by a single 5-ton van without any 30-cwt vans at all. Ten extra 8-ton van-days would be necessary in the peak month, when delivering to the three areas together. This is summarised as a table in Figure 8:12.

Journey-days for the whole region. The total number of journey-days required for delivering to the whole of the Midlands region would be reduced by combining small van journeys into larger ones. The actual number of journey-days required for each area are shown as the tables in Figures 8:13 and 8:14; calculations were based upon estimated distances and corrected journey times.

Number of 8-ton van-days = journey time frequency×load frequency.

Vehicle requirement	Number of drop points	Corrected journey time	Utilisation % time	Utilisation % load	Journeys per month Off-peak	Journeys per month Peak
One 8-ton van	7	515 min	86	97	2	4
One 30-cwt van	1	286 min	100	63	$\frac{1}{2}$	1

Figure 8:11 LOCAL DELIVERY VEHICLES IN AREA SH

PREPARING DISTRIBUTION PLANS

Area	Main town	Off-peak month				Peak month				Ratio of off-peak to peak
		Total cases	\multicolumn{3}{c}{Journey days}	Total cases	\multicolumn{3}{c}{Journey days}	
			30-cwt	5-ton	8-ton		30-cwt	5-ton	8-ton	
SH	Shrewsbury	830	1	—	2	1680	1	—	4	$\frac{1}{2}$
WV	Wolverhampton	1240	1	—	3	3720	—	1	9	$\frac{1}{3}$
MW	Welshpool	210	—	1	—	750	—	—	2	$\frac{1}{3}$
	All areas Theoretical	2280	2	1	5	6150	1	1	15	$\frac{2}{5}$
	Practical	2280	—	1	5	6150	—	1	15	$\frac{2}{5}$

Figure 8:12 VEHICLE REQUIREMENTS FOR THE THREE AREAS

Monthly journey-days by area. The journey-days required for the whole region was the summation of the requirements for each area. The number of 8-ton vans required in the peak month was nearly three times as many as the number required for an off-peak month, but some of the smaller vans were redundant and they should be overhauled as necessary.

Vehicle requirements

The number of vehicles that was required for operating the regional distribution system was found by considering the number of journey-days for each vehicle size divided by the number of working days in a month. A 22-day cycle was a condition for each month then the vehicle requirements were calculated.

Off-peak month requirements of vehicles

For 30-cwt vans $\quad \dfrac{\text{Journey days}}{\text{Cycle days}} = \dfrac{16}{22} = 0.73$

For 5-ton vans $\quad \dfrac{\text{Journey days}}{\text{Cycle days}} = \dfrac{4}{22} = 0.18$

PREPARING DISTRIBUTION PLANS

For 8-ton vans $\quad \dfrac{\text{Journey days}}{\text{Cycle days}} \quad = \dfrac{37}{22} = 1.70$

These vehicle requirements are shown in Figure 8:15. The figures had to be rounded up and combined so that the requirements were:

Off-peak period = 1 30-cwt van and 2 8-ton vans.
Peak period   = 1 30-cwt van and 5 8-ton vans.

It was decided to operate a basic vehicle fleet of one 30-cwt van and two 8-ton vans throughout the year and to supplement them during November by hiring three 8-ton vans.

Area	Number of drop points	Journey times		Off-peak month					
		In area (min)	Journey frequency	Number of cases	8-ton loads		Time required		
					Drop frequency	Journey days	Number of van days		
							30-cwt	5-ton	8-ton
B	24	910	1.6	1 520	3.8	6.1	1	–	6
BU	15	765	1.3	1 130	2.8	3.7	1	1	3
CV	20	885	1.5	1 250	3.1	4.7	1	1	4
WR	9	570	1.0	870	2.2	2.2	1	–	2
SH	8	545	1.0	830	2.1	2.1	1	–	2
WV	17	780	1.3	1 240	3.1	4.1	1	–	4
MW	6	480	0.8	210	0.5	0.4	2	–	–
ST	10	760	1.3	1 070	2.7	3.5	3	–	3
DE	11	745	1.3	1 210	3.0	3.9	2	1	3
LE	11	725	1.2	1 100	2.7	3.3	2	–	3
NN	13	805	1.4	1 320	3.3	4.6	–	1	4
PE	9	790	1.3	950	2.4	3.2	1	–	3
All	153	8 760	15.0	12 700	31.7	41.8	16	4	37

Figure 8:13 JOURNEYS TO THE MIDLANDS REGION: OFF-PEAK MONTH

PREPARING DISTRIBUTION PLANS

Area	Number of drop points	Peak month					
		Number of cases	8-ton loads		Time required		
			Drop frequency	Journey days	Number of van days		
					30-cwt	5-ton	8-ton
B	24	5030	12.5	20.0	–	–	20
BU	15	3220	8.0	10.4	2	–	10
CV	20	4270	10.7	16.0	–	–	16
WR	9	1860	4.6	4.6	–	1	4
SH	8	1680	4.2	4.2	1	–	4
WV	17	3720	9.3	12.1	1	–	12
MW	6	750	1.8	1.4	2	–	1
ST	10	2250	5.6	7.3	2	–	7
DE	11	2460	6.1	8.0	–	–	8
LE	11	2390	6.0	7.2	1	–	7
NN	13	2610	6.5	9.1	1	–	9
PE	9	2080	5.2	6.8	1	1	6
All	153	32320	80.5	117.1	11	2	104

Figure 8:14 JOURNEYS TO THE MIDLANDS REGION: PEAK MONTH

Month	Vehicle requirements			Total capacity (8-ton loads)
	30-cwt	5-ton	8-ton	
Off-peak	0.73	0.18	1.70	1.963
Peak	0.50	0.09	4.75	4.909

Figure 8:15 MONTHLY VEHICLE REQUIREMENTS

8:4 SELECTING THE VEHICLES

Planning the delivery function of a distribution system must continue beyond the establishment of vehicle requirements and consider how the vehicles should be selected and acquired. A systematic approach is excellent for deciding the number and the locations of supply points and planning the delivery of goods, and it can be used for selecting vehicles too. It is necessary to investigate the vehicles that are available and to select ones that satisfy the delivery requirements.

The original plans will have considered the vehicle requirements for optimal deliveries; next, specific vehicles have to be selected with reference to design, types, personnel and operating instructions. These factors will be involved when comparing the size of vehicles with journey-loads, or body design with unit load handling methods. The best balance will be a practical one that includes other factors too, like expected vehicle life and fluctuations in the volume of goods delivered.

Planning vehicle operations depends upon the vehicles that are selected. For example, when delivering palletised goods, the dimensions of the pallets and vehicle bodies must be compatible in order to obtain good space utilisation. Also, the ease of loading and unloading will affect the delivery time utilisation. The requirements for trunking and local deliveries must be considered together, because it is advantageous to standardise vehicles and equipment whenever possible.

Vehicle planning standards

Standardising operational times is a great assistance to vehicle planning, because planning standards can be used to develop synthetic times without resorting to physical testing. The use of planning standard times was illustrated in Section 8:3 with the problems of making local deliveries.

Planning standards help to stabilise the variable time factors of vehicle delivery operations. They can be used for comparing one vehicle with another when making selections, as well as developing multi-operational times synthetically.

Periodically, planning standards must be reviewed in order to bring them up to date and to improve the efficiency of the vehicles selected. Planning standards have to be tested in operation in order to see if the estimated times are viable and to find what correction factors are necessary otherwise.

Vehicle operating times are affected by restrictions to load capacities and delivery procedures; consequently, the overall efficiency, economy and control of them will be affected too. In the same way, estimated work contents will vary with changes in operating times or the number of drops. The stan-

PREPARING DISTRIBUTION PLANS

dard conditions observed when setting planning standards must be generally applicable or they will be liable to vary in a dynamic situation.

Allowances must be made for exceeding the standard times and this can be done by making the times generous and the time in hand at the end of a job will be a reward for safe planning.

Recommending the vehicles

The number of vehicles that will be required in a system has been covered in the chapters on routing, scheduling and preparing distribution plans. In practice, these factors in combination can cause the original numbers to be modified slightly, especially when there are peaks of demand during the year. The estimates can represent basic fleet requirements and supplements can be added from time to time as circumstances change.

Vehicle size and type. Vehicle recommendations are presented with specifications, usually, and they result from examinations of economic delivery loads and vehicle design characteristics. The economic load may be defined by weight or by volume and it provides the best utilisation of the delivery time available.

It is wise to standardise on vehicle size and type, because the advantages in maintenance, operating control and driving will outweigh the disadvantages of losing a few minutes, or loading one or two fewer goods.

Vehicle manning. The normal manning of vehicles can be expressed in terms of the numbers, experience and qualifications of personnel.

Vehicle types. Each type of delivery needs the right type of vehicle, and operational experience is the best qualification for recommending vehicle types. Types of vehicle differ according to wheelbase and body design which are fairly standard to all makes and models of vehicles. A closed body design gives good weather protection, but a flat-deck is easier to unload and it has a slightly greater load capacity. The compromise between these two types of vehicle is an open body with a roof which is detachable.

Recommendations based upon operating experience have the advantage of being particularly suitable for producing realistic plans. The assistance of vehicle agents or other operators will be valuable if personal experience is lacking.

Vehicle capacities. The capacities of vehicles depend upon the volume of goods to be delivered, but it is advisable to recommend the largest size that can be operated safely. As a precaution, it is preferable to recommend vehicles that are too large rather than exactly right for the volume of goods.

PREPARING DISTRIBUTION PLANS

Simplification of fleet management is a strong reason for recommending vehicles of similar capacities.

Delivery costs. The method of delivery that is recommended must take into account the value of the goods to be delivered. The proportion of selling prices that is contributed by distribution increases with the bulkiness of goods. For example, over 50 per cent of the price of sand is contributed by transport costs, 40 per cent of coal prices, around 30 per cent of vegetable prices, but less than 2 per cent of the price of cigarettes, foodstuffs or office machines.

Delivery distances. Road vehicles are suitable for short and medium hauls, rail for long distances, ships or canal barges for bulky, non-perishable goods, pipelines for liquids or gases and aircraft for valuable or very perishable items. Road vehicles are the most flexible, because body designs are available for nearly all commodities.

Full details of road vehicle costs are to be found in the *Freight Transport Association Yearbook* and it is recommended to all fleet operators. Average annual vehicle operating costs in Britain are £1900 for 3-tonners and £2500 for 6-tonners. These figures are based upon running 200 miles per week and carrying 800 tons a year; driver only; wages, fuel lubricants and maintenance; garaging, repairs, and licensing, and refer to flat-deck vehicles. The individual items of vehicle operating costs are listed below:

1   *Wages*   depend upon the type of vehicle and area, and also upon working hours
2   *National Insurance*   compulsory contributions
3   *Accident insurance*   to cover vehicle, goods and third parties
4   *Establishment*   standing charges including administration and supervision
5   *Licences*   vehicle and traffic operating licences
6   *Depreciation*   the vehicle capital cost spread over its working life
7   *Running costs*   fuel, oil, tyres and batteries
8   *Repairs*   all garage work needed to keep a vehicle running

Vehicle operating costs. The average cost of operating a 10-ton rigid tipper in England is shown in Figure 8:16 as an aid to planning vehicle selection. The individual costs are specific to this type of vehicle, but this example is presented in order to show all the items that must be included. The cost per mile, excluding overheads, is £0.14 for this 10-ton tipper.

In comparison, the cost per mile for operating a 30-cwt van for 25 000 miles per annum is £0.07; for a 5-ton flat truck £0.10; for a 15-ton articulated lorry £0.16; and for a 20-ton tanker £0.21.

PREPARING DISTRIBUTION PLANS

ANNUAL COSTS		£/year	Pence/mile
Standing costs			
Wages (40 hours per week)		630	2.52
National insurance		55	0.22
Accident insurance		220	0.88
Administration		740	2.96
Licences		200	0.80
Depreciation		400	1.60
	Sub-total	2245	8.98
Running costs			
Fuel		660	2.65
Lubrication and servicing		35	0.14
Tyres		160	0.63
Maintenance and repairs		400	1.60
	Sub-total	1255	5.02
Total costs		3500	14.00

Cost per week for 50 weeks a year = £70
Cost per hour for 40 hours a week = £1.75
Cost per mile for 25 000 miles a year = £0.14

Figure 8:16 OPERATING COSTS FOR 10-TON TIPPER TRUCK

Transport efficiency. Increasing the efficiency of vehicle operations will reduce the number of vehicles required for a given throughput of goods and it will reduce the operating cost per ton transported. Both savings help to narrow the gap between the producers and consumers of goods. Narrowing the gap will encourage industrial specialisation, manufacturing in larger volumes and increasing the size of markets.

8:5 TRANSPORT MANNING

The personnel for manning the transport section of a distribution system must be technically qualified to control traffic activities or to operate the

PREPARING DISTRIBUTION PLANS

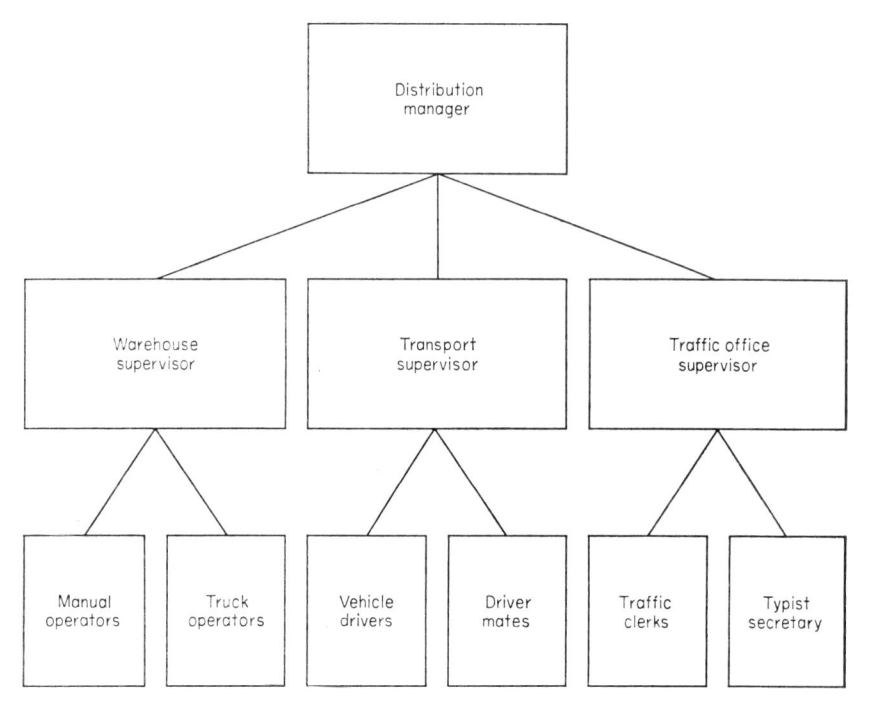

Figure 8:17 STAFF ORGANISATION FOR DISTRIBUTION

vehicles. Relationships between the different distribution sections are presented as an organisation chart in Figure 8:17.

Management

Each person in charge of a transport section in Britain has to have a transport manager's licence after 1971. The purpose of this licence is to attach a degree of personal legal responsibility to designated Transport Managers who control vehicle operations. In this manner, it is hoped to stimulate a greater concern for the condition of vehicles in the interest of road safety.

This responsibility of transport managers covers the licensing of drivers, operating legal hours and the keeping of proper records. It is an administrative duty rather than a technical one; the holder must arrange for tests and overhauls and prevent breaches of the law. A transport manager may be a part-time title, but a licence is obtainable only by passing a test or examination. The licence is the personal property of the holder and it is not attached to any particular post.

PREPARING DISTRIBUTION PLANS

The responsiblity of a transport manager to his company differs with circumstances. The following is a list of general responsibilities:

1. Controlling directly vehicle drivers and transport personnel
2. Administrating delivery schedules and vehicle routes
3. Monitoring the delivery function
4. Supervising vehicle maintenance, repair and testing
5. Acquiring the knowledge and passing a transport manager's test
6. Keeping records of driving hours
7. Servicing and garaging the vehicles
8. Implementing training schemes for drivers
9. Organising transport activities
10. Arranging the payment of wages and bonuses to personnel

Office staff

The documentation and book-keeping related to transport operations should be maintained by the staff of the traffic office. They will be clerks, in most cases, who are responsible to the transport manager. Duties include processing the paperwork that is necessary for controlling delivery operations, orders, invoices and goods delivered. There may not be sufficient work for employing a traffic clerk full time and manning the office will depend upon the size of the fleet and its operations.

Drivers

Each vehicle on the road must have a driver and, in some instances, a driver's mate. A driver must possess a current goods vehicle licence and he will be responsible to the transport manager and will act in accordance with the law. The general duties of drivers are:

1. To drive and maintain vehicles as instructed
2. To keep records of vehicle activities
3. To report accidents, delays and vehicle faults
4. To comply with the regulations concerning hours, vehicle loading and operation, unloading and waiting restrictions, reporting accidents and observing the highway code

Recruitment

The recruiting of staff must be included with selecting vehicles when planning a distribution system, because the two are complementary. Recruitment starts with the preparation of job specifications and advertising for the personnel required. Applicants must be interviewed in order to select those that satisfy requirements. Then, the successful applicants have to be instructed about their duties and given training as necessary. Finally, the transport section must be manned so that it becomes operational.

9 CONTROLLING DISTRIBUTION

Controlling is the present aspect of managing a system. The past aspect is organising and the future is planning. Organisation involves arranging factual things, like people, materials, machinery and other resources, systematically. Planning involves preparing the resources for future utilisation. Control is the key to managing, because it involves comparing the actual results with the plans and initiating adjustments whenever necessary.

Proper control is impossible without plans that provide meaningful standards for judging results. The closer that the results approach the plans, the easier it is to control activities. Therefore, good planning is essential for controlling a system effectively.

Managing a distribution system starts with establishing the distribution policies which will be the overall plans for the complete system. They form the framework within which the distribution system is organised and they are the responsibility of the persons with overall control of the system. Broadly speaking, the policies for a distribution system establish the framework for warehousing and delivering the goods. The organisation chart in Figure 8:17 shows the basic activities of the system in terms of the personnel responsible for them. The managerial level is at the top of the structure and it controls the supervisory level below. Supervisors are junior managers who control the operating level at the base.

There are three basic activities of the distribution function and plans for controlling them are reflections of the tripartite nature of distribution itself. The plans for controlling distribution are multi-purpose, being concerned with marketing and production as well as distribution.

9:1 TRIPARTITE ORGANISATION OF DISTRIBUTION

The control and organisation of distribution are pulled in three directions by the needs of marketing, production and distribution in its own right. Nowadays, distribution has outgrown its passive role under the direction of the sales force and has become an active management function helping to achieve overall company objectives. A big factor in current trends is the realisation that the control of distribution extends beyond the movement of goods alone. The eyes of managers are being opened to the fact that scientific techniques are available for analysing complex problems like routing and scheduling vehicles, or controlling costs.

Modern distribution

The number of permutations for distributing goods is multitudinous, due to the wide choices of warehouses, vehicles, delivery routes, order frequencies or customer locations. Successful solutions must be developed scientifically and logically; intuition is insufficient on its own. However, all techniques are ineffectual if used in isolation without purposeful management control. Control starts with an organisation that is based upon feasible objectives.

Distribution objectives

The basic objective of distribution is to provide an agreed standard of service to customers. This standard varies enormously; for example, from daily deliveries for frozen foods to annual deliveries for fireworks. Some customers put a great importance upon regular supplies, others on convenience or on variety. From the distribution point of view, the service offered must be matched by its cost and it is necessary to perform a joint budgeting exercise with customers so that these two objectives for successful distribution are agreed mutually. In effect, the market has to be disciplined to decide the economic level of service that is acceptable. Objectives must not be set in isolation without considering the overall policies; for example, a company wants the largest profit and not the largest number of sales. Similarly, distribution provides a service to customers which is for their benefit and not for the company's convenience.

Need for compromise

In many instances, there is a straight-line relationship between cost and the level of service; in other words, the better the service the more it costs. A balanced compromise is the only successful solution. Unless marketing, production and distribution realise that their objectives conflict, there will be an unstable situation when one of the three gets out of line. An organisation based upon tripartite objectives has a good chance of success, because it will be designed to optimise compromises anyway. When operations are well organised, they become more reliable as tested routines develop. Routine procedures beget consistency which is an essential feature of good service.

Effective organisation

Establishing an effective organisation takes a long time, but it is well worth the waiting, both from the viewpoints of better service and lower costs. When operations are well organised, people know exactly what to do and this gives them more confidence, which improves their efficiency. Good organisation overcomes conflicts and it is valuable for showing the right channels for delegating authority and for implementing accountability.

When responsibility for distribution is divided, practical difficulties arise and conflicts begin. One advantage of incorporating distribution into the functional management structure of a company is better decision making and another is improved coordination while yet another is centralised control of the distribution function. No organisation can be truly effective without realistic objectives and they are the prime requisite for control.

9:2 CONTROLLING DISTRIBUTION COSTS

The organisation structure that is used for controlling the staff provides the best framework for controlling the costs. Authority is greatest at the top of an organisation and authority is another name for accountability. The value of the assets that managers control is a good measure of their authority and accountability. Logically, accountability must apply to liabilities as well as to assets and there is a case in favour of organising cost control along the same lines as staff control. Costs are related to the different physical resources of the company and the scale of values is shown by the pyramid structure in Figure 9:1 for the outputs of manufacture.

In order to breathe life into an organisation structure, it is necessary to inject some financial blood from the sale of products. Costs are a drain on the system, flowing in the opposite direction to the incomes. Since the flow lines of incomes and costs are similar, they can be compared on equal terms at specific places in the structure. Comparisons take the form of balance sheets that show the financial state as profit or loss. At any point, the results of balancing income with cost contributes to the total company profit or loss. The amount of income that flows down to a structural level is expressed by its budget which shows the limit of expenditure for operating at that level.

The picture of the corporate nature of a company financial system helps to put incomes and costs into perspective. Costs need control because they drain the income "life blood" from the economic system and it is essential to know something about the different types of cost.

Fixed costs are controlled by senior management, because they represent the contribution of capital investments to the cost of operations. They include sites and buildings, or plant and equipment. Investments are incurred irrespective of the operations that are performed or the products that are manufactured and distributed.

CONTROLLING DISTRIBUTION

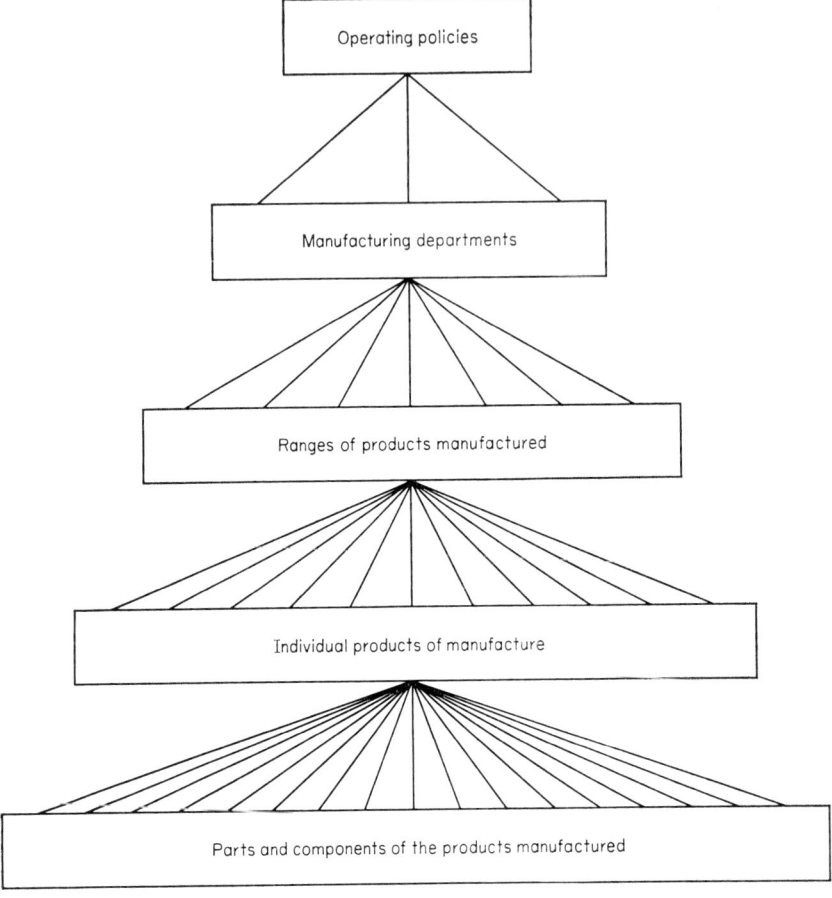

Figure 9:1 ORGANISATION FOR COST CONTROL

Variable costs depend upon the activities of a company, because they arise from doing things, like manufacturing, selling or distributing products. Costs that vary with throughputs include materials, labour and direct operating costs.

Sometimes it is difficult to call a cost either fixed or variable, but this is less important than forgetting to include it in the balance sheet at all. The locations of operations that contribute to the cost of products are called *cost centres* and sources of income are called *profit centres*. The costs and incomes from these centres must be balanced together in order to determine the economic status of the company.

Control by balancing costs with incomes can be exercised at any place in the structure. The incomes are budgets in most departments and control means preventing the costs from exceeding the budgeted allowance. Controlling costs within a budget is a sign of responsible accountability, but this is not realised by every manager, unfortunately. Irresponsible people believe that a budget is bottomless and forget that exceeding the budget is a drain on company reserves. If this drain becomes excessive, the company may become bankrupt and the irresponsible people will lose their jobs.

Performance ratios

In distribution, control can be exercised by comparing the ratios of the budget and the costs for each activity. With experience, costs can be related to the distribution resources in order to exercise control. Five effective performance ratios are:

1   Cost contribution per customer
2   Cost contribution per delivery journey
3   Cost contribution per vehicle
4   Cost contribution per depot
5   Cost contribution per product distributed

Performance ratios are useful for indicating the least costly items, or showing the operations that need streamlining.

A ratio is more meaningful when it is examined on its own, because specific cost reductions and improvements can be seen more readily, but they can be masked by average figures. The consistency and performance of individual costs are more important than averages. The use of ratios compares related factors and it provides a useful efficiency measure.

Profit margins

Subtracting the costs of resources from the sales income leaves the *gross profit* and subtracting production overheads from it results in a *net profit or loss*. Distribution is one of the overheads that decides whether the overall result is a profit or loss.

Larger profits result from reducing the overhead costs, which include stockholding and transport operations. Both are related, because operating more vehicles reduces the stockholding costs, since some of the stock is held in transit. Stockholding costs money; therefore, stocks should be turned over as rapidly as possible, particularly in the case of deteriorating goods.

When the interest on capital borrowed is 10 per cent, keeping stock in a warehouse for one year adds another 10 per cent to its cost without adding value. This is the same as saying that the profit margin is reduced by 10 per cent, or the price of the goods has increased by 10 per cent How many people are willing to pay more for last year's goods?

Standard costing

In simple terms, standard costing is a method of estimating the amount of money that will have to be spent in order to perform operations in the precise way that they were planned. It is a powerful tool for controlling operations, remembering that control is the action of correcting operations that get out of line with plans.

The principles of standard costing and budgetary control are similar but the former refers to operations specifically and it is more appropriate for controlling distribution costs.

Standard costing in practice. The first step is to produce as accurate a budget as possible for the given period of time. The throughput of goods will have been forecast by the sales office and the task of standard costing is to estimate all the separate costs of distributing the throughput forecast. The next step is to compare the expected income with the costs estimated and to decide on the budget to be allowed. Estimates must be based upon the standard costs of materials, labour, machinery and direct overheads.

Standard costs are evaluated at the end of each accounting period for distribution operations, by comparing the budgeted costs with the actual costs. Variances must be noted and steps taken to control them better in the next period.

The use of standards in conjunction with budgets provides a comprehensive accounting service that includes the following controls for distribution

1   Control of performance
2   Control of warehousing
3   Control of transport operations
4   Control of labour costs
5   Control of overheads

In addition, standard costing is a sound basis for estimating, a method for evaluating savings, a reliable source of comparing information and a valuable starting point for cost reductions. There is an inherent benefit of standardisation: it is the reduction of variety which is always costly to maintain.

9:3 CONTROLLING DISTRIBUTION STOCKS

The generally accepted meaning of stock control is the establishment of

CONTROLLING DISTRIBUTION

upper and lower levels of stock and for reordering more stocks in order to maintain equality. An important factor is knowing when to order so that stocks are neither too low nor too high. Thus, there are three levels to be considered for controlling stocks and they are shown in Figure 9:2.

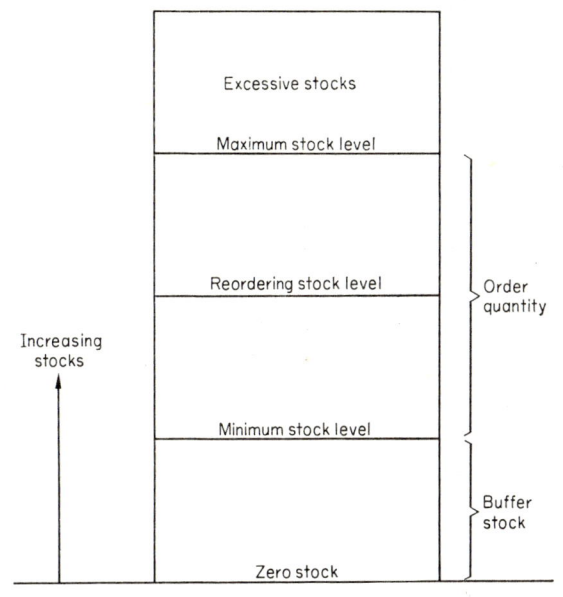

Figure 9:2 STOCK LEVELS

Methods of stock control

Any method of stock control is defined by two parameters; the order quantity and the reordering level. In a dynamic situation like distribution, a third parameter has to be included, namely the fluctuations in throughput.

Parameters can be determined by inspired guesswork, or by establishing predetermined stock levels or by scientific appraisal. The drawback to guesswork is that success or failure cannot be measured and it depends upon wide experience for good results. Predetermined stock levels are set in advance, for example by setting time limits for stock utilisation based upon standard throughputs. The scientific approach optimises the variables that affect the stock levels at certain times. Some of the variables are:

1 Delays in supplying goods to warehouses
2 Variations in customer requirements
3 Fluctuations in handling times
4 Deterioration of goods held in stock
5 Varying quantity discounts

CONTROLLING DISTRIBUTION

6   Costs of placing orders
7   Returns on capital secured as inventory
8   Variations in warehousing costs
9   Differences in order lead times
10 Acceptable risks of stock-outs

The reordering quantity depends upon the cost of holding stocks and the cost of replacing stocks. In the first instance, costs are reduced by holding minimal stocks and in the second instance, replacement in bulk quantities is cheapest. Optimising must aim at finding the best compromise between these two stock quantities.

A general equation for determining the reordering quantity (ROQ) with the least cost is:

$$ROQ = \sqrt{\frac{(2\ a\ t)}{c}}$$

where
a = the cost of placing an order
t = the throughput in a given time period
c = the cost of storing an item for this time period

The reordering level is a measure of the time that will elapse before reordering stock. Ideally, the replacement stock should arrive just as the buffer stock is finished and the reordering level will be equivalent to the throughput during the lead time for the order. The buffer stock is a variable and it is impossible to guarantee that any buffer stock will be adequate.

The reordering level (ROL) can be found, with reasonable accuracy, by examining records of past throughputs for similar periods of time. The probability of future throughputs can be calculated by statistical analysis and the minimum and maximum stock levels defined at the appropriate risk level. A general equation can be used when the buffer stock is known and it is the following one:

$$ROL = Sn + \sqrt{nB}$$

where
  S = mean stock throughput for the period
  n = order lead time (weeks)
  B = buffer stock for one week
$\sqrt{nB}$ = buffer stock for the lead time (weeks)

Buffer stock is needed for two reasons; firstly, to cover the lead time and, secondly, to guard against the stock-out risk. This risk can be forecast only

CONTROLLING DISTRIBUTION

when the throughput follows a standard pattern, which is unlikely in distribution systems.

Variable throughput makes it advisable to use mean throughputs for similar periods in the past, preferably moving averages.

Failure to predict demand makes stockholding necessary, particularly holding a buffer stock in order to cope with unexpected increases in throughput. The size of the buffer stock reflects the amount of risk expected, or the effectiveness of forecasting. Supply is controllable within certain limits only and they can create a situation of stock peaks and troughs repeatedly. Stocks rise to a maximum after receiving a replenishment, then fall slowly as they are utilised. This situation is shown graphically in Figure 9:3 as a saw-tooth pattern.

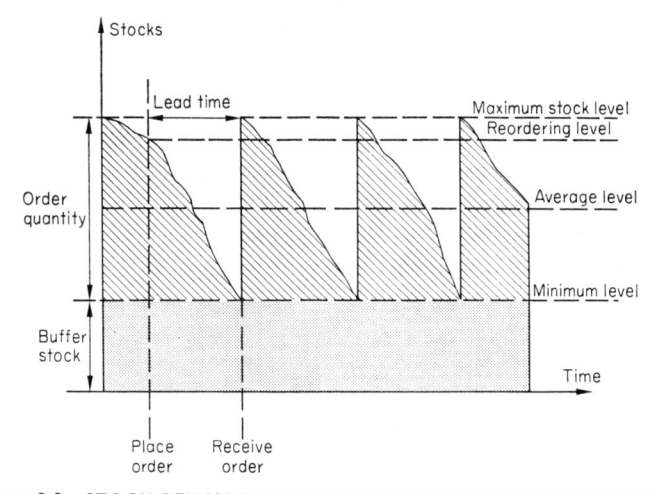

Figure 9:3 STOCK BEHAVIOUR PATTERN WITH CONSTANT DEMAND

Normal stock patterns have a fixed buffer stock and a fluctuating operating stock, and deciding the best method of stock control starts with examining supply and demand.

Stock control principles

A simple stock control procedure can be operated by one man, using record cards and making decisions according to current needs. As stocks increase, control becomes more complicated and rules must be made to ensure stockholding safety. There are three principles which govern these rules:

1   Small stocks incur least costs

CONTROLLING DISTRIBUTION

2   Stock-outs are costly
3   Bulk replenishments save money

Conflicts between these principles have to be overcome by balancing costs and savings. Optimal compromises will be found by experimenting and using logic. The success of stock control is an agreement that the overall stocks are no more than the combined total needed for replenishing each item on its own.

Timing orders. The reordering level must be at the stock level that just allows the order lead time to elapse before the replenishment is needed. Assuming that the forecast demand is correct, the buffer stock will be untouched before the replenishment arrives.

It follows that the reordering level of stock equals the demand forecast for the lead time plus the buffer stock. Of necessity, the buffer stock is too large when forecasting is accurate and too small when forecasting is uncertain.

Stock-outs. Running out of stock must be avoided and can be prevented by forecasting stock-outs. The diagram in Figure 9:4 shows the probable

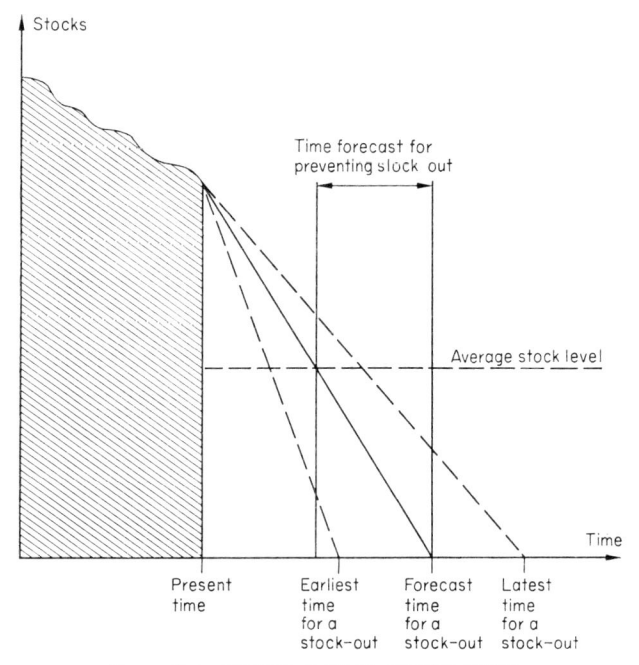

Figure 9:4 CONTROLLING STOCK-OUTS

CONTROLLING DISTRIBUTION

time when a stock will run out. The earliest and latest times will be based upon practical estimates and they will be measures of the forecasting error. The advantage of this diagram for control purposes is that it indicates the time for an expected stock-out at each stock level according to the accuracy of forecasting.

Economic order quantity. Two types of cost are associated with stockholding; firstly, the actual cost of holding the stocks and, secondly, the cost of ordering stocks that includes placing the order, receiving the replenishment and inspecting it. As the size of an order increases, the cost of holding it increases directly while the cost per unit of ordering decreases. These operating costs in combination determine the economic order quantity that conforms to the least total cost. Deciding the economic order quantity is shown graphically in Figure 9:5.

The cost of stockholding may increase at different rates according to the needs for holding different sizes of stock. As a result, the cost of stockholding line on the graph in Figure 9:5 will be stepped downwards whenever there is a cost reduction that is geared to order size. Then the curve for total cost will have a minimum for each order size range and the economic quantity will depend upon the order size/cost ratio and the reordering level.

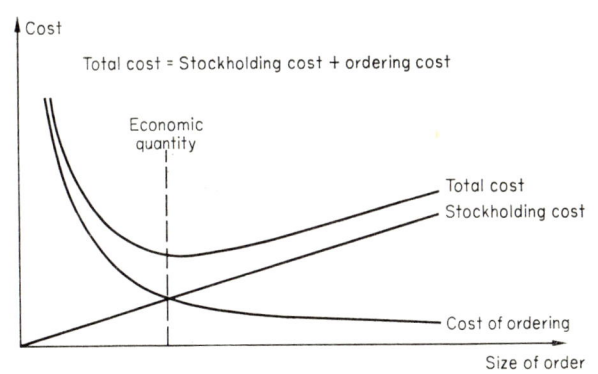

Figure 9:5 ECONOMIC ORDER QUANTITY

Visual presentation of the relationships that have to be optimised before making decisions for controlling distribution can be valuable for day-to-day control. They are easy to follow and serve as progress reminders when kept on the office wall.

9:4 CONTROLLING RESULTS GRAPHICALLY

Methods of controlling a distribution system must be related to cost control, but practical people find it easier to understand costs that are expressed

CONTROLLING DISTRIBUTION

in charts rather than as figures in a ledger. For the man who wishes to keep control over the results of distribution, presenting cost graphically has a great value and the Z-chart provides a form that is superior to any other.

The three cost figures that are essential for control purposes are the current costs, the cumulative costs of the present operating year and the moving annual total which shows costs for the previous twelve months. A Z-chart can show the three costs at the same time, which allows a direct comparison to be made between costs for the current twelve months and those for the operating year. It shows that current costs are part of a continuous series.

Usually, costs are plotted on a Z-chart monthly, because a month is a convenient period for reviewing distribution operations; however, control is a continuous process. Effective control is exercised by considering the actual costs when compared with the budgeted costs. The Z-chart is really a continuous picture of performance, each year being like a film sequence. Orders received, invoices issued, distribution costs and profit or loss can be recorded on Z-charts, because they present all the basic information that is needed for cost control purposes.

Z-chart construction

Units have to be chosen for the chart and throughput per month is a convenient one for distribution. The horizontal axis shows months and the vertical axis throughput which is directly proportional to cost usually. An example of the throughput for a corn merchant distributing wheat to millers is presented for a full year in Figure 9:6.

All the lines on this chart are black, but the chart will be made more effective in practice if they are shown in different colours.

Removing seasonal effects

The moving annual total (MAT) is the total throughput for the last twelve months; therefore, it will discount any seasonal fluctuations. In each twelve month period, all months of the year are included and the MAT line shows the annual state of affairs up to date. In Figure 9:6 the annual tonnage is dropping gradually from August to December and it is a trend that the distributor needs to investigate, because the MAT line should be roughly level normally. The MAT line is a barometer of performance month by month.

The cumulative line presents the total throughput for the current year up to date and, obviously, it will be similar to the moving annual total at the end of December. It shows the progressive result for the current year. Since the cumulative total follows seasonal movements, control comparisons can be made only with a complete graph for each year concerned. This is

CONTROLLING DISTRIBUTION

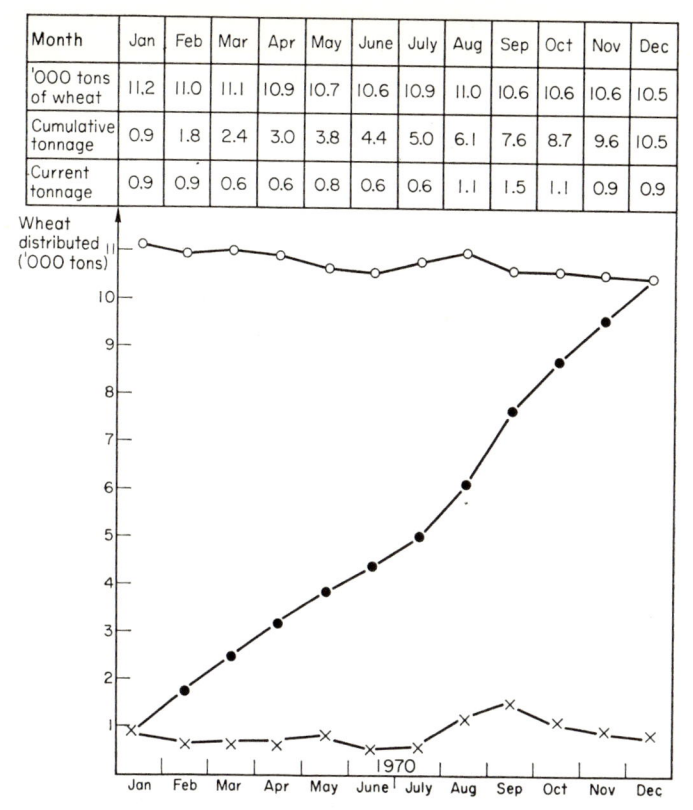

Month	Jan	Feb	Mar	Apr	May	June	July	Aug	Sep	Oct	Nov	Dec
'000 tons of wheat	11.2	11.0	11.1	10.9	10.7	10.6	10.9	11.0	10.6	10.6	10.6	10.5
Cumulative tonnage	0.9	1.8	2.4	3.0	3.8	4.4	5.0	6.1	7.6	8.7	9.6	10.5
Current tonnage	0.9	0.9	0.6	0.6	0.8	0.6	0.6	1.1	1.5	1.1	0.9	0.9

Figure 9:6 Z-CHART FOR WHEAT DISTRIBUTION
Key to throughput: O = MAT, ● = cumulative, X = monthly

a disadvantage which is removed by using a NAT line which keeps the controller in touch with affairs throughout the year.

Current affairs

The current line at the bottom of a Z-chart shows monthly results and it can jump about in some situations. The current monthly throughput has little meaning on its own. Therefore, it has little value for control purposes although it is useful for providing details.

Trends

When the current and MAT lines are studied together the reasons for trends become more apparent. The trend line shows the result of the previous twelve months and the results for succeeding months must be as good as previous months or it will not be uniform. Comparing a number of different factors can be done with MAT lines alone. Where a distribution cost total includes

CONTROLLING DISTRIBUTION

several products, it is useful for the MAT lines to be presented on the same chart. Differences in performance will be seen readily, and the chart gives the incentive that is needed for arresting falling trends or for stimulating rising ones. Removing seasonal effects gives a visual sense of security that is difficult to attain by other control methods.

Moving annual averages

When a trend for a number of years is required, as for the annual prices of wheat or the wages of workers, moving annual totals are useless. In such a case, it is usual to take the average for the period, and repeating this successively over a long period of time will provide data for a moving annual average graph. A long term graph can show a planner the probable trends for future supplies or throughputs.

Planning with Z-charts

The trends shown by a Z-chart provide a yearly view of affairs that put

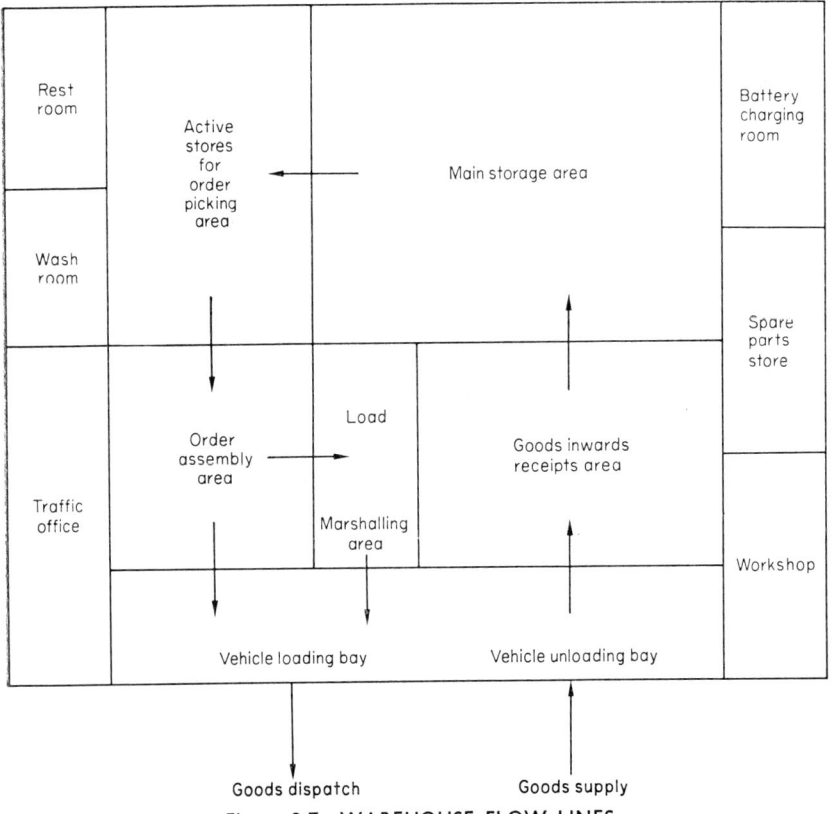

Figure 9:7 WAREHOUSE FLOW LINES

CONTROLLING DISTRIBUTION

day-to-day events in their right perspective. The MAT lines on a Z-chart are essentially guides for planning, showing the attitudes to adopt after comparing similar trends in the past. Trend patterns allow comparisons to be carried out month by month so that an up-to-date indication of fluctuations in the results is obtained for preparing plans. The Z-chart is one of the most valuable aids for planning and control ever devised.

9:5 WORK STUDY FOR CONTROLLING DELIVERIES

Distribution is a difficult field for work study, particularly delivery operations. Warehousing costs can be reduced by method study and work measurement in much the same way as production operations. Flow process charts are valuable for showing the movement of goods in warehouses according to a planned sequence of events. A warehouse layout is shown in Figure 9:7 in order to illustrate the basic flow lines.

Applying work study to transport operations is problematical, because work targets are impractical, supervision is impossible and control is indirect. Incentives are essential for raising productivity and setting standards is necessary for judging results, but standardising delivery operations is very difficult. Basically, the efficiency of delivery can be measured in terms of low cost, good service and least time.

Observing work activities provides the input of information and operational vehicle schedules form the output for implementation. Collecting information is a task that can be done by junior staff or trainees and its purpose will be twofold, firstly, to gather factual evidence and, secondly, to allow inexperienced persons to learn the job of delivering goods.

An oil distribution company obtained 4000 observations of delivery work in six months and they were treated statistically in order to determine standard times for the distances driven and for the products carried. These times were used in order to develop an incentive payment scheme for the vehicle drivers without restricting their cooperation. The scheme still allowed the drivers to plan their own load construction and unloading sequences, but they objected to the new scheme. After a while, the scheme was accepted and the manager believes that the original objection was against the measure of control that had been established over the drivers for the first time.

Traffic engineering

The different design characteristics of vehicles can be utilised for improving the flow of traffic. Factors that contribute to road congestion include vehicle lengths and widths, turning circles, speeds and the acceleration of vehicles. Analysing these details helps to improve the construction and layout of roads, particularly their dimensions, corners and accessibility at junctions or private entrances and parking facilities.

CONTROLLING DISTRIBUTION

Improving traffic conditions is a continuous process, because problems are ever changing and plans for solving them must be adaptable and dynamic. A methodical approach is beneficial for overcoming conflicts. Industrial engineers use a step by step procedure for solving dynamic problems methodically which is shown as a schematic diagram in Figure 9:8.

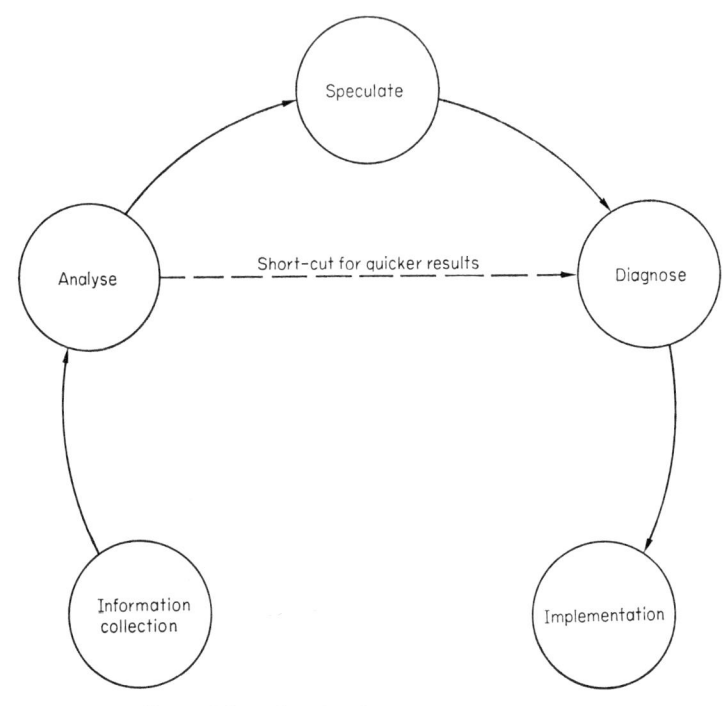

Figure 9:8 METHODICAL PROCEDURE

The implementation of plans for solving problems starts with the collection of information, then analysis can diagnose troubles immediately, or speculation can make suggestions for improving things. Adopting a methodical approach gives a greater insight into the contributing factors so that the plans developed for implementation have the best chance of success.

Traffic congestion problem. The area supervisor of the Public Works Department of an Indian state had received many complaints from road users about the congestion on a particular road. The large number of complaints suggested that the road was carrying more traffic than it could handle and the immediate answer considered was to widen it. However, the budget was

CONTROLLING DISTRIBUTION

committed for the next three years and a plan as expensive as widening the road was out of the question.

Information. The methodical approach was adopted for reducing the traffic congestion and the following items of information were collected:

1 Traffic densities as number of vehicles
2 Traffic variety as different types of vehicle
3 Destinations of vehicles
4 Routes and locations served by the road
5 Average speeds of travel
6 Places of restricted flow
7 Journey frequencies of vehicles
8 Number of destinations along the road
9 Volume of goods carried
10 Number of passengers

Analysis. The facts collected were analysed in order to determine patterns for the volume of traffic, direction of flow and positions of bottlenecks. An immediate diagnosis of the trouble was a bad corner where the road deviated to avoid a factory. The sketch map in Figure 9:9 shows that the situation was aggravated by the junction of a minor road at the corner and opposite the factory entrance.

Road flow times showed that realigning the road to avoid the factory

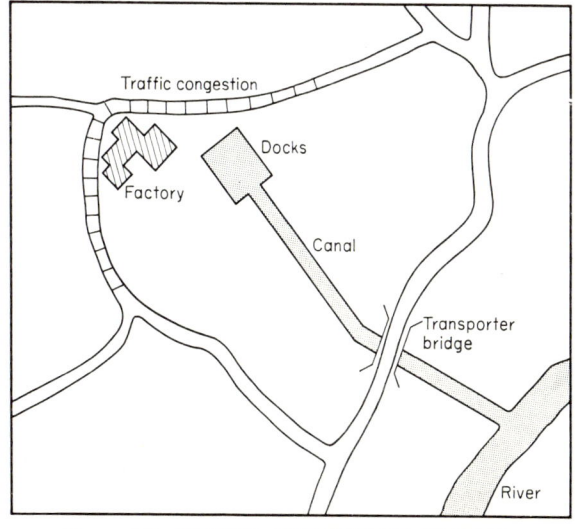

Figure 9:9 TRAFFIC CONGESTION PROBLEM

would alleviate the traffic congestion in this area. Since immediate answers may not be the best answers, the procedure continued by speculating on the ideas analysed.

Speculation. Following the observation that the bad corner was responsible for the greatest congestion on the road, suggestions were made for removing the bend and for improving the junction. Other items of information were looked into more closely and it was found that over half the vehicles using this road could use alternative roads and erecting clearer signboards might redirect some of the traffic away from this road in order to relieve the congestion.

Diagnosis. The immediate diagnosis was to remove the corner in some way or another, but the diagnosis after speculation was to divert some of the traffic via alternative routes. The reason for traffic congestion at the bad corner was obvious, but the reason for vehicle drivers using the congested road in preference to others was not so apparent.

Questioning drivers produced the revealing information that many of them used the road in order to avoid the unpredictable delays at a transporter bridge on a more direct road. Therefore, the reasons for these delays were investigated and were found to be due to the passage of shipping along a canal to the docks. Also, it was found that the operator of the transporter bridge was given excessive time warnings for raising the bridge, due to the uncertain time for each ship to move from the main river to the bridge.

Implementation. Improving the waiting time at the bridge required better coordination of shipping and traffic flows, but a new bridge or a tunnel for the road would avoid delays entirely.

Finance for redesigning the road over the canal was unavailable and controlling traffic flows was considered instead. A schedule of activities had to be prepared and it was found to be easier to control the shipping than the road traffic. Timetables for the passage of ships reduced individual delays to a minimum and a more precise warning system to the bridge operator ensured that the bridge was raised only for the duration of a ship passing under it.

Implementing the plan took a little while, but it had cost the minimum of money for relieving the traffic congestion on another road. The most favourable solutions are rarely obvious and a methodical investigation is necessary in order to obtain a better solution for the least cost.

Studying transport operations

Many transport problems are political due to the regulations that beset transport operations; others are human or organisational and work study applied confidently can help to solve them successfully. Collecting the information for controlling transport operations is tedious and involves much travelling along routes with the drivers. This procedure requires being accepted by the men and explaining to them the benefits that they will derive from improving the system. The amount of tedious work can be reduced with random sampling of the operations in order to develop standard times. The standard times necessary for controlling transport operations include:

1   Vehicle running times
2   Loading times per unit carried
3   Vehicle maintenance: constant times
4   Paperwork for traffic control: constant times
5   Customer drop times

The units for measurement, apart from time, are distance run, unit delivery costs and number of items loaded. Work study obtains standard times by observing operational times and recording them with a stop-watch, then they are corrected for normal conditions by multiplying the observed time with an effort rating. On the international scale, normal working is rated at one hundred and slow or easy work is rated at less than this figure, while fast or energetic work is rated above it. In this way, observed times are reduced if they are considered easy to achieve and increased if they are difficult. Normal time represents the time for doing a job of work that can be kept up steadily all day; in other words, a fair day's work for a fair day's pay.

Rating vehicle drivers. The work of a driver is within his own control, largely, and he must feel a personal responsibility of working well. Consequently, the work of driving a vehicle is rated above one hundred, usually. Industrial engineers use ratings between 110 and 120, as a rule, when drivers are conscientious.

When a driver is idle, it means that he has saved time somewhere on the journey; it is difficult to prepare schedules based upon running times only, for this reason. It is wise to study two vehicle drivers at a time, in order to gain their confidence and to double-check the times.

When controlling transport operations with standard times, observing times alone is inadequate unless they are related to distances travelled and loads carried. Standard times based upon bad days are preferable to ones studied on good days, because encouragement is given only when the apparently tight times are achieved by the men.

Standard delivery times. Work study was performed on vehicles that were

CONTROLLING DISTRIBUTION

Work elements	Overall time of driver (minutes)	Standard time (minutes)	Comments
1 *Loading van at depot*			
Check data on load sheet on departure	1.01	1.09	Rough check only before loading vehicle
Check vehicle load and correct errors	1.74	1.87	
Make corrections	0.84	0.91	
Close van doors	0.38	0.41	
Report to traffic office	1.04	1.12	
Enter cab and make up log book	1.38	1.49	
Sort delivery sheets and decide the route	3.19	3.50	Can be done while van is being loaded
Start vehicle and drive to depot gate	2.67	2.93	
Sub-total		13.32	Before leaving depot
2 *Returning to depot*			
Drive to unloading bay	0.78	0.84	
Unload empty pallets	1.64	1.79	With forklift truck
Complete journey sheet and refuel vehicle	4.45	4.79	
Fill in vehicle log	3.81	4.12	
Report to traffic office	2.98	3.21	
Sub-total		14.75	After returning
3 *Servicing the van*			
Check oil, water and battery	2.33	2.54	
Inflate tyres	4.23	4.60	
Wash down van	22.65	24.77	
Sub-total		31.91	Daily service of van
Grand total time spent at depot		59.98	For one journey

Figure 9:10 STANDARD DEPOT TIMES FOR A VEHICLE DRIVER

used for delivering cased goods to retail customers in England. All the operations were studied from loading the vehicles to making drops to customers. Where applicable, percentage time allowances were added for rest periods and for fatigue.

Loading times. Orders were assembled on pallets and the pallets were loaded into 5-ton vans with fork-lift trucks. Standard times were expressed as minutes per pallet loaded and as minutes per foot travelled with a fork-lift truck.

The sum of elements of loading and unloading a pallet resulted in a standard work time of 1.344 minutes and the rate of travel for the fork-lift truck was 0.0058 minutes per foot. Therefore, the time allowed for loading a pallet in the assembly area, transporting it 200 feet to the vehicle and unloading it into the vehicle was equal to $1.344 + (200 \times 0.0058) = 2.504$ minutes per pallet.

Journey times. A complete journey comprised loading palletised goods into a van, transporting the goods by road, dropping them at the premises of customers and returning to the depot. Drop times varied according to the size of orders, but the standard times presented in Figure 9:10 were based upon an urban route involving five drops with a 5-ton van.

Drop times. The goods were unloaded by hand at customer drop points and wheeled into the premises with a sack truck for small deliveries; larger multiple deliveries were handled with the customer's fork-lift truck. Standard drop times for delivering cased goods to customers are shown in Figure 9:11.

Summary

Work study is used for investigating the way that jobs are performed in order to improve the utilisation of existing resources. This kind of improvement is far less costly than investing more capital. An improvement that applies to transport operations is that it is a good idea to underload vans, because the number of journeys in a week can be almost doubled. Work loads can be equalised by organising a delivery rota for the drivers.

The biggest advantages of performing work study are the reduction of wasted effort and the increase in effective time utilisation.

CONTROLLING DISTRIBUTION

Drop elements	Observed time (minutes)	Standard time (minutes)	Allowed case time (minutes)
1 *Single case delivery*			
Collect case, carry into store, hand over and get signature	3.61	3.90	3.90
2 *Sack truck delivery*			
Remove sack truck from vehicle, pick order of three cases, load cases on truck, transport into store and return empty	0.48 1.80 7.22	0.52 1.98 7.80	
Sub-total		10.30	3.43
3 *Off-loading with customer's truck*			
Pick order of six cases, load onto truck	1.06 0.71	1.15 0.77	
Sub-total		1.92	0.32
4 *Small multiple delivery*			
Offload three cases and carry into store one at a time	6.63	7.26	2.42
5 *Large multiple delivery*			
Book into warehouse Prepare for offloading Pick order of 110 cases Transfer cases to pallets Transport pallet into store	3.64 2.82 3.65 6.12 2.41	3.93 3.08 3.96 6.60 2.62	
Sub-total		20.19	0.18
Grand total for all deliveries		43.57	Mean case time 2.05

Figure 9:11   STANDARD DROP TIMES FOR A 5-TON VAN

10 A SUCCESSFUL DISTRIBUTION SYSTEM

Ambition plays a large part in determining a successful distribution system, because success depends upon personal yardsticks. Success is relative. The measures for it must be based upon the objectives of the plans and the degree to which they are achieved. Therefore, the amount of control that has to be exercised over a distribution system shows how successful it is.

The control of a distribution system is measured by the resemblance of the operating results to the plans that were prepared for them. A very ambitious man will prepare very ambitious plans and attaining them will be easily recognised. Fortunately, different people have different ambitions and this helps to keep distribution in proportion and prevent the proverbial "rat race."

Success depends upon the ability of managers to manage well, supervisors to supervise well and operators to operate well. Each person in the distribution system must be integrated with the others, because its success will be proportional to the joint effort put into it. Fairness is the moral key to success. Being fair is putting as much effort into a job as the benefits taken out of it. Management includes everybody in the organisation, from the managing director down to the office boy and its continued existence depends upon teamwork.

People are like water, because they determine their own levels. Ambitious men rise to the surface on the shoulders of the multitude who make up the pool of society. These men stay at the top when they look after the people below them. A good manager realises the potentials of his staff and he helps them to flow into their correct levels. The success of managing depends upon the coordinated efforts of all the staff, upon the ability to plan activities and upon the expertise in controlling them effectively.

Distribution success

A successful distribution system achieves the desired levels of service needed by the customers and keeps down the operating costs to a minimum. These two opposing objectives are optimised by balancing one against the other and selecting the most satisfactory compromise.

Planning is the activity of establishing the objectives, and planning for

A SUCCESSFUL DISTRIBUTION SYSTEM

success means setting the objectives within the sights of the people involved. The objectives must demand a little more effort than is being expended now. Bettering current achievements is another way of achieving success. It gives that feeling of satisfaction which comes from knowing that a job has been done well.

Distribution successes give pleasure when they result from effective plans, concerted efforts and a well-managed system. The outward appearances of a successful distribution system are happy customers, smiling shareholders and a cheerful staff.

10:1 SUCCESSFUL CONTROL OF DISTRIBUTION

The control of distribution includes reducing investments and operating costs. Each person in a distribution system is responsible for incurring some of the costs and their accountability depends upon the authority vested in them. Investment costs are the larger and they must be spread over the greatest number of items as possible, in order to increase their unit value. Planning distribution resource investments in this way provides the most strategic benefits.

Strategic investments

Investments that are planned for reducing risk are strategic in nature. The benefits from investing in distribution resources are widespread throughout the company and stretch well into the future. Moreover, it is difficult to measure the rate of return on this capital, because benefits, although real, may be delayed or they may be difficult to relate to any specific activity. These chacteristics make distribution unattractive when deciding to invest on a "rate of return" basis. In order to overcome investment competition within the company and to help the distribution manager to concentrate upon providing the best customer service, it is a good idea to put aside a proportion of the planned investments for distribution. Around 5 per cent of marketing or production capital expenditures will be appropriate in many companies.

A suitable method of apportioning strategic investments applies handicapping percentages that are based upon management's estimation of the benefits or earning power of each investment. Allotting percentage handicaps is a critical decision making exercise and each must be considered on its own merits.

Choice of distribution channels

The cost of distribution must bear a direct relationship to the basic price of the goods distributed. The budgeted costs must cover the cost of warehousing, delivering and order processing, at least. These costs must be related to throughputs, except when there are additional sales promotion costs that are independent of throughputs.

In the eyes of customers, the quality of the distribution service reflects the quality of the goods and certain distribution costs may be a worthwhile sales investment.

Planning requirements

Two important requirements of successful planning are the abilities to think widely and communicate well. Information systems for developing operational plans must be scientific and based upon three fundamentals:

1 Setting effective objectives
2 Formulating strategies for attaining the objectives
3 Deciding the best courses of action

The flow of information needed for planning a distribution system starts with collecting environmental information that describes the social, political and economic environment for planning. The next type of information required refers to competitive activities and explains past performances. Additionally, internal company information is required in order to discover its strengths and weaknesses. The flow of information required for distribution planning is shown schematically in Figure 10:1.

Planning information bypasses the lines of authority and responsibility in an organisation, because it flows along the lines of communication. It shows trends over long periods, smooths out small details and prepares for the future of distribution. Efficiency and service levels are important for planning.

Control information follows organisational lines and it covers shorter periods of time. It is more detailed than the information required for planning and it is oriented towards the actual operating results. Cost results are most important for control.

Qualitative data includes statistical observations of the service levels, the community standing of the company, industrial and public relations activities and market appreciation values.

Quantitative data refers to the volume of sales, all the distribution costs, the market share, the delivery times and the resources utilised.

Value of the planning information. This depends upon the relevance of the information collected and how up to date that it is. Analysing the informa-

A SUCCESSFUL DISTRIBUTION SYSTEM

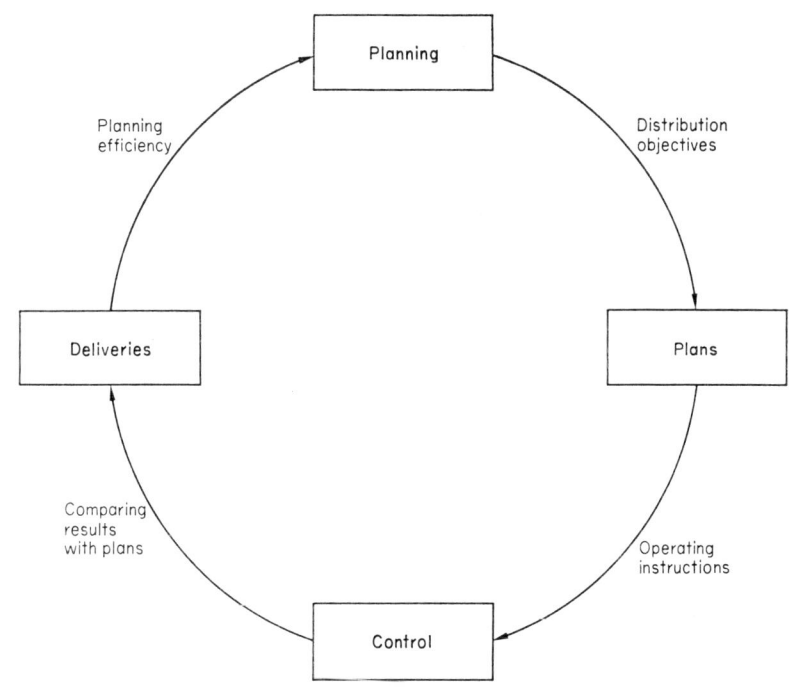

Figure 10:1 DISTRIBUTION INFORMATION SYSTEM

tion improves its value, provided that the recommendations developed are reported to the people who can use it for the company's benefit. Competitive activities influence the distribution service provided by the company and awareness of them is necessary for timely strategic plans.

Value is the ratio of service to cost and distribution value is uncertain without good records of the costs for distributing each product. All the factors that affect these costs must be discovered and the conditions for success must be clearly defined and communicated to the staff.

Communications

Information systems can be made more effective by analysing all the data received in terms of the needs and problems of distribution. Grapevine information is inevitable and it can be useful provided that it is kept in context. The basic features of information that is conveyed by "the grapevine" must be understood, so that they can be converted into profitable use. These features are:

1   People talk most about recent events
2   People talk about things that affect them
3   People talk about things that they believe

A SUCCESSFUL DISTRIBUTION SYSTEM

4 People working together share the same grapevine
5 People on the same organisation level will be on the same grapevine, usually

Creative thinking is necessary for improving activities and a checklist for making improvements is shown in Figure 10:2.

```
1   Are there other uses?
2   Can anything be adapted for other purposes?
3   Can the design be improved?
4   Can anything be modified?
5   Can the range be increased or is it too wide?
6   What substitutions can be made advantageously?
7   Can the components be rearranged successfully?
8   Are the sequences correct?
9   Can savings be made by combining things?
10  What is the value of each item and can it be improved?
```

Figure 10:2 CHECKLIST FOR IMPROVING DISTRIBUTION

Successful strategic planning

In order to be successful, strategic planning must include an inward search of the current distribution practice in order to evaluate its strong points and its limitations. A broad look around the environment will help to recognise factors that can strengthen the service levels and to identify obligations of the company and the customers. Strategic planning prepares for the future and makes control more effective. Strategic planning procedure:

1 Forecast the environment
2 Define the objectives
3 Outline the strategy
4 Plan the organisation
5 Decide the resources required
6 Measure the operating results
7 Evaluate the performance

Method for analysing distribution

The control of operations is improved by studying cost fluctuations over a

A SUCCESSFUL DISTRIBUTION SYSTEM

long period of time; this is important when it is impossible to compare them with other operations. Fluctuations that reduce in size are a sign of improving control. The difference between the smallest and largest values in a sample is a measure of their variance and the smaller the variance the better the control.

Analysing distribution operations and measuring the variances provide a procedure for controlling the system successfully:

1   Sample the operation by observing the activities and recording a representative number of results
2   Calculate the mean value for the sampled results
3   Determine the range of variance for the results
4   Calculate the control limits for the sample mean and the variance range
5   Control all activities within the limits calculated when conditions are the same

Limits of control

The limits for controlling a number of operations can be calculated when they are based upon the statistical law of probability. According to this law, the probability of an event occurring again depends upon the number of times that it has already occurred. When a certain result has been observed once in ten times, it can be expected to occur in future once multiplied by the probability factor for ten which is the size of the sample observed. Tables for probabilities based upon random sampling are available for obtaining this factor.

For a sample of five results, the probable limits for the mean are ± 0.58, which is the same as saying that the mean of any sample observed under similar conditions will be no greater than 0.58 above the mean for the original five results, nor will it be smaller than 0.58 below mean.

The limits for control purposes can be determined mathematically and they are valuable for planning a distribution system. Results can be plotted on a time scale to show the mean value and the range of variances.

Mean for a sample $= \bar{x}$
Range of variances $= R$
Probability of the mean: $A = \pm 0.58$
Probability of the range: $D = 1$ to $E = 2.12$

Upper control limits
For the mean $= \bar{x} + AR$
For the range $= ER$

A SUCCESSFUL DISTRIBUTION SYSTEM

Lower control limits
For the mean $= \bar{x} - AR$
For the range $= DR$

The use of these control limits will be illustrated with a practical example.

Controlling vehicles. A public carrier believed that it was uneconomic to operate large vans in a certain delivery area. Five large vans were operated in the area and the capacities of their loads were observed on a certain day in order to decide if they were being utilised economically. The observed percentage loadings of the five vans were:

$$
\begin{array}{c}
73 \\
77 \\
75 \\
72 \\
73 \\
\hline
\end{array}
$$

Total 370%

Mean $\bar{x} = 74\%$ and range $R = 72$ to $77\% = 5\%$

Control limits. It would be the upper control limits that determined the greatest percentage loading that could be expected and it would help to decide if a smaller size of van should be operated.

Upper control limits
Upper mean loading
$= \bar{x} + AR$
$= 74 + (0.58 \times 5)$
$= 74 + 2.90$
$= 76.9\%$
Greatest range of variance
$= ER$
$= 2.12 \times 5$
$= 10.6\%$

Solution. The expected upper mean loading of the vans was 76.9% and the greatest range of variance about this mean was 10.6%. Assuming that half this variance would be above the mean, the greatest loading for the vans that could be expected was:

$$\frac{76.9\% + 10.6\%}{2} = 82.2\%$$

Provided that the same conditions prevailed, the carrier could operate smaller vans with 82.2 per cent of the present capacity and increase the operating economy correspondingly. Obviously, the accuracy of the results would be increased with a larger sample.

10:2 SUCCESSFUL WAREHOUSING PLANS

Probably, there are as many reasons for having a warehouse as there are different products to be warehoused. There are three general reasons that override the others and they are economic, operational and service reasons.
Economically, warehouses provide the opportunity to purchase in bulk or at a time when prices are favourable. At the warehouse, goods can be stored until they are required in different quantities by the customers.
Operationally, the goods stored provide a buffer against fluctuations in demand and the warehouse provides the facilities for processing orders according to demand.
Service is provided by warehouses, since the goods are held at places that allow delivery times to comply with the requirements of customers.

Total cost of distribution

Distribution is a complex function that includes the number, sites and sizes of warehouses, vehicle routes and schedules, resource investments and control activities. Each element can be designed singly, but it is better to plan them in unison, because the interactions between them must be coordinated for successful implementation.

The total cost of distribution is illustrated graphically in Figure 10:3 and it shows the component costs which include warehouse fixed costs, warehouse stockholding costs, trunking costs and local delivery costs. The requirement for the least cost of the first three components is fewer warehouses, but local delivery costs are minimal with more warehouses. The optimum will be the least total distribution cost.

The least total cost can be improved by streamlining local deliveries, by building less expensive warehouses, by holding fewer stocks or by reducing the number of trunking deliveries. The slopes of lines in Figure 10:3 depend upon specific costs, but this shows a method for comparing costs in order to optimise the total cost of distribution.

Warehouse siting

The optimal site for a warehouse depends upon the number and locations of other warehouses in the distribution system, upon the locations of customers allocated to the warehouse and upon the total cost of handling goods. The practical approach allows each of these factors to be considered both singly and together for a number of different sites. It has the advantage of considering a number of known sites and compares the ones that satisfy the cost and service limits feasibly.

A SUCCESSFUL DISTRIBUTION SYSTEM

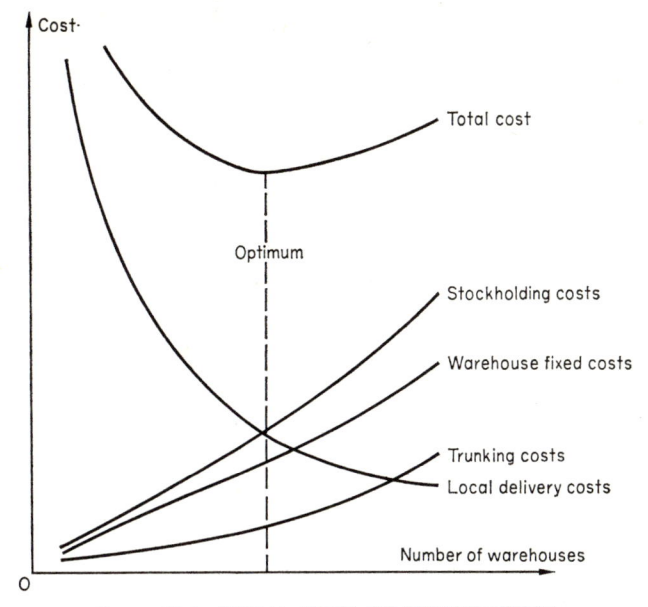

Figure 10:3 TOTAL COST OF DISTRIBUTION

The chief disadvantage is the extra work involved of considering sites that may not be feasible. An alternative approach is the theoretical one that assumes that a warehouse can be sited anywhere within the distribution area under consideration. This is a flexible approach, but specific costs have to be examined later.

Collecting data. Starting with customers, demand data is needed for reducing the number of customers to manageable limits in terms of the vehicles and delivery times. The market demand is dynamic and sales forecasts are more valuable than sales records. Examining the market helps to establish the service levels required.

Cost data that is relevant to the service levels must be collected. Warehousing costs are fixed or variable and they depend upon the warehouse location and its throughput of goods. Delivery costs include both trunking and local delivery costs.

Developing plans. When there is a choice of known sites for a warehouse, the alternative advantages and disadvantages can be compared by simulation. Simulation allows many different factors to be examined in potential rather than in fact. Interactions cause fluctuations in cost and service level so that their effects have to be optimised.

A SUCCESSFUL DISTRIBUTION SYSTEM

A useful method for developing warehouse siting plans involves heuristic programming. Heuristics are a set of rules for attaining objectives feasibly, but not necessarily optimally. The use of practical knowledge and commonsense heuristically can produce good warehouse locations quickly and economically.

Theoretical methods for siting warehouse consider the distribution area as a whole and the method of finding a centre of demand was described in Chapter 4. General sites are adaptable and they can be utilised according to particular requirements. It is easier to forecast changes in demand and operating methods than it is to forecast technological changes. Nevertheless plans must be made on the basis of the greatest certainty, and the more uncertain a situation the more flexible the plans must be.

Implementation. Plans for warehouse sites have to be implemented effectively for successful distribution and it is important to study all reactions to the plans beforehand. This is the essence of strategic planning, because a plan is tested for robustness under different conditions. Testing for robustness is sometimes called sensitivity analysis.

An illustration of the reaction of the total distribution cost to differences in warehouse site is shown in Figure 10:4. The least costly site depends

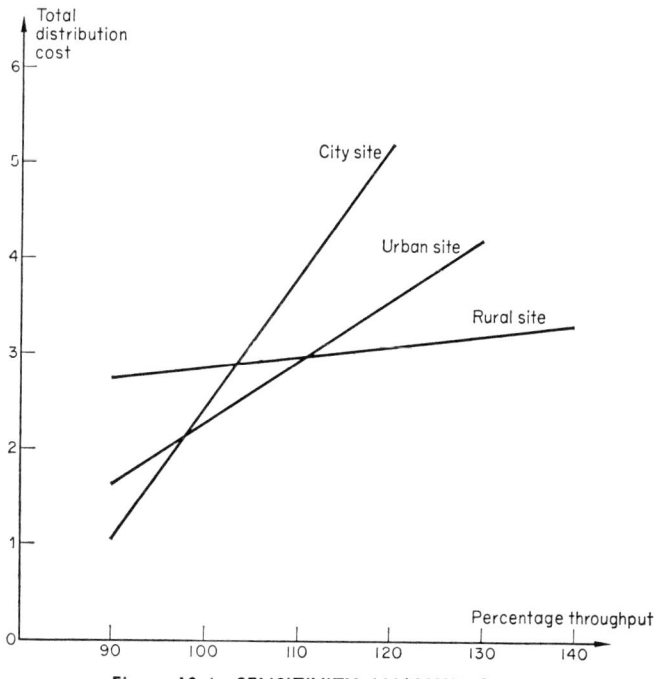

Figure 10:4 SENSITIVITY ANALYSIS CHART

upon the throughput and each site is optimal for different throughput ranges.

The sensitivity analysis chart in Figure 10:4 covers a single time span, but graphs have to be prepared for other times too, in order to plan dynamically. A decision to select a particular warehouse site is far reaching, possibly for twenty years or more, and it is wise to estimate the future costs when studying the reactions within a system. Different variable factors can be compared with the sensitivity analysis chart, for example different delivery vehicles or routes on a unit cost basis or a time basis.

In the chart, the total distribution cost is relative and the throughput is expressed as percentages of the current volume. It can be seen that a city site is preferable if throughput is declining, but a rise of 10 to 20 per cent favours an urban site and above this increase a rural site should be selected.

Dynamic planning. Distribution parameters change with time and it is necessary to determine the length of the planning period in order to prepare dynamic plans.

The time span depends upon the cost of setting up and closing down a warehouse and upon the accuracy of the forecasts. Decisions to change the site of a warehouse cost least money if the establishment time is short. After a short while, property depreciates least and the cost of improvements is small. When forecasts are good or future conditions seem fairly certain, the time span for strategic plans can be longer and they will be more accurate than when forecasting is poor or conditions are uncertain.

The data required for dynamic planning is similar to that described already, but information for forecasting the delivery resources for the length of the plan is needed in addition to current data. Estimates will be required also of the costs involved in setting up and closing down warehouses. Comparisons are more relevant if these additional costs are discounted back to the current time, so that interest costs and appreciation values are included.

The dynamic siting method starts by deciding the optimal site for a warehouse, currently. Then, the cash flows for successive years can be calculated and the total distribution cost for the period determined. Next, the optimal cost sites for the changes forecast throughout the period need to be analysed in the same way. Alternative total costs for the planning period must be compared in order to decide which is the best.

Successful warehouse siting. The best sites for warehouses provide the best service to customers in terms of delivery times and the least cost for delivering goods.

Making sound decisions requires careful planning which has been based upon good forecasts and relevant experience. However, a knowledge of scientific planning methods ensures that the practical expertise available is guided to produce optimal plans.

10:3 SUCCESSFUL DISTRIBUTION COST REDUCTION

The cost of distributing goods can contribute up to half total product cost and reducing distribution costs is a sure way of bringing down prices. Unfortunately, distribution costs have continued to rise since the Second World War and reducing them is the concern of everybody today.

A successful distribution system is one that has been implemented using all the ways open to it for reducing warehousing and delivery costs. Different reasons for rising costs affect different companies and a summary of the basic reasons will be given now in order to offer some advice.

Changing order patterns

Increased competition and better availability of materials have encouraged companies to offer better service to their customers and this has changed many customer order patterns. Better service requires improved inventory management, but it has resulted in customers demanding more frequent deliveries. Consequently, order quantities are getting smaller and buffer stocks are being pushed back closer to the factories than markets. More frequent ordering raises the cost of distribution, because suppliers have to deal with more orders for the same volume of throughput.

Increasing product variety

Trends indicate that customers order a greater variety of goods, too, when the service level improves. Greater variety increases the amount of handling in a distribution system and steps have to be taken to reduce it. One method is to make warehouses more specialised in order to cut down the number of varieties handled; alternatively, handling procedures can be standardised so that they are the same for several different products.

Selling more effectively

Improved selling techniques, aided by greater customer spending, have increased distribution throughputs. Greater throughputs need more expensive handling methods, larger warehouses and better vehicles. In addition, pressures to reduce prices have forced suppliers to distribute more directly to retail outlets. This reason for increased distribution costs reflects the importance of coordinating all the elements of a system. It is an old saying that the strength of a chain is the strength of the weakest link, and the strength of effective selling is the strength of the delivery service that supports it.

A SUCCESSFUL DISTRIBUTION SYSTEM

Price restrictions

Legal action to restrict prices justifies price differentials and discounts more than ever in order to encourage people to buy. When profit margins are small, it is the largest cost budgets that are slashed first and this means distribution in most instances.

Competitive strategies

Many companies improve their market share by outperforming their competitors in terms of better customer service or product availability. The benefits to customers of reduced inventory and better handling, shift the onus for these activities on to the distributor and the requirements of distribution are changed accordingly. When marketing realises that a flexible and reliable distribution system improves its selling efforts, the advantage of strategic planning will be highlighted.

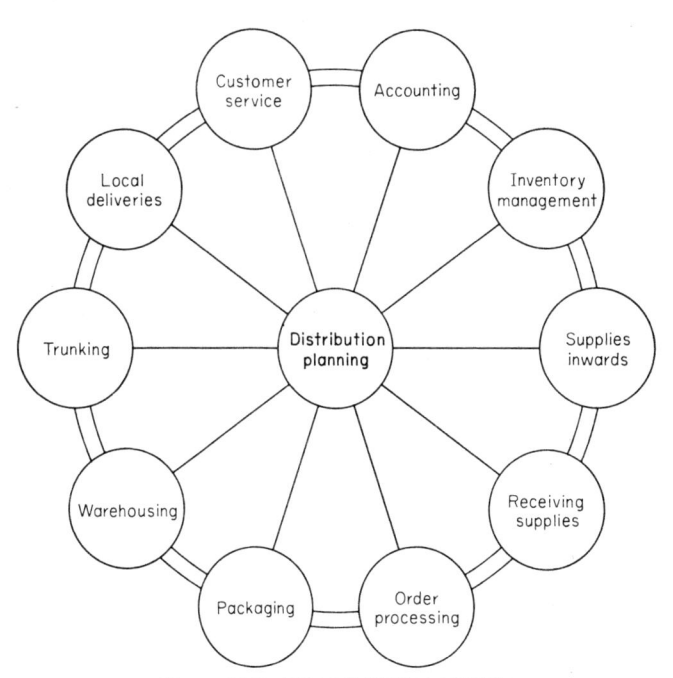

Figure 10:5 DISTRIBUTION WHEEL

The basic reasons for increased distribution costs are interrelated and they can be shown as a distribution wheel in Figure 10:5. Distribution planning at the hub unites the activity spokes which are interrelated at the rim. Each of the activities contributes to the total distribution cost and identifying or measuring the size of the cost spokes is useful for analysing problems of this nature.

Flow charting

Specific distribution systems can be analysed with the aid of flow charting. Flow charting is a simple graphical method for portraying individual throughputs and costs as the goods flow around the distribution system. Flow lines suggest the different channels and methods of delivering that can be used as well as the costs that are contributed by each activity and their relative importances.

The wheel of distribution in Figure 10:5 is composed of a number of activity wheels, really, because each activity is the hub of related operations or sub-activities. Taking local deliveries out of the chart and looking at it in more detail can show the individual costs of delivering to each customer, or the costs of operating each vehicle. It is important to know how these costs react to changes in the system as well as identifying them.

Local delivery costs fall as the number of warehouses increases and, up to a point, the total distribution cost reduces too. However, the costs of increasing the number of warehouses are large compared with the local delivery savings and the total cost starts to rise after the optimum has been reached.

Inventory investment

Customer service is measured in terms of delivery time and delivery times can be reduced by carrying more inventory. The shorter the delivery time, the better the service, but the inventory investment increases disproportionately. It has been known for the inventory to double in size when trying to reduce the delivery time by 10 per cent.

Capital investment

The most dramatic cost reductions are achieved from long-term capital investment savings. To attain them, a change in the number of the locations of warehouses may be necessary, or a change from owning the vehicles to hiring them. Long-term savings can be planned in phases, but short-term savings can be implemented immediately. When returns on capital can be spread over long periods, the length of time affects the cost of capital investments.

Total cost reduction

A realistic method for reducing the total cost of distribution determines the total operating costs of the existing system, before calculating what it would be if the system operated at its greatest efficiency.

In this way, every cost reduction is put into action with the existing resources and without further investments. These savings provide yardsticks for measuring the returns on any proposed capital investments.

Economic planning

It is exciting to plan a new distribution system, but all investments have to be justified to the shareholders. The impact of plans on profits and returns on capital are the true tests of success.

Quite often, the economic differential between operating the present system more efficiently and investing money in a new system is too small to justify the investment. Improving the existing system has a further advantage; it provides an opportunity for the distribution manager to demonstrate that cost reductions can be attained quickly by a universal procedure that can apply to other functions of the company too.

Inventory control

Reductions in inventory carrying costs can be large in relation to the savings from other distribution activities. Distribution has been described as the movement and storage of goods, but a recent American interpretation is the strategic replacement and utilisation of inventories. Inventories tie up capital for varying lengths of time and the cost of this investment affects the total cost. For many years, companies have charged the investment in stocks at bank rate plus 1 per cent. Recent opinions consider that it should be charged according to the "opportunity cost of capital." For example, other company investments may be earning an annual return of 15 per cent and further investment there can be more economic than investing in a distribution improvement that will have a return of less than 10 per cent.

Economically, inventory reductions must rank first for reducing the total cost of distribution and simplifying the system comes second. In practice, it is difficult to rank one above the other, because they are interrelated and it is better to tackle them both together.

10:4 MONITORING DELIVERY SERVICE

Controlling a distribution system successfully depends largely upon the quality of the information that is available for comparing with the plans. The communications cycle presented in Figure 1:5 shows that feedback is required for learning how the plans and instructions have been put into action. The feedback needs to be monitored in order to initiate any adjustments that may be necessary. Actions are initiated by the ideas of people with authority, but these ideas have to be converted into plans before they can become instructions for performing work activities. The process is a continuous one that is initiated successively by the feedback that stimulates new ideas.

A SUCCESSFUL DISTRIBUTION SYSTEM

Monitoring the delivery service provides the feedback of information for planning a distribution system and the data acquired must include delivery costs, levels of delivery service and performance of delivery operations.

Delivery data

The flow of data depends upon the composition of the system and the availability of data decides the method of monitoring it. The monitoring method should be kept as simple as possible in order to prevent confusion and to ensure that everyone understands it.

Data required

1. Delivery costs including:
   Vehicle operating costs
   Goods in transit insurance
   Wages of personnel for vehicles
   Traffic office charges
   Administration overheads
   Hire charges
   Interest on capital
2. Delivery service including:
   Lead time between order receipt and delivery
   Order sizes and frequencies
   Load capacities and sizes
   Unloading facilities at drop points
   Customer research information
   Public relations
3. Delivery operations including:
   Vehicle operating specifications
   Planning standards for work activities
   Duties of traffic personnel
   Drop times and restrictions
   Driving speeds and road conditions
   Operational times

Data for monitoring the system must be filed for reference purposes when updating operations continually. It provides a bank of information for checking delivery efficiencies, controlling the cost of operations and planning future developments.

Delivery cost monitoring

In a distribution system for delivering cased goods to British customers, the flow of data is shown schematically in Figure 10:6. Deliveries were

A SUCCESSFUL DISTRIBUTION SYSTEM

planned by industrial engineering consultants who recommended that leased, hired and carriers' vehicles should be used in different situations.

The schematic diagram shows the flow of data from its sources to the distribution manager for control purposes. The basic sources were journey load sheets, vehicle records and invoices from the carriers.

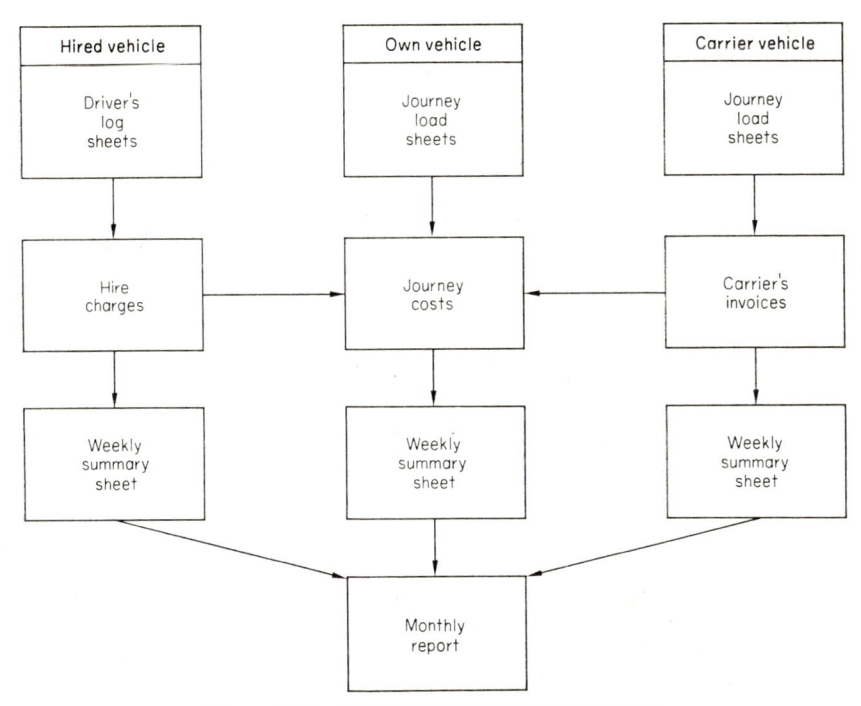

```
┌─────────────────┐   ┌─────────────────┐   ┌─────────────────┐
│  Hired vehicle  │   │   Own vehicle   │   │ Carrier vehicle │
│   Driver's      │   │    Journey      │   │    Journey      │
│     log         │   │     load        │   │     load        │
│    sheets       │   │    sheets       │   │    sheets       │
└────────┬────────┘   └────────┬────────┘   └────────┬────────┘
         ↓                     ↓                     ↓
┌─────────────────┐   ┌─────────────────┐   ┌─────────────────┐
│      Hire       │→  │    Journey      │  ←│    Carrier's    │
│    charges      │   │     costs       │   │    invoices     │
└────────┬────────┘   └────────┬────────┘   └────────┬────────┘
         ↓                     ↓                     ↓
┌─────────────────┐   ┌─────────────────┐   ┌─────────────────┐
│     Weekly      │   │     Weekly      │   │     Weekly      │
│    summary      │   │    summary      │   │    summary      │
│     sheet       │   │     sheet       │   │     sheet       │
└────────┬────────┘   └────────┬────────┘   └────────┬────────┘
          ↘                    ↓                    ↙
                     ┌─────────────────┐
                     │     Monthly     │
                     │     report      │
                     └─────────────────┘
```

Figure 10:6 MONITORING DELIVERY COSTS

Individual operating costs were combined into journey costs for the delivery vehicles and the summaries were prepared weekly. The weekly summary sheets were used to make the monthly operating report for the manager. The monthly report also contained quarterly cumulative averages and an annual total, so that Z-charts could be produced for controlling deliveries. Forms for each of the information types were printed and they formed the medium for the flow of data.

Delivery service monitoring

The flow of data for monitoring the service level to customers was similar to that for monitoring cost. The sources of information were the customer orders. Information from the orders was used for preparing journey load sheets, delivery sheets for the supply companies and records of orders out-

A SUCCESSFUL DISTRIBUTION SYSTEM

standing. These summaries were incorporated into a monthly operating report which the manager compared with the cost report in order to optimise them.

The flow of order data is shown schematically in Figure 10:7. Once again, printed forms were used for conveying the data. The monthly reports for delivery cost and service had similar formats for facilitating control.

Examples of the forms for monitoring delivery cost and service are presented in an appendix at the end. Forms are a convenient medium for the flow of distribution information which is used in conjunction with bin or pallet cards for tracking the flow of goods through warehouses. A central filing system allows every item in the system to be recorded and its whereabouts shown at different stages in the system.

Records

The information in a distribution system is specific always and it is important to examine and appraise every data item for control and planning purposes. Every item needed by the distribution manager, either directly or indirectly, must appear in the monitoring method. Not only must they appear, but they must appear in the right places, meaningfully. Subsequently,

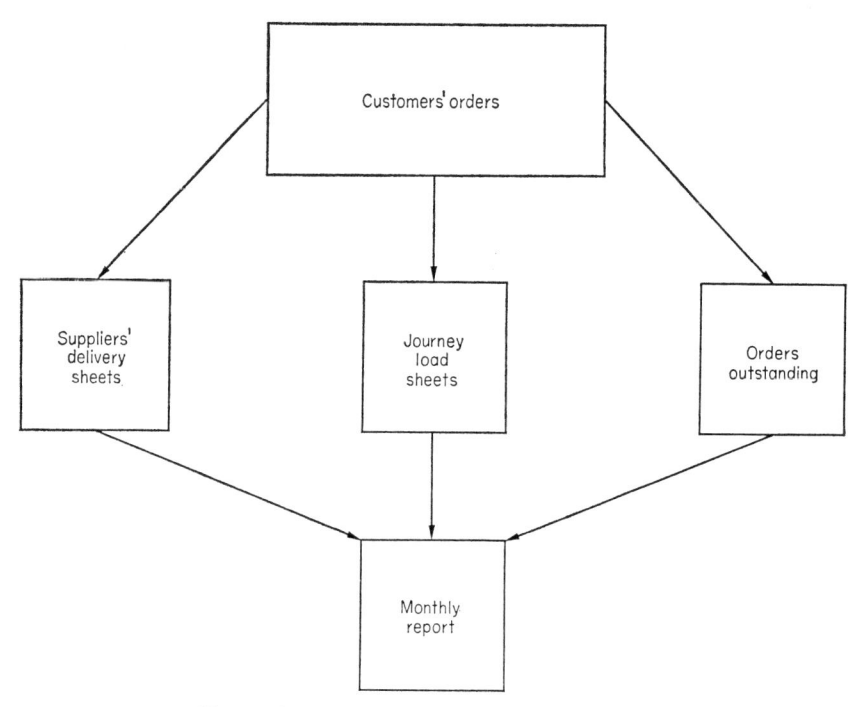

Figure 10:7 MONITORING DELIVERY SERVICE

all the calculations must be written down and a list of the items incorporated should be recorded too. Then, the two lists can be compared and one will supplement the other and prevent items being overlooked, or items being included when they are superfluous.

The value of the systematic approach to planning a distribution system cannot be stressed too strongly.

10:5 FROM PLAN TO REALITY

All people become engrossed in work that they find interesting and it is difficult to stop at times. This comment applies to planning in particular because everyone likes preparing something new. Plans require knowledge and experience, both of which are expensive to acquire. Therefore, knowing when to stop planning can save money. Once again, it is a case of optimising the savings that can accrue from planning with the costs involved. Initially, the savings from planning are large, but later they diminish until the break-even point is reached. That is the time to concentrate on controlling results instead of planning for them.

Control takes over when the plans are put into action. The implementation of plans starts with understanding the objectives and learning about the resources that are required and available.

Objectives for implementing a distribution system. These are dual purpose, namely, to provide the greatest service at the least cost. Naturally, there will be conflicts between these fundamental requirements unless there is realistic control which allows the system to function harmoniously. The optimal strategy for distributing goods provides the greatest customer service for the least operational cost. However, terms of reference for the service have to be defined clearly otherwise it will be impossible to measure its effectiveness.

Implementation commences with selecting the distribution strategy that will provide the greatest level of service to customers, while control implies comparing the actual results, particularly costs, with those planned for the selected strategy and making adjustments when necessary.

Implementing distribution plans

The more that is known about a plan in action, the easier it will be to implement it effectively.

Sometimes trials or simulations provide useful information about behaviour patterns and it is less costly to test a plan in this manner. The simulations can use models of the system, usually in the form of networks or schematic diagrams. In some cases, a plan can be tested by writing a report and submitting it to the people concerned. Then, it should be discussed at a meeting in order to smooth out any difficulties that could develop into practical problems.

Whatever the method chosen for testing a plan, testing will improve it and make it more acceptable in practice. When the proposals for implementing a plan have been accepted by the persons with authority, it becomes necessary to design functional controls for the system including methods for monitoring the activities. Acquiring information can be as simple as by "word-of-mouth," or as sophisticated as using an analogue computer.

Controlling the system

Coordinating activities and helping them to conform with the objectives are the essence of control. Adjustments have to be made whenever changes occur or the objectives are modified.

It has been suggested that long term plans are rarely achieved in practice, because they are continually revised as conditions change.

The control of distribution is prone to change regularly when it is considered that its objectives are compromises between marketing and production needs. Consequently, distribution plans must be adaptable and the distribution manager must be resilient to withstand pressures from both directions. Strictly speaking, distribution is part of the marketing function, which is responsible for promoting sales and for satisfying customers. Obviously, controlling distribution is difficult and it will cause concern in many companies, particularly those oriented towards marketing consumer goods. It is estimated that the cost of distribution exceeds 20 per cent of the sales price of all goods and reaches 50 per cent in a few cases. Consequently, it is vital to control distribution costs strictly in order to satisfy the needs of both producer and consumer.

Need for realistic costs

Any attempt to make a mathematical matrix for determining distribution costs will be confused by the large number of overheads that are difficult to allocate realistically. There is a great variance among these overhead costs; hence, the effective life of the matrix will be short. Also, some costs, like research or advertising, are general and cannot be allocated fairly to one specific operation.

It may be necessary to completely revise the information systems used by an organisation in order to introduce realistic procedures for allocating overhead costs and attaining better control of the distribution system.

Analysing distribution costs

Analysis means breaking down a system into its component parts, examining

A SUCCESSFUL DISTRIBUTION SYSTEM

them and recommending improvements. The fundamental components of distribution are warehousing and delivering and they can be subdivided successively into their basic elements. Allocating costs to these components is essentially a form of standard costing which is a valuable technique for controlling complex costs.

It is reasonable to consider distribution as being a process for costing purposes when breaking it down into its standard components; then more realistic records can be kept and the actual costs can be compared with the standard costs for better control.

When the elemental costs for distributing goods are understood and trusted, they can be examined more readily and control of the distribution system will be really effective. Subsequently, comparisons can be made more easily between the actual and planned costs for different delivery areas, different types of order, different warehouses and different vehicles. Improvements or deteriorations can be measured more quickly, targets can be set more realistically and the distribution function will be organised more practically.

Using computers to control distribution

It is believed by some people that distribution is a confused area for some managers, but identifying its elements precisely can assist them to provide better organisation and control. Classifying its elements provides a framework for this purpose and a computer code using numerical language is a realistic framework for most control purposes. Code numbers can be given to products, operations and customers, then relating the costs and quantities to these codes will integrate the distribution system more effectively. A computer imposes discipline and consistency on the system and this ensures that every relevant factor is considered, provided that it has been included in the original program.

Complete distribution system

Developing a functional organisation structure for a company is the first essential when analysing the complete distribution system, since it will indicate the importance of distribution in relation to the rest of the organisation. Then, lines of authority and responsibility can be defined so that managers know where to collect relevant information and how authority is delegated.

Overall solutions: Distribution problems have more than one fundamental form and they must be considered as being composed of integrated factors in order to find effective solutions. It follows that optimal solutions must apply to the overall system. Teamwork is essential for stimulating individual

A SUCCESSFUL DISTRIBUTION SYSTEM

ideas and developing interpretations into a composite solution, otherwise recommendations will be incompletely effective when implemented.

Investigating distribution problems

Investigations commence with the collection of information, but there has to be a purpose for making each investigation otherwise some of the information collected will be irrelevant. Sometimes distribution problems involve routes between different warehouses, depots or drop points and it may be useful to develop a network which can be developed as the guidelines for the distribution system.

Computer programs

Programs have been written for vehicle routing and scheduling, for site selection and for load utilisation. The approach to vehicle routing and scheduling is a general one, so that the programs can handle different problems by changing the restrictions.

The number of depots in a distribution system can be classified in various ways, for example by numbers and types of customer, product or vehicle; then different routes can be compared until an optimum is found. When many thousands of customers are involved, it may be advisable to group them into clusters according to their geographical locations. A computer program that includes all the variables of a distribution system will produce an optimal solution, because an exhaustive search of all the possible permutations and combinations of routes will be made. The biggest limitation is identifying all the variables and programming them in computer language.

Restrictions to routing and scheduling vehicles

All transport problems involve restrictions of similar kinds and they can be grouped into seven basic kinds:

1 *Availability of vehicles.* What are the alternatives? How many vehicles are available? What are their types and what are the operating limits? Are the vehicles owned or can they be hired?

2 *Capacity of vehicles.* Is load capacity restricted by weight, volume, time or the nature of orders? What kinds of load can be transported?

3 *Availability of drivers.* How many? What are the driving restrictions? Can deliveries be made to areas away from their bases? Are mates required? What licences are required?

4 *Speed restrictions.* What are the speeds of vehicles? What are the traffic congestions on roads? What time allowances are required for meals, maintenance and breaks in journeys?

5 *Time restrictions.* What are the times for loading and unloading? What are working hours? What are the hours for delivering to different drop points?

6 *Service restrictions.* What service level is expected by customers? What are the customer service restrictions? Can orders be accumulated? What happens in the case of non-delivery?

7 *Scheduling restrictions.* What is the life of a vehicle schedule? What sequences have to be observed? How often can schedules be reviewed? Is there sufficient information available?

Distribution problems

The systematic approach to solving distribution problems can be summarised as follows:

1. Study the whole system
2. Find the causes of problems
3. Analyse the system into components with reference to the different problem causes and planning objectives
4. Develop a framework for the system under consideration and make sure that it is consistent with the objectives, the information available and the operating precepts
5. Utilise the most accurate operating methods available and review the results regularly
6. Simplify the system as much as possible in order to arrive at effective procedures for the whole system rather than just part of it

Reality of plans

In practice, plans must be both short term and long term, so that the distribution manager is prepared for all eventualities. Systematic planning is the most effective, because plans are developed in conjunction with the objectives for controlling and operating the system. Experience in the fields of distribution was bought at high cost by the pioneers, but present-day managers can benefit less expensively by taking advantage of this experience intelligently.

Implementing plans is the most costly part of planning a distribution system. Therefore, implementation must be considered carefully and every cost must be evaluated against its savings or the service that it provides.

Some companies regret their enthusiastic investments in distribution systems that were poorly planned. Automation is very expensive and it has many advantages, but it is better to evaluate investments in terms of the "return on capital" and compare them with the cost of improving the present system. It is easy to be wise after the event, but it is wiser to remember that it is economic to think before investing money.

People take a pride in the things that they control, whether a forklift truck, a road vehicle or a large distribution warehouse; normally, these

A SUCCESSFUL DISTRIBUTION SYSTEM

things represent their livelihood. This is an essential requirement for their cooperation and using it will help to improve efficiency. It is wise to give instructions in terms that are fully understood, then the actions will be more effective. Putting plans into reality means using good communication which, in turn, produces full cooperation.

The true effectiveness of distribution plans depends upon the quality of their management. The quality of management that is needed for managing distribution function includes flexibility, leadership, respect and sound experience. Above all, managing means organising well, controlling firmly and planning realistically. Systematic training and development of personnel ensures that the distribution system will be maintained at a high level of effectiveness.

APPENDIX

Forms for Monitoring Deliveries

APPENDIX

Form 1

VEHICLE TIME SHEET										
Depot		Week		Date		Vehicle registration number			Form 1	
Driver		Mate				Vehicle type				
DAY	Vehicle hours					Deliveries			Clock hours	
	Warehouse	Delivery	Slack	Repair	Total	Orders	Drops	Cases	Miles	Driver	Mate
Mon											
Tues											
Wed											
Thurs											
Fri											
Sat											
TOTAL											

APPENDIX

VAN CONTRACT HIRE—WEEKLY RETURN					Form 2	
Depot		Week			Date week ending	
Vans Registration number	Type	Speedo reading			Van days	
		End	Beginning	Weekly mileage	Operational	Maintenance

APPENDIX

WEEKLY SUMMARY OF CARRIER'S DELIVERIES & CHARGES CARRIER'S NAME					Form 3	
Depot		Week		Week ending		
Date	Journey load	Total orders	Total drops	Total cases	Estimated charges £	Actual invoices £

APPENDIX

Form 4

WEEKLY SUMMARY OF OWN VEHICLE TIME SHEETS

Depot   Week   Date week ending

Vehicle number	Type	Vehicle hours					Deliveries				Clock hours	
		Warehouse	Delivery	Slack	Repair	Total	Orders	Drops	Cases	Miles	Driver	Mate

APPENDIX

Form 5

MONTHLY DELIVERY COSTS FOR 19___

Item	Delivery information	Monthly 1	2	Cumulative 3	Monthly 4	5	Cumulative 6	Monthly 7	8	Cumulative 9	Monthly 10	11	12	Annual total 13
1	Number of vans operated													
2	Number of van-days													
3	Total mileage													
4	Miles per van													
5	Cost per van-mile													
6	Gross operating hours													
7	Operating hours per van													
8	Operating costs for own vans													
9	Number of customer orders													
10	Number of drops													
11	Number of cases													
12	Average cases per order													
13	Average miles per drop													
14	Number of days booked by drivers													
15	Number of days booked by mates													
16	Traffic office costs													
17	Van hire costs													
18	Carriers charges													
19	Other expenses													
20	Total delivery cost: own vans													
21	Total delivery cost: hired vans													
22	Total delivery cost: carriers													
23	Number of orders: own vans													
24	Number of orders: hired vans													
25	Number of orders: carriers													
26	Cost per order: own vans													
27	Cost per order: hired vans													
28	Cost per order: carriers													
29	Total cost of deliveries													

APPENDIX

Form 6

ORDERS RECEIVED AND DELIVERED

Depot .... Week .... Date ....

| DAY | Carried forward | | Orders received | | Total load | | Deliveries | | | | | | Overdue | |
| | | | | | | | Own transport | | Carriers | | Total | | | |
	Orders	Cases	Orders	Cases	Orders	Cases	Orders	Cases	Orders	Cases	Orders	Cases	Orders	Cases
Mon														
Tues														
Wed														
Thurs														
Fri														
Sat														
TOTAL														

APPENDIX

Form 7

ORDERS RECEIVED FROM SUPPLY COMPANIES																
Depot		Week						Week ending								
		Brown		Cambridge		Goodness		Lincoln		Stoney Cross		Weston		Daily total	
DAY		Orders	Cases	Orders	Cases	Orders	Cases	Orders	Cases	Orders	Cases	Orders	Cases	Orders	Cases
Mon															
Tues															
Wed															
Thurs															
Fri															
Sat															
TOTAL															

APPENDIX

Form 8

ORDERS OUTSTANDING FROM SUPPLY COMPANIES ON FRIDAY OF EACH WEEK

Depot _____   Period _____   Date _____

Week ending	Brown		Cambridge		Goodness		Lincoln		Stony Cross		Weston		Weekly total
	Orders	Cases	Orders	Cases	Orders	Cases	Orders	Cases	Orders	Cases	Orders	Cases	
Total Orders													
Cases													
Average Orders													
Cases													

APPENDIX

Form 9

ANNUAL DELIVERIES BY SUPPLIERS 19___

Item	Delivery information	1	2	3	Cumulative	4	5	6	Cumulative	7	8	9	Cumulative	10	11	12	13	Annual total
1	Brown: orders received																	
2	number of cases received																	
3	orders outstanding																	
4	number of cases outstanding																	
5	Cambridge:																	
6																		
7																		
8																		
9	Goodness:																	
10																		
11																		
12																		
13	Lincoln:																	
14																		
15																		
16																		
17	Stony Cross:																	
18																		
19																		
20																		
21	Weston:																	
22																		
23																		
24																		
25	Total number of orders received																	
26	number of cases received																	
27	number of orders outstanding																	
28	number of cases outstanding																	

APPRECIATION

The help given by members of the following organisations, in one way or another, to acquire the knowledge that is presented in this book is greatly appreciated.

Anglo-American Tobacco Company
Applied Management Practice Limited
Associated Electrical Industries
Beechams Limited
British Leyland Motor Corporation
Brooke Bond Limited
Caltex Oil Companies
C. G. Chantrill & Partners
Chrysler International
College of Marketing
Distillers Company (Distribution) Limited
Dodge Brothers Limited
Egerton Agricultural College
Fertilizer Corporation of India
Ford Motor Company
General Electric Company
General Engineering Company
Glaxo Laboratories
Government of India
Hindustan Lever Limited
Hindustan Motors Limited
Institute of Works Managers
Institute of Work Study Practitioners
International Labour Office
Lansing Bagnall Limited
Marshall Brook & Partners
National Institute for Training in Industrial Engineering
Operational Research Society

APPRECIATION

Parke Davis Limited
Pyrethrum Board of Kenya
Sterling Drug Corporation
Texaco Oil Company
University of Edinburgh
Wolverhampton Polytechnic
Woolwich Polytechnic
Yale & Towne Manufacturing Company

INDEX

Analogue siting 68–9
Analysis of distribution 16–17
  marketing considerations 17
  method 18
  production considerations 16–17
Assignment of vehicles
  to routes 106–10
  delivery schedules 110
  linear programming 107–10

Bar charts 25–6
Branch line system 71, 89
Budgetary control 38–9
  objectives 39
  preparation of budget 38–9
Buffer stock 164–5
Bulk delivery vehicles 112
  scheduling 130–2

Capital investment 192
Centres of demand 27–30
  case study 28–30
  costs 27–8, 30
  map coordinates 28–30
Chain of distribution 1–2
Communications 4–6, 182–3
  circle 5–6
  creative thinking 183
Computers 199, 200
  computerised routing 102–3
  programs 200
Control effectiveness 65–6
Control of distribution 157–78, 180–6
  communications 182–3
  control of costs 159–62
  control of stocks 162–7
  controlling results graphically 167–71
  distribution objectives 158
  limits of control 184–6
  method of analysis 183–4
  modern distribution 158
  planning requirements 181–2

Control of distribution—*continued*
  strategic investments 180
  strategic planning 183
  tripartite organisation 157–9
Correlation analysis 41
Cost centres 160
Cost reduction 190–3
  capital investment 192
  changing order pattern 190
  competitive strategies 191–2
  flow charting 192
  improved selling techniques 190
  increasing product variety 190
  inventory control 193
  inventory investment 192
  price restrictions 191
  total cost reduction 192–3
Costs:
  centre of demand 27–8, 30
  delivery costs 31–2, 102–3, 152, 194–5
  distribution costs 27–8, 77–82, 126, 159–62, 186, 190–3, 198–9
  operating costs 64–5
  overhead costs 82–4
  transport costs 27
  vehicle operating costs 153
Creative thinking 183
Customers:
  cost of keeping customers 53–4
  customer service 54
  location 141
  order analysis 53–4
  order frequencies 141
  order sizes 141
  rationalisation 53–4
  research 12

DARSIRI method of value
  analysis 45–8, 56
Delivery costs 31–2, 102–3, 152
  monitoring 194–5
Delivery distances 152–3

215

INDEX

Delivery method 65
Delivery planning 30-3, 55, 113
  basic data 31
  optimising costs 31-2
Delivery problems analysis 55-60
  basic steps 56
  reduction of delivery time 59-60
  route engineering 56-9
Delivery ratios 77
Delivery scheduling 110-24
Delivery service, monitoring of 193-6
Delivery system and distribution planning 12-13
  customer research 12
  number of vehicles required 13
  simplest system 12-13
Delivery time, reduction of 59-60
Delivery vehicle rating 95-110
Delivery vehicle scheduling 112-14
  bulk delivery vehicles 112
  journey planning calculation 113-14
  methods 112-14
  objectives 112
  planning deliveries 113
  planning standards 114, 115
  scheduling charts 113
Demand centres 27-30
Depot siting 85-7
Design of distribution system 18
Distribution costs 27-8, 77, 82, 159-62, 186
  and lead time 81-2
  and number of sites 77-82
  balancing 27-8
  cost reduction 190-3
  fixed costs 159
  mathematical analysis 78, 178-9
  optimisation example 79-81
  performance ratios 161
  profit margins 161-2
  savings 126
  standard costing 162
  variable costs 160
  variations 78
Distribution network 52, 53
Distribution operations 8
Distribution plans 125-56
  economic deliveries 125-8
  local delivery resources planning 132-50
  selection of vehicles 150-3
  transport manning 153-6
  trunking deliveries 128-32
Distribution performance 15
Distribution service, improvement of 15-16

Distribution system, the, 1-20
  delivery system 12-13
  distribution operations 8
  functional distribution 1-4
  objectives of distribution 7-8
  organisation of management functions 4-7
  planning principles 13-20
  warehousing 8-12
Drivers 155
  rating of 175
Drop shipment 55
Drop times 177, 178

Economic deliveries, planning of 125-8
  combined routing and scheduling plans 127-8
  distribution cost savings 126
  distribution rationalisation 126-7
  route planning 125-6
Economic order quantity 167

Flow charting 192
Forecasting:
  demand 40
  good forecasting criteria 42-3
Fork-lift truck operatives 34-5
Freight Transport Association Yearbook 152
Functional distribution 1-4
  distribution chain 1-2
  value of distribution 2-4
Functions of distribution 62, 63
Future of distribution 25-8
  balancing distribution costs 27-8
  bar charts 25-6
  economic factors 26-7
  transport costs 27

Graphic control of results 167-71
  current affairs 169
  moving annual average 170
  moving annual total (MAT) 168-71
  removal of seasonal effects 168-9
  trends 169-70
  Z-charts 168-71

Heuristic programming 188

Implementation of distribution plans 197-202
  analysis of costs 198-9

216

INDEX

Implementation of distribution—*continued*
  computers 199, 200
  control of system 198
  distribution problems 200, 201
  objectives 197
  realistic costs 198
  reality of plans 201–2
  restrictions to routing and scheduling vehicles 200–1
Inventory control 193
Inventory investment 192
Iso-cost contour maps 67–8

Journey planning 105–6, 113–14
  analysis of routes 106
  distribution areas 105
  graphical planning 119–20
  increased journeys example 105–6
  journey effectiveness 105
  journey scheduling 118–20
  manual planning 118–19
  mechanical handling 106
  service level 105
Journey times 143–4, 177

Lead time and distribution costs 81–2
Leadership 6–7
Line theorem 69–71, 74
  application 74
  branch line system 71, 89
  loop line system 71, 89–90
  two and three demand location systems 70–1, 88–9
Linear programming, assignment method 107–10
Load capacities of vehicles 142
Loading times 177
Local delivery resources
  planning 132–50
  areas 143–4
  cased goods example 133
  collection of information 136–9
  delivery frequency 134
  distance and times 134
  journey times 143–4
  planning deliveries 133–6
  planning standards 139–42
  procedure 136, 137
  routes 135
  unloading time 135
  vehicle capacities 135–6
  vehicle journey calculations 142–5
  vehicle requirements 136, 145–50

Location of supplies for distribution 61–6
  control effectiveness 65–6
  delivery method 65
  functions of distribution 62, 63
  level of service 64
  nature of product 64
  operating costs 64–5
  planning of resources 65
  supply sites 62–4, 66
  warehousing method 65
Logistics of distribution 51–3
  network 52, 53
  regions 51–2
  supply of market 52, 53
Long-term planning 17
Loop line system 71, 89–90

Management functions, organisation of 4–7
  bond of communication 4–6
  leadership 6–7
Market demand analysis 40–60
  changing demand 41–2
  concept of demand 40–3
  correlation analysis 41
  criteria for good forecasting 42–3
  customer rationalisation 53–4
  delivery problems analysis 55–60
  distribution logistics 51–3
  elasticity of demand 40–1
  forecasting demand 40
  market research 40
  normal demand 43
  ordering cycle 47, 49–51
  patterns of demand 43
  planning for market demand 54–5
  value analysis 43–7
Market research 40
Marketing considerations and distribution 16–17
Monitoring delivery
  service 193–6
  cost monitoring 194–5
  delivery data 194
  forms 203–12
  records 196
Moving annual averages 170
Moving annual total (MAT) 168–71

Objectives of distribution 7–8, 158
Operating costs 64–5
Operational programming 120–4

217

INDEX

Order analysis 53–4
Order lead time 75–6
Ordering cycle 47, 49–51
　elements 49–50
　order processing 50–1
Overhead costs 83–4
Overnight stops 101

Pallet handling times 35–6
Performance ratios 161
Pin and string method 100
Planning for market
　demand 54–5
　delivery planning 55
Planning priciples for
　distribution 13–20
　analysis of distribution 16–17
　basic components 13–15
　design of system 18
　distribution performance 15
　distribution systems 13–14
　improvement of distribution service 15–16
　long-term planning 17
　short-term planning 17–18
　systematic method of resources planning 18–20
Planning requirements 181–2
　control information 181
　planning information 181–2
　qualitative data 181
　quantitative data 181
Planning standards 114, 139–42, 150–1
　customers 141
　inaccuracies 115
　load capacities of vehicles 142
Plant size and factory siting 82
Price restrictions 191
Product variety 190
Production considerations and distribution 16–17
Profit centres 160
Profit margins 161–2

Rationalisation of distribution 126–7
Records 196
Recruitment of staff 155–6
Regions of distribution 51–2
Reordering level (ROL) 164
Reordering quantity (ROQ) 164
Route distances, estimation of 103–4
　optimisation example 103–4
Route engineering 56–9

Routing delivery vehicles 95–110, 125–8
　area boundaries 98
　computerised routing 102–3
　development of routes 99–101
　estimation of route distances 103–4
　factors affecting routing 98–9
　journey planning 105–6
　long routes 101
　optimal routes 97–8
　overnight stops 101
　pin and string method 100
　remote areas 101
　restrictions 99, 200–1
　review of routes 98
　routing facts 96–7
　scientific routing 96–8
　staging points 101
　sub-area group method 100–1
　transfer depots 101
　variable factors 98–9

Savings theory 102
Scheduling charts 113, 130–1
Scheduling of deliveries 110–24, 127–8
　general forms of problem 111
　journey scheduling 118–20
　operational programming 120–4
　requirements of good scheduling 116–18
　scheduling vehicles 112–14, 200–1
　vehicle utilisation 115–16
　vehicles required 115–16
Selection of vehicles 150–2
Selling techniques 190
Short-term planning 17–18
Siting according to demand 69–71
　line theorem 69–71, 74
Siting methods 66–9
　analogue methods 68–9
　exhaustive search method 66–7
　iso-cost contour maps 67–8
　systematic search methods 68
Staging points 101
Standard costing 162
Standard times 33–8
　delivery times 175–7
　schematic procedure 36–8
　truck handling times 34–6
Stock control 162–7
　methods 163–5
　parameters 164
　principles 165–7
　timing of orders 166
　variable throughput 165

218

INDEX

Stock-outs 166–7
Strategic planning for
 distribution 21–39, 183
 benefits 32–3
 budgetary control 38–9
 coordinated centres of demand 28–30
 future of distribution 25–8
 graphs 22–3
 need for planning 21–3
 objectives 24–5
 planning deliveries 20–3
 planning in practice 31
 scale of planning 23–4
 Synthetic standards 33–8
Sub-area groups 100–1
Supply points, siting of 61–74
 complex siting problems 71–4, 90–4
 location of supplies for distribution 61–6
 methods of siting 66–9
 siting according to demand 69–71
Supply sites, selection of 75–94
 delivery ratios 77
 depot siting 85–7
 distribution costs 77–82
 example of procedures 86–94
 number of sites 75–82
 number of vehicles 76
 order lead time 75–6
 supply areas 76–7
 total demand 76
 variable factors of siting 82–5

Three demand locations systems 70–1, 88–9
Transfer depots 101
Traffic engineering 171–4
 congestion problem 172–3
 methodical approach 172–3
 information 173
 analysis 173–4
 speculation 174
 diagnosis 174
 implementation 174
Transport costs 27
Transport efficiency 153
Transport managers 154–5
Transport manning 153–6
 drivers 155
 management 154–5
 office staff 155
 recruitment 155–6
Transport operations, study of 174–7
 drop times 177–8
 journey times 177

Transport operations—*continued*
 loading times 177
 rating vehicle drivers 175
 standard delivery times 175–7
Truck loading times 34–6
 fork-lift truck operations 34–5
 pallet handling times 35–6
Trucking deliveries, planning of 128–32
 cycle duration 131
 number of vans 129
 routing vans 129
 scheduling bulk deliveries 130–2
 scheduling rules 132
 trunking conditions 129–30
 trunking to depots 129–30
Two demand locations systems 70, 88

Unloading time 135

Value analysis 43–7
 DARSIRI method 45–8
 for service quality 44–5
 for warehouse 45
 practice of analysis 46–7
Value of distribution 2–4
Variable siting factors 82–5
 overhead costs 83–4
 plant size and factory siting 82
 production output 85
 site location 82–3
 siting problems 82
 transport requirements 84–5
 variations in demand 83
Vehicle journey calculations 142–5
 application to problem 144–5
 journey times 143–4
Vehicle requirements 145–50
 for areas 146–8
 journey-days for whole region 146, 148–9
 monthly journey-days by area 148
 off-peak month requirements 149–50
Vehicle selection 150–3
 capacities 152
 delivery costs 152
 delivery distances 152–3
 manning 151
 operating costs 153
 planning standards 150–1
 recommendation of vehicles 151–3
 size and types 151–2
 transport efficiency 153

INDEX

Vehicle utilisation 115–16
  delivery capacity 116
  efficient operation 116

Warehouse siting 186–90
  collection of data 187
  development of plans 187–8
  dynamic planning 189
  heuristic programming 188
  implementation 188–9
Warehousing 8–12, 65, 186–90
  automatic warehouses 10
  example 10–12

Warehousing—*continued*
  ideal solution 9–10
  influence on plans 8–10
  mechanical warehouses 10
  simple warehouse 10
  siting 186–90
  strategic planning 8–9
Work study for controlling
  deliveries 171–8
  study of transport operations 174–7
  traffic engineering 171–4

Z-charts 168–71, 195